The Biosphere

D0881409

The Biosphere

2nd EDITION

IAN K. BRADBURY

Department of Geography, University of Liverpool, UK

JOHN WILEY & SONS

Chichester • New York • Weinheim • Brisbane • Singapore • Toronto

Other Wiley Editorial Offices

John Wiley & Sons, Inc., 605 Third Avenue,
New York, NY 10158-0012, USA

Wiley-VCH Verlag GmbH
Pappelallee 3, D-69469 Weinheim, Germany

Jacaranda Wiley Ltd, 33 Park Road, Milton,
Queensland 4064, Australia

John Wiley & Sons (Asia) Pte Ltd, 2 Clementi Loop #02-01,
Jin Xing Distripark, Singapore 129809

John Wiley & Sons (Canada) Ltd, 22 Worcester Road
Rexdale, Ontario, M9W 1L1, Canada

Library of Congress Cataloging-in-Publication Data

Bradbury, Ian K., 1944–
    The biosphere / Ian K. Bradbury. — 2nd ed.
        p.   cm.
    Includes bibliographical references and index.
    ISBN 0-471-98549-X
    1. Ecology.   2. Biosphere.   3. Paleontology.   I. Title.
QH541.B697   1998
577—dc21   98-36447
                                                     CIP

British Library Cataloguing in Publication Data

A catalogue record for this book is available from the British Library

ISBN 0 471 98549 X

Typeset by MHL Typesetting Ltd, Coventry.
Printed and bound in Great Britain by Bookcraft (Bath) Ltd.
This book is printed on acid-free paper responsibly manufactured from sustainable forestry
in which at least two trees are planted for each one used for paper production.

I ANN

Contents

Preface to 1st Edition

An understanding of how our environment works and how it responds to human activities requires some knowledge of living organisms and ecological systems. Yet many students enter higher education to pursue environmentally centred courses with little or no training in the life sciences. This book is written primarily for such students, but also for anyone without a biological training who is seeking a basic understanding of the biosphere. In England and Wales (but not in Scotland) we retain a narrow – and increasingly indefensible – curriculum for 16–18 year olds whose minds become compartmentalized quite early. An unfortunate result is that subjects not taught in the last two years of secondary education are frequently regarded as inaccessible, and this applies particularly to the sciences. This book attempts to introduce the basic functional features of the biosphere so as to make one component of our natural environment more accessible to the non-specialist. No assumptions are made about biological – or chemical – knowledge beyond what might be reasonably regarded as 'everyday', and there are certainly no prerequisites in terms of courses successfully completed.

In practically all institutions offering degree-level work in geography, students are required to study some aspects of the physical environment. Geographers traditionally accept they must know something about the composition of the Earth and the processes that shape its surface, and frequently acknowledge that hydrology and atmospheric phenomena are also part of the deal. With the 'living world' there appears to be less certainty; a tendency exists to regard that part, labelled 'biology', as a separate, and somewhat alien, discipline. However, geographers are concerned with an impressively wide range of subject matter requiring at least some knowledge of organisms and ecology. In addition to the Earth's natural systems such topics include environmental history, land form development, climatic change, environmental impact assessment, agricultural practices, pollution and resource conservation. Unfortunately, basic biological principles relevant to such topics are all too frequently neglected by geography students, and also their teachers. Consequently, the level of understanding is sometimes more superficial than is desirable. It is hoped that this review of some fundamental concepts, with its emphasis on functional aspects, will provide a foundation for the study of those issues of concern to geographers and others engaged in environmental studies.

In deciding what to include in this text I was guided chiefly by what I felt I would like my own students to know about, and also by the sorts of questions they frequently ask. Of course, opinions will differ concerning the choice of subjects, the relative amounts of time spent on each and the arrangement of the chosen material. As far as structure is concerned, I have tried not to introduce a topic without first providing some background necessary for its understanding. Due consideration has been given to topics such as aquatic ecosystems and decomposition, frequently given short shrift in 'biogeography' texts, but which are central to an understanding of the biosphere. On the other hand I have made little reference to regional-level distributions of the biota – i.e. biogeography *sensu stricto* – because this subject is well treated elsewhere for a similar audience.

One of the major problems in producing an elementary treatment of life processes is that there always appear to be exceptions to generalized statements of principle. Accordingly, a great many more caveats might have been justified than actually appear. However, my aim was to establish a set of workable frameworks without obscuring the points of central concern. There was a similar problem in deciding just how much vocabulary – much of it likely to be new – to include, and again compromises were necessary.

Many environmental texts conclude with a 'human impact' chapter. I have avoided this practice, partly because such chapters are usually too short to be satisfying, but chiefly because human activities tend to affect the rate and degree of 'natural' processes rather than differing from them in kind. To reinforce this principle, some major environmental problems are mentioned where relevant processes are being discussed.

During the preparation of chapter drafts, I relied heavily on the critical comments of others; most were asked because of their particular expertise, but some provided a non-specialist view. For their valuable time, support and guidance I am extremely grateful to Christopher Beadle, Mary Benbow, Andrew Charlesworth, Julian Collins, Stephen Cuttle, John Goad, John Goode, Angus Gunn, Adrian Harvey, Ann Henderson-Sellers, Peter James, Meriel Jones, Cedric Milner, Heather Paterson, Christopher Paul, Philip Putwain, Judith Quinn, Barbara Rouse, Marjorie Sullivan, David Thompson, Ken Walton and Bernard Wood. Of course, responsibility for the finished product lies with the author.

Special thanks are due to Paul Smith, who drew all the diagrams, and to Ian Qualtrough and Suzanne Yee, who were responsible for photographic work. Appreciation is expressed to the Trustees of the National Museums and Galleries on Merseyside for granting access to the collections of the Liverpool Museum and to Eric Greenwood, Keeper of the Liverpool Museum, for facilitating the reproduction of material. Philip W. Phillips, Curator of Palaeontology at the Liverpool Museum, is warmly thanked for much invaluable guidance and advice. Thanks are also due to Iain Stevenson of Belhaven Press for his encouragement and support and to Vanessa Harwood who competently oversaw the final stages of production.

Preface to 2nd Edition

In preparing a new edition I have taken the opportunity to rewrite the whole book using the framework which appeared to meet with general approval in the 1st edition. The major addition is a new section (Part Four) devoted to spatial aspects of the biosphere. Despite comments in the earlier preface about the satisfactory treatment of this aspect elsewhere I, and others, felt the lack of a geographical perspective to be a shortcoming. Part Four has also allowed inclusion of some important topics, such as change and disturbance, which do not fit comfortably into other parts of the text. In addition, a couple of chapters have been transposed and two others amalgamated. The aim is to provide an accessible overview of functional, historical and geographical aspects of the biosphere, particularly for students in geographical and environmental disciplines who have limited background in the life sciences. Again, the emphasis is on functional aspects in order to provide a foundation for more advanced study.

I am very grateful to Sandra Mather, Graphics Unit Director, Department of Geography, University of Liverpool, for her skills and her patience, and to Suzanne Yee and Ian Qualtrough who contributed to the drawings and also figure prominently in the photo credits. Julian Collins again read chapter drafts. Zoe Gibbs read the complete first draft and made a lot of very useful suggestions. Later, the text benefitted from a close reading by Karin Fancett who identified a number of errors and imperfections. In thanking them all for their contributions I take full responsibility for the deficiencies that remain.

Part One

THE UNITY OF LIFE

The main purpose of the first part of the book is to emphasize the unity of life, because all organisms, whatever their size and shape, wherever they live and whatever their lifestyle, share certain features. They share aspects of chemistry, they are all made of cells, they all reproduce, they all require energy, and all are the product of evolutionary processes. However, there is also enormous diversity in the living world. Accordingly, this set of chapters deals also with the various ways in which organisms can be categorized.

These chapters provide some essential background which will make the topics introduced later much more accessible. They also introduce some essential vocabulary. The first chapter deals with important levels of organization in the biosphere, while those that follow consider the chemical basis for life, genes and reproduction, evolution, the classification of organisms and energy and life.

1
Levels of Organization

The term *biosphere* is variously defined, but it is used principally in two ways. Perhaps most commonly, the biosphere is defined as the zone in which life occurs, including the totality of life on Earth. It is common to regard the Earth's near-surface environment in terms of the lithosphere (the solid Earth), the atmosphere, the hydrosphere and the biosphere. Sometimes this scheme is represented as a series of overlapping circles, with the overlaps between the biosphere and the other components signifying the association of life with water, the atmosphere and part of the lithosphere. Sometimes, however, the term biosphere is used to refer only to the sum total of the organisms on the planet. Some have described it as 'the green envelope' or 'green skin' at the Earth's surface. In this book the term *biota* is used to refer to living organisms in general, while 'biosphere' is employed when the intention is to convey an impression of living organisms interacting with their physical environment.

Although there may be problems in agreeing a close definition of 'biosphere', that is not important. More important is the set of ideas inherent in the biosphere concept. This concept recognizes that organisms are functional entities, processing energy and matter, and that the entire biota, together with its physical environment, can be regarded as a single system. In thinking about the biosphere it is helpful to use a reference framework of organizational levels, some of which are real entities while others are rather abstract. These levels of organization are now dealt with individually.

The Cellular Structure of Organisms

All organisms are made up of *cells*. The cell is a fundamentally important unit of biotic organization; cells can be regarded as the modules of which organisms are constructed. Also, it is within cells that life processes occur. Frequent reference will be made to cells in the first part of the book, because some understanding of cellular processes will considerably enhance understanding of functional aspects of the biosphere.

Some organisms, bacteria and amoeba for example, consist of just one cell (Figure 1.1). They are known as *single-celled* or *unicellular* organisms to distinguish them from all other, *multicellular* organisms. The number of cells in multicellular organisms varies

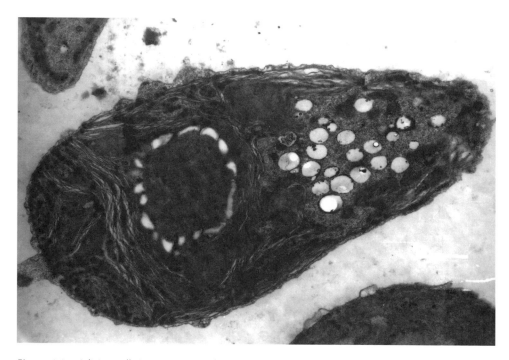

Figure 1.1   *A living cell. A transmission electron micrograph (× 20 000) of a unicellular eukaryote, the marine alga Dunaliella parva. Most of the left-hand part of the cell is occupied by the chloroplast; the lighter areas in the right-hand area are small vacuoles; the nucleus is located in the upper middle part of the cell. (Picture courtesy of Julian Collins)*

enormously, but for a large mammal it is hundreds of billions.[1] Cells are essentially microscopic entities, meaning they cannot be discerned with the naked eye, although there are some notable exceptions to this generalization. Because of their very small size, cell dimensions are usually expressed in micrometres (one micrometre, 1 μm, is just one-millionth of a metre, or 1×10^{-6} m). Bacterial cells are typically between 0.5 and 1.0 μm in diameter, whereas a human egg cell has a diameter of about 100 μm. The living part of a cell is called the **protoplast**, and it is made up of **protoplasm**. All cells from a multicellular organism have certain features in common, even though they look very different under the microscope and perform their own specialized functions. Cells from particular kinds of organisms have characteristic features. The cells of plants, fungi and bacteria, for example, are surrounded by a **cell wall**. Much of the interior of plant cells is typically occupied by a **vacuole**, a fluid-filled cavity in which water and essential substances are stored and to which cellular wastes are deposited. Aggregations of cells of broadly similar appearance and function are called **tissues**. **Organs** are parts of an organism which have a well-defined morphology and function, the heart and liver for example.

On the basis of cell type, all organisms are categorized as either **prokaryotes** or **eukaryotes**. This is a fundamental distinction and we will use the terms, and the

---

[1] 1 billion = 1000 million, i.e. 10^9.

adjectives *prokaryotic* and *eukaryotic*, many times in this book. All multicellular organisms and some unicellular organisms are eukaryotic. The only prokaryotic organisms are those commonly known as bacteria. For now it is worth noting that, compared with eukaryotic cells, prokaryotic cells are simpler in structure. They contain none of the subcellular structures, called *organelles*, that are characteristic of eukaryotic cells. These structures include the nucleus, the mitochondrion and the chloroplast. Prokaryotic cells are smaller than eukaryotic cells, reproductive processes in prokaryotes do not involve the fusion of two cells, and prokaryotes preceded eukaryotes on Earth by nearly 2.5 billion years.

Organisms

The most obvious level of biotic organization is the individual organism. Many familiar organisms, particularly animals, appear to be discrete entities both morphologically and functionally. For some organisms, however, morphological and functional boundaries are far from clear. This applies particularly to those organisms which form colonies. For example, many perennial plants appear to be physically discrete above ground, but the individual stems are connected below ground. Even apparently distinct individuals such as trees may form connections between their root systems. Certain organisms, ants for example, display such a high degree of social organization, even though they are not physically connected, that the notion of the 'individual' might be questioned. Despite these important qualifications, however, the individual organism provides a key point of reference in discussing organization in the biosphere.

Populations

A *population* is defined as a group of organisms of the same species living within a prescribed area. We could refer to the population of tigers in a national park in India, the population of oak trees in a forest, or the human population of a certain country. The population is a major focus of study in ecology and evolution. Population characteristics of interest include size (abundance), changes in abundance over time (Figure 1.2), age structure, the physical factors and biotic interactions that control abundance, and migration. Population size is a function of the rate at which new individuals are born (natality), the rate at which individuals die (mortality), and also the rate at which individuals move in or out of the prescribed area. Understanding what factors influence these rates is a key area of ecological research, and it is one with major implications for conservation, natural resource management and the control of pest populations.

Communities and Ecosystems

Populations do not naturally occur on their own, but co-exist with other populations to form ecological *communities* (Figure 1.3). Unlike cells, which demonstrably exist as well-defined units, the community is a rather abstract level of organization. What is

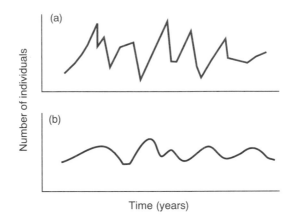

Figure 1.2 *Changes in the size of populations (abundance) over time. Two hypothetical examples are shown. (a) A population which fluctuates widely over short time periods. Changes could be due to differences in weather. (b) A population with fairly regular oscillations around an equilibrium level. The population appears to be regulated in some way*

Figure 1.3 *A community. Any group of organisms living together can be referred to as a community. (Photo, the author)*

meant here is that communities do not normally exist as physically discrete entities like individual cells with clearly defined boundaries. Boundaries around collections of plants and animals are drawn arbitrarily, although natural features may suggest their location as in the case of oceanic islands and ponds. Human activities tend to compartmentalize the landscape, enabling boundaries to be drawn more easily. This is particularly obvious with agricultural fields and forest plantations. However, even communities that seem well defined spatially are subject to movements of organisms in and out of them. Although there may be good practical reasons for demarcating communities, in general the biosphere is best considered as being continuously variable in space, both in terms of the physical environment and community composition.

Despite the fact that ecological communities are not discrete entities, the concept of the community as an assemblage of populations is still valid and, rather like the term 'biosphere', it is the ideas conveyed that are really important. The term community is widely used, and the organization of communities is another major focus of ecological study. Moreover, as particular types of environment in different geographical areas often support organisms which have a degree of morphological similarity and functional equivalence, we can refer informally to 'community types', for example a sand dune community and a heathland community.

The remarks made about the ecological community apply also to the ***ecosystem,*** the term used for a community of organisms together with the physical environment with which it is interacting. The term ecosystem was introduced by British ecologist Arthur Tansley in the 1930s to emphasize the various functional interactions between organisms and between organisms and their physical environment. Expressions such as marine ecosystem, freshwater ecosystem, tropical forest ecosystem and agricultural ecosystem are commonly used, implying that each type has certain distinguishing features of structure and function. Understanding the organization of these various ecosystem types requires observation and experimental work, either in what seem to be good representatives of the type, or in artificial situations which approximate the 'natural' environment. The Earth's terrestrial environment is conventionally divided up into a handful of zones, known as ***biomes***, each with its own distinguishing combination of climate and major life forms, particularly the types of plants that are dominant. A biome (e.g. the tundra biome or the hot desert biome) covers an extensive geographical area and shows a degree of homogeneity. However, as with communities and ecosystems, we should regard the demarcation of biomes as a rather arbitrary process.

2

Chemical Composition of the Biota

Organisms require chemical substances for structure, function, protection, interaction with other organisms, and for storing and transmitting information. The number of substances produced collectively by organisms must run into millions, and yet the total weight of any organism consists of just a few key chemical groups. These are introduced and briefly discussed in this chapter, emphasizing their role in the biosphere.

Chemical Elements and Life

The raw materials for life are the *chemical elements*. Each chemical element is symbolized by one or two letters (a capital is used if there is only one letter and for the first letter if there are two). For many elements, e.g. carbon (C), nitrogen (N), phosphorus (P) and magnesium (Mg), the symbol is, or begins with, the first letter of the English word, but for other elements, e.g. lead (Pb), potassium (K) and mercury (Hg), the symbol is derived from another language, usually Latin. There are a little under one hundred naturally occurring elements, although a few more can be made artificially.

The element most closely associated with life is undoubtedly carbon, which makes up around 45 per cent of the biota's dry weight. ('Dry' weight, rather than 'wet' or 'fresh' weight, is used because, although water is essential for life, it does not really form part of the chemical structure of an organism, and its content is so variable.) Atoms of carbon combine strongly with those of hydrogen, oxygen, nitrogen and sulfur to form a huge variety of stable substances. The dry weight of plants, which make up most of Earth's living biomass, typically consists of around 95 per cent carbon, hydrogen and oxygen. In addition, a number of other elements are essential for all organisms, including nitrogen, sulfur, phosphorus, potassium, calcium and magnesium. A few elements, e.g. silicon and boron, are required by certain types of organisms but not by others. The metabolic role of some elements which appear to be essential for at least some organisms remains unclear: tin is such a case. The following list contains most of the 'biotic' elements.

C carbon
O oxygen
H hydrogen

N nitrogen	Na sodium	Fl fluorine
P phosphorus	Fe iron	I iodine
K potassium	Co cobalt	Si silicon
S sulfur	Cu copper	B boron
Ca calcium	Zn zinc	Mo molybdenum
Mg magnesium	Cl chlorine	Sn tin
Mn manganese		

For many of these elements, the amounts required are tiny, often accounting for less than 0.001 per cent of the weight of an organism. Such elements are accordingly referred to as **micronutrients** or **trace elements**. However, concentration should not be equated with importance: if an element is required, however tiny the concentration, living processes will be impaired if it is not present. Another principle is that while an element may be essential in tiny concentrations, it may become toxic at higher concentrations. Copper and zinc are good examples of such elements.

Elements which are not essential for metabolism may also be found within organisms. Plants take up non-essential elements through their root systems while animals may consume such elements in their food. Non-essential elements may be benign, but some, lead and cadmium (Cd), for example, are very toxic at low concentrations. The discharge of potentially toxic elements, and their fate in the environment, is therefore a matter of considerable concern. Plants and microorganisms can be very sensitive indicators of the chemistry of their local environment. Indeed, one technique of geological exploration involves the analysis of plant tissues to evaluate the likelihood of finding precious metals near by. Moreover, plants and microorganisms which take up and tolerate unusually high concentrations of potentially toxic elements may be used to lower the concentration of these elements in soil and water. The movement of chemical elements back and forth between organisms and their environment is known as **biogeochemical cycling**. Because this process is so central to the functioning of the biosphere, a whole chapter is devoted to it in Part Two.

The Substances of Life

Some Definitions

Before introducing the major classes of biotic substances a few basic definitions are reviewed. First, elements (or, more strictly, the atoms of elements) combine with each other in characteristic ratios to form **molecules**. Formally defined, a molecule of a particular substance is the smallest part of that substance which can exist independently and still retain the properties of the substance. Molecules are represented by their **molecular formulae** in which the number of atoms of each element is indicated by the subscript following the element symbol. The molecules of some substances are made up of atoms of a single element. The molecular forms of oxygen and nitrogen both consist of a pair of atoms, and they are symbolized as O_2 and N_2 respectively. A molecule of the gas methane, which contains one atom of carbon and four atoms of hydrogen, is represented by CH_4. Similarly, a molecule of glucose, which consists of six atoms of carbon, twelve atoms of hydrogen and six atoms of oxygen appears as $C_6H_{12}O_6$. Note that the numbers of atoms in a molecule of glucose can be divided by six to derive what is called the *empirical formula* (in this case CH_2O), which simply shows the proportions in which the different atoms occur. For methane, the molecular formula and the empirical formula are obviously the same. In some cases, the same molecular formula can be shared by more than one substance. For example, a number of sugars have the same molecular formula as glucose. These sugars differ in the arrangement of atoms, which causes them to have different properties. The configuration of atoms in a molecule is represented diagrammatically by a *structural formula*.

Another term to be aware of is *chemical compound*, which is defined as a substance in which there are two or more elements combined in fixed proportion by weight. Thus the substances methane and glucose are compounds, while oxygen and nitrogen are clearly not.

The terms 'organic' and 'inorganic' are in such common use that further comment may seem unnecessary. In fact, these terms are difficult to define accurately. Organic chemistry is concerned with all carbon-based compounds, including those produced synthetically, while inorganic chemistry deals with substances in which carbon is absent or not prominent. But 'organic' is used also in the sense of 'biotic', and this is how it is used in this book. Thus 'organic processes' are those which occur in living organisms, and 'organic matter' refers to material of biotic origin. In contrast, inorganic processes should be those that do not involve living organisms. To confuse the issue, we sometimes talk of 'inorganic nutrition' when referring to essential mineral elements such as phosphorus and potassium.

Water

Earlier it was explained why 'dry weight' is used when referring to an amount of biotic material. There are occasions, however, when the water content of tissues is of interest, as for example, during an experiment to determine the response of an organism to dehydration. Water is of course absolutely essential for life. All biochemical processes occur in water. In fact biochemical reactions often involve either the addition of water (*hydrolysis*) or the formation of water molecules (*condensation*). Water is used as a medium in which substances are transported around plants and animals and waste substances are released. In addition, the evaporative loss of water from an organism brings about surface cooling, which is an important mechanism for preventing overheating.

Proteins

Proteins are so central to living processes that we can regard them as synonymous with life itself. Proteins are present in every living cell where they perform a wide variety of vital roles. Differences between organisms are closely associated with differences in their proteins. Indeed, analysing proteins provides a means for determining relationships between organisms, which is very important for elucidating evolutionary histories and for classification. Most importantly, proteins are associated with their role as ***enzymes***. Enzymes are essentially catalysts which regulate the numerous chemical reactions which make up an organism's metabolism. Biochemical reactions controlled by enzymes often involve either the hydrolysis or condensation reactions mentioned above when considering water. Importantly, enzymes are not consumed during the reactions they control. The digestion of food provides a very familiar example of enzyme-mediated activity. In addition, vital cellular processes such as photosynthesis and respiration involve a sequence of chemical reactions, each controlled by a specific enzyme, and each resulting in a fairly small change in the structure of the chemical molecules involved. A series of chemical reactions of this sort is known as a ***metabolic pathway***.

In addition to their role as enzymes, proteins perform a variety of other vital functions. Antibodies, which provide our bodies with protection against foreign substances, are mainly protein; muscle fibres are rich in protein, which is why animal flesh is such an excellent source of dietary protein; hoof, hair, nail and cartilage are also largely protein. Proteins are not normally used to provide energy, but if the principal sources of energy, i.e. carbohydrates and fats, are in short supply protein may be metabolized for this purpose.

Chemically, proteins are very large molecules with complex structures. However, all proteins are composed of just 20 or so quite simple substances called ***amino acids*** which are linked together by chemical bonds. (The general term for a long chain of chemical units is ***polymer***, while the process of linking the component units together is ***polymerization***.) All amino acids contain nitrogen, which on average contributes about 14 per cent to the weight of protein, and some amino acids contain sulfur or phosphorus as well. Strictly, proteins are made up of amino acid *residues* because in the linking of two amino acids a molecule of water is produced in a condensation reaction. The term ***peptide*** refers to any string of linked amino acids.

Just 20 amino acids are sufficient to allow for an almost incomprehensible variety of proteins. If all proteins contained 200 amino acid residues (a typical size), the number of different sequences possible would be 20^{200}! The sequence of amino acids defines the primary level of organization of a protein. However, their structure is rather more complex: cross-linkages between side groups of amino acids link peptides together so that protein molecules form a variety of three-dimensional structures.

Lipids

The ***lipids*** perform a variety of functional, structural and energy-storage roles in the biota. The most abundant, and certainly most well-known lipids are the fats and oils. Traditionally, the distinction is that fats are more or less solid at 'normal' temperatures (around 20°C) while oils are liquid, although fat is now frequently used to refer to both. In general, fats are associated with animals while oils are associated more with plants, although the oils produced by many fish provide an exception to this generalization. The oils extracted from the seeds and fruits of some types of plants, e.g. olives and corn, are very familiar household items.

Fats and oils are made of substances called *triglycerides*. A triglyceride consists of a molecule of a substance called **glycerol** and three *fatty acid* molecules. There are a number of different fatty acids and different combinations of fatty acids give rise to different triglycerides. A fat or oil from a particular part of an animal or plant may well contain a mixture of triglycerides.

Fats are not the only type of lipid of importance. The **waxes**, which are made from fatty acids and **alcohols**, form surface films on plant leaves and fruit and also on animal fur and feathers. Waxes confer protection, particularly against desiccation and wetting and against the invasion of pathogenic agents.

Carbohydrates

Carbohydrates are universally present in living organisms. The simplest carbohydrates, known as **monosaccharides**, contain between two and seven carbon atoms, with six the most common number. The most familiar and abundant monosaccharide is **glucose**, which plays a vital role in energy metabolism. Another monosaccharide is *fructose*, which is found in the nectar of flowers and is a major ingredient of honey. But glucose and fructose are just two of a large number of naturally occurring monosaccharides. *Disaccharides* are composed of two monosaccharide units (or residues) linked together. 'Table sugar' is the disaccharide **sucrose**, which is made up of a molecule of fructose and a molecule of glucose. For commercial purposes, sucrose is extracted principally from sugar beet, a temperate plant with sugar stored in a bulbous underground organ, and sugar cane, a grass of tropical origin. Sucrose is very abundant in nature because it is the principal form in which organic substances are transported within plants. Another disaccharide, **lactose**, is the principal sugar in mammalian milk. Lactose is made from glucose and another monosaccharide, **galactose**. Some carbohydrates assembled from three, four or five monosaccharide units are also found naturally and, like monosaccharides and disaccharides, are known as sugars. However, they are not as abundant as the monosaccharides and disaccharides.

Molecules of the carbohydrates mentioned so far are comparatively small, being composed of one, or a very few monosaccharide units. But there is another, extremely important group of naturally occurring carbohydrates. These are composed of very much larger numbers of glucose units and are referred to as **polysaccharides**, or simply non-sugar carbohydrates.

The two most abundant polysaccharides in nature are **starch** and **cellulose**. Although these two substances are based on glucose they differ greatly in their chemical properties and in their biological roles. Chemically, starch is a mixture of two glucose-based polymers in which the glucose units are linked in different ways. The result is that starch has a branched structure. Starch is produced by plants for energy storage. The concentration of starch varies between different parts of the same plant, it varies over time and it varies between plant types. Seeds and underground plant organs are often rich in starch, reflecting their role in the storage of energy for later use. Starch from cereal grains and certain root and tuber crops such as potatoes and yams contributes a large proportion of the energy intake for an overwhelming majority of the human population.

Cellulose is unquestionably the most abundant substance in the biota. Chemically, cellulose differs from starch in forming long, unbranched strands. Also, the alignment of bonds differs between starch and cellulose. As a consequence, starch and cellulose have very different properties, and different enzymes are required to break down these two polymers to their component sugar units. Like starch, cellulose is manufactured by plants, but, unlike starch, it is a structural rather than an energy-storage carbohydrate. Cellulose is found principally in the walls surrounding plant cells. Here, it enables the cell to resist swelling from internal water pressure and it gives the plant structural rigidity. As a plant ages, more and more cellulose is laid down in its cell walls. Cellulose, as cotton and as paper, and as a major ingredient of wood, plays an important role in our everyday lives. *Glycogen* (sometimes informally called 'animal starch') is another polysaccharide based on glucose units. It is the major energy-storage carbohydrate of mammals and is found chiefly in muscle cells and in the liver.

Lignin and Other Structural Substances

Lignin, a chemically complex substance, is synthesized by plants and it is found in cell walls along with cellulose (Figure 2.1). As plants age, increasing amounts of lignin are manufactured. Most of the interior wood in the trunk of a tree is actually dead material, a complex mixture of lignin, cellulose and other polymers. Lignin is very resistant to decay

Figure 2.1   *Woody plant tissue is largely composed of a mixture of cellulose and lignin. Cellulose is the most abundant biotic compound on Earth. (Photo, the author)*

because only certain organisms produce the enzymes necessary for its breakdown. ***Chitin*** is a tough, nitrogen-containing polysaccharide which is found in the cell walls of fungi and the exoskeletons of insects. The chitin of animals is impregnated with calcium which strengthens it still further. ***Calcium carbonate*** ($CaCO_3$) is a structural and protective compound for a variety of organisms, notably those with 'shells'. The hardness and strength of the internal skeletons of animals are largely due to calcium salts and other minerals that are deposited in the bone matrix.

Secondary Metabolites

The substances mentioned so far collectively make up the greater part of the dry weight of the living biota. But organisms, particularly plants and microorganisms, produce a huge variety of other substances which do not appear to be involved in their own growth, development and reproduction. Such substances are accordingly known as ***secondary metabolites***, or secondary products. The majority of such substances appear to play a role in protecting organisms from other organisms, often as feeding deterrents. In addition, some secondary metabolites are released into the environment where they inhibit the development of other, potentially competing organisms.

Because secondary metabolites are 'bioactive', they may be put to good use, perhaps for medicinal purposes or for pest and disease control in crops and livestock. In fact, many of the medicinal drugs in common use were extracted originally from plants or other organisms. The extinction of species therefore results in the loss of potentially valuable biochemical resources, so providing a quite pragmatic argument for the conservation of biotic diversity.

The Nucleic Acids

The ***nucleic acids***, like proteins, practically define life on Earth. The nucleic acids are introduced here rather than at the beginning of this section, simply because the topics that follow build logically on some appreciation of their structure and function. There are two nucleic acids to consider, ***deoxyribonucleic acid (DNA)*** and ***ribonucleic acid (RNA)***, both of which are present in every living cell. Essentially, DNA carries all the information, in chemically coded form, necessary for the functioning of the cell and the development of the organism while RNA serves to translate this information into action, principally through the synthesis of proteins. As DNA is passed on from generation to generation, it also provides the basis for the inheritance of characteristics and the continuity of life.

Chemically, DNA is made up of units called ***nucleotides*** (Figure 2.2). Each nucleotide is itself formed from three smaller units, a five-carbon ***sugar*** (ribose), a ***phosphate*** group, and a ***nitrogenous base***. There are four different nitrogenous bases in DNA: their names are ***adenine***, ***thymine***, ***guanine*** and ***cytosine*** and they are often symbolized as A, T, G and C respectively.

Nucleotides are linked together by chemical bonds between the sugar unit of one nucleotide and the phosphate group of the adjacent nucleotide. The result is a nucleotide strand. However, DNA exists as a double-stranded molecule, with the two strands

(a)

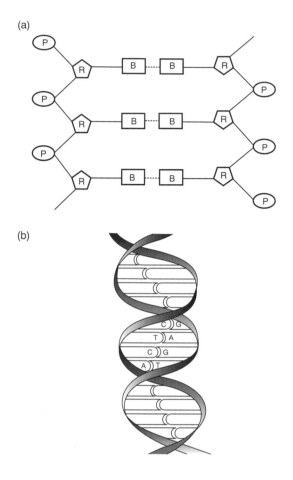

(b)

Figure 2.2   *A segment of a DNA molecule. (a) DNA consists of nucleotides, each of which is made up of a phosphate group (P), a sugar (ribose) molecule (R) and a nitrogenous base (B). The bases are adenine (A), thymine (T), cytosine (C) and guanine (G). (b) The whole structure is twisted round itself to form the familiar double helix*

running in opposite directions (Figure 2.2). The nitrogenous bases of the two strands face each other and they are linked by comparatively weak hydrogen bonds. Very importantly, adenine only links with thymine while guanine only links with cytosine. Adenine and thymine, and guanine and cytosine, are thus said to be ***complementary base pairs***. The DNA molecule is twisted around its own axis to form a structure known as a ***double helix*** (Figure 2.2). An analogy sometimes used to assist appreciation of DNA structure is that of a ladder with rope sides and rigid rungs. Chemically, each side of the 'ladder' is made of the sugar and phosphate groups while each 'rung' consists of a complementary pair of nucleotide bases. The elucidation of DNA structure, in the early 1950s, is generally acknowledged to be one of the most important advances ever in the history of the life sciences, and it led to the award of Nobel prizes to three scientists, James Watson, Francis Crick and Maurice Wilkins.

There are important differences between RNA and DNA. In RNA, the nitrogenous base *uracil* takes the place of the thymine in DNA, and is therefore the complementary base for adenine. Also, RNA is a single-stranded, not a double-stranded molecule. In addition the sugar molecules are slightly different.

The Relationship between DNA, RNA and Proteins

The vital point about DNA is that the sequence of nucleotide bases forms a chemical code, known as the *genetic code*, that appears to be universal for all known life forms. A particular sequence of three adjacent nucleotide bases (on one side of course), known as a *triplet*, specifies a particular amino acid. The order in which amino acids are linked together, and hence the type of protein ultimately produced, is directly related to a sequence of base triplets. Actually, there are 64 different base triplets (they can be thought of as 'words'), which is many more than the number of amino acids, but the same amino acid may be coded for by more than one triplet. Also, some triplets code for the 'stopping' of amino acid sequencing. So, as an example (using just the first letter of the nucleotide base), the sequence of triplets CCA–AAG–CGG specifies a different amino acid sequence from the sequence of triplets AAC–GCC–ACG. As the difference between types of protein is primarily a function of difference in amino acid sequence, it is essentially the variation in nucleotide sequences that is the basis for variation between organisms.

The DNA does not do the 'work' of protein synthesis. That is the function of RNA. RNA molecules 'read' the information stored in coded form on the DNA, then carry this information to the sites in the cell where proteins are synthesized, and orchestrate the sequencing of amino acids in the correct order for the production of proteins as specified by the piece of DNA that is 'read'. Three different types of RNA, with different names, are involved in these processes.

Here we show in outline how proteins are manufactured according to instructions carried on DNA molecules and the roles of the different types of RNA in this process. Protein synthesis is generally described as a two-stage process. The two stages are called *transcription* and *translation*. Transcription involves the 'reading' of the chemical code on the DNA. This requires the 'unzipping' of the DNA molecule and the synthesis of a strand of *messenger RNA (mRNA)* of complementary base sequence. A special enzyme is involved in this process: it moves along the DNA strand, identifies the nucleotide base it encounters, and adds the appropriate complementary base to produce the mRNA strand. The mRNA strand then migrates to the *cytoplasm* from the nucleus where the DNA is situated. (This does not apply to bacteria because they have no nucleus.)

The translation stage involves the ordering of amino acids as specified by the sequence of triplets on the strand of mRNA. A sequence of three bases on a mRNA strand is called a *codon*. The site of protein synthesis is the *ribosome*, which is made up of another type of RNA, *ribosomal RNA (rRNA)*, and protein. Ribosomes, which occur in groups, connect with the mRNA (Figure 2.3). Molecules of yet another type of RNA, *transfer RNA (tRNA)*, which have a characteristic shape (Figure 2.3), pick up amino acids in the cytoplasm and convey them to the ribosomes. There is a specific type of tRNA molecule for each type of amino acid. The tRNA molecules have a triplet of unpaired bases, called an *anticodon*, at one end, and it is here that they link with the mRNA molecule. On the ribosomes, the sequence of amino acids is therefore related to the ordering of tRNA molecules, which in turn is controlled by the order of

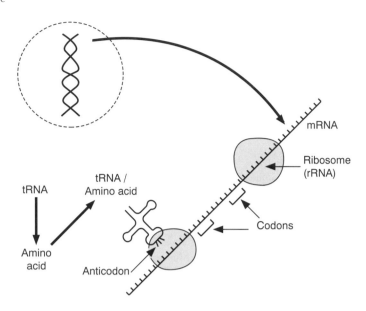

Figure 2.3   *Schematic representation of protein synthesis at the ribosomes in a eukaryotic cell. Information stored on DNA in the nucleus is carried into the cytoplasm by complementary strands of messenger RNA. Within the cytoplasm, specific transfer RNA molecules pick up the amino acids and hand them on to ribosomal RNA. At the ribosomes they are joined to a lengthening peptide chain. Note the characteristic shape of a transfer RNA molecule. The sequence of amino acids is determined by the order of base triplets (codons) on the messenger RNA strand*

base triplets on the mRNA strand. Ribosomes move along the mRNA strand, and as each triplet of bases is passed, the amino acid hauled into position by its tRNA molecule is attached to the lengthening chain of amino acid residues. When the tRNA molecule hands over its amino acid it is free to pick up another molecule of the same type. Several polypeptide chains may be manufactured simultaneously on a mRNA molecule.

In outline then, this is how the coded information of DNA molecules is first read, and then translated into action. Of course, this account begs all sorts of questions about what it is that controls which bits of DNA that are read and at what stages of the cell's life. Despite the complexity of the processes involved, however, it is not difficult to appreciate that the types of protein present in a cell are closely related to the detailed sequencing of bases on the DNA, or more specifically those bits of the DNA that are read. This last caveat is necessary because in most cells only a proportion, often a tiny proportion, of the DNA library is read during the cell's lifetime. Furthermore, the same bits of DNA are not read in every cell of a multicellular organism, and different bits may be read at different times in the cell's life. This is why cells, and the tissues and organs they comprise, perform different functions. The amount of information stored in the DNA of a cell is enormous. It is estimated that within the nucleus of a human cell there are a staggering 3000 million (i.e. 3 billion) bases, and within a comparatively simple bacterium the number is likely to be a few million. In summary, therefore, developmental and functional processes in cells and organisms are determined ultimately by the information stored on molecules of DNA. As discussed in the following chapter, DNA is transmitted from parent to offspring during reproduction, thus ensuring the continuity of life.

3

Genes, Chromosomes and Reproduction

The final section in the previous chapter summarized the process by which proteins are manufactured in the cell according to a chemical code held by DNA molecules. It is DNA that determines how an organism grows and develops, and it is DNA that is passed on, as *genes*, to offspring. The transmission of genes from cell to cell is essential for growth and reproduction. Some of the key mechanisms involved in this process are outlined here, and they provide some necessary background for the discussion of evolution which follows in the next chapter.

Genes and Chromosomes

In chemical terms, genes are fragments of DNA, but in terms of what they do, genes prescribe all the characteristics of an organism, including its pattern of development, its appearance and its function. They do so primarily by 'ordering' the manufacture of proteins, as described earlier (Pages 17–18). Genes are also the units of heredity, passed on during reproduction from parent to offspring. The same genes are present in every cell of a multicellular organism and collectively make up the *genome* of that organism. Although all the cells of a single organism contain the same genetic information, different parts of the genome are expressed in different cells according to the specialized functions they perform. One of the great achievements of molecular biology in the 1990s has been the 'sequencing' of all the genes of a few life forms. This was done first for certain bacteria and viruses, which have relatively few genes. The first eukaryotic organism whose gene sequence was analysed was a yeast which has some 6000 genes made up of over 12 million DNA base pairs. (For comparison, humans have roughly 70 000 genes and 3 billion base pairs.)

Chromosomes

In a eukaryotic organism, genes are carried on thread-like structures called *chromosomes* which are located within the cell nucleus. The chromosome comprises a single DNA molecule together with some protein. Chromosomes are commonly likened to rods, but it is only when a cell nucleus is dividing that they appear as such. In prokaryotic cells (bacteria), which have no nucleus, the DNA molecule usually appears as a loop, attached at one point to the cell membrane. There is not usually any associated protein, and in fact the term 'chromosome' is not always used.

In eukaryotic cells, the chromosomes occur in twos, known as ***homologous pairs***. With the exception of sex-determining chromosomes, each homologue of a pair is effectively identical in appearance. Essentially, each chromosome of a homologous pair carries genes that code for the same general structures and functions. The genes occur in the same order on each chromosome of the pair so that each gene has a specific location (the ***locus***). There are, however, usually alternative 'versions' of each gene, which are called ***alleles***. The alleles that occur at the equivalent locus on a homologous chromosome pair may well be different. So, if we use a letter to represent a gene, we could say that it exists either as *A* or *a*. This gene could therefore be present on a homologous chromosome pair as *AA*, *Aa*, or *aa*. The sex chromosomes may differ considerably in appearance. In eukaryotic species, either males or females carry a pair of identical sex chromosomes, whereas individuals of the other sex carry one of each type. In humans it is the female that carries identical sex chromosomes.

Each eukaryotic species has a characteristic number of chromosome pairs per nucleus, and the size and shape of chromosomes also varies between species. Humans have 23 chromosome pairs and 46 chromosomes in all (but there are 24 *types* of human chromosomes because of the two sex chromosomes). If an organism has different alleles at the equivalent locus on homologous chromosomes, it is said to be ***heterozygous*** for whatever trait is determined by those genes. But if identical alleles are present on a chromosome pair the individual is described as ***homozygous*** for the specified trait. Alleles that are expressed are described as ***dominant***; those that are not expressed are termed ***recessive***. Most characteristics are determined by a number of genes, and they may well be located on more than one chromosome.

Cells and organisms with the full complement of chromosome pairs are called ***diploid*** while those with only one chromosome of each pair are called ***haploid***. The diploid number is symbolized by $2n$, the haploid number by n. So, for human cells, $2n = 46$ and $n = 23$. Diploid and haploid cells therefore carry two sets and one set of chromosomes respectively. The cells that make up the bodies of most familiar higher plants and animals are diploid, i.e. both homologues of each chromosome are present. The process of cell division giving rise to 'daughter' cells with exact copies of chromosomes as the 'mother' cell is called ***mitosis***, and the dividing cell can be either diploid or haploid.

At some time during the life cycle of all types of sexually reproducing organisms, haploid cells are produced from diploid cells. This type of division, in which the chromosome number is halved, is termed ***meiosis***. The necessity for such a 'reduction' division should be quite obvious when we consider the alternative. If the sperm and the egg (the sex cells, or ***gametes***) each carried two sets of chromosomes, fertilization would produce a cell with four sets of chromosomes. And every subsequent fertilization would result in a doubling of the number of chromosomes. So a reduction division is essential in order for the diploid number to be restored upon fertilization. Meiosis also ensures that each 'daughter' cell contains one or other 'version' of each type of chromosome.

For higher plants and animals the reduction division takes place just prior to the formation of the sex cells. All other cells are therefore diploid. But this is not the case with every type of organism. For example, the 'bodies' of mosses are composed of haploid cells, and the diploid part of their life cycle is very inconspicuous. It is a characteristic of fungi that following fertilization (which is not very common incidentally) the first cell of the new generation undergoes a meiotic division.

All plants undergo an ***alternation of generations*** between haploid and diploid phases. The haploid generation is called the ***gametophyte*** and the diploid generation is called the ***sporophyte***. In some plant types the two generations exist as independent entities, but in others they remain closely associated. Mosses are somewhat unusual in that the gametophyte is the more conspicuous generation. For seed plants, the sporophyte is dominant while the gametophyte is very tiny and short-lived, and its development takes place on the sporophyte generation. For the flowering plants this is within the floral organs. The principle of alternation of generations is demonstrated in Figure 3.1 using a fern as an example. In this type of seedless plant it is the sporophyte which is dominant.

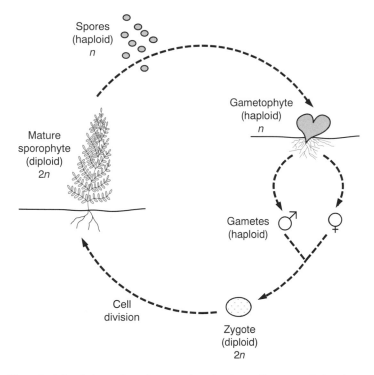

Figure 3.1 *The principle of alternation of generations in plants. The example is a fern, a type of seedless plant. The drawings are not to scale. The sporophyte (diploid) generation is the larger and longer-lived phase while the gametophyte (haploid) generation is tiny. Note that the two generations are independent, which is not the case with most plant types*

The Division of Cells

Growth and reproduction clearly require cell multiplication. Although it may seem a little illogical, the process by which this is brought about is known as *cell division*. The reason for this is that one cell splits before the formation of a new membrane separating the two cells. Division of a prokaryotic cell, i.e. a bacterium, occurs by *binary fission* (Figure 3.2). First the single DNA molecule is copied, usually quite early in the cell cycle. Later the DNA copies separate, and a membrane is completed around each so that two, genetically identical, independent cells are formed.

For eukaryotic organisms, cell division is a little more complex. In describing this process we concentrate on the chromosomes because it is here that the genetic information is located. Strictly, we are concerned with the division of the nucleus rather than the cell. This is because a nucleus, where the chromosomes are located, can divide without the formation of two new cells. In some kinds of organisms the formation of multinucleate cells is normal at certain stages in the life cycle. For simplicity, however, the term cell division is used here, but with the understanding that nuclear division can occur independently of cell division.

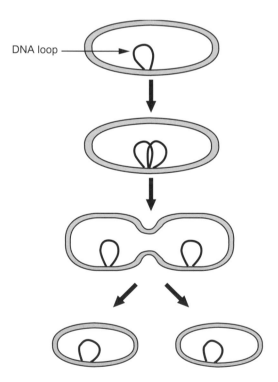

DNA loop

Figure 3.2   *The reproduction of a prokaryotic cell. As all prokaryotes are unicellular, this division, called binary fission, produces new organisms. The DNA, which exists as a single molecule, is copied and later the cell divides*

Mitosis

When cells divide mitotically, two new cells are formed, each with the same number of chromosomes as the original nucleus and each of identical genetic constitution. Mitosis must therefore involve the copying of the DNA on the chromosomes. Before it is copied, the DNA molecule is 'unzipped', and two new strands of DNA with complementary base

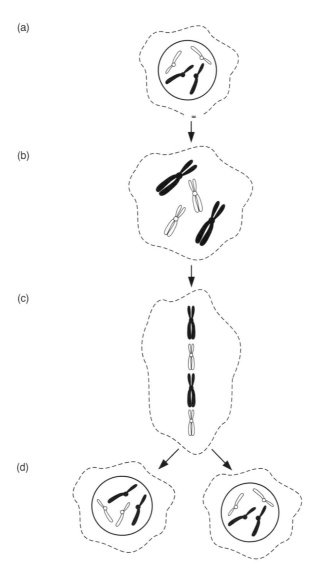

Figure 3.3 *The behaviour of chromosomes during mitosis. In this example the diploid number (2n) is four. (a) Chromosomes prior to duplication. (b) Chromosomes have duplicated, but remain joined. (c) Chromosomes 'line up' prior to separation. (d) After separation there are two 'daughter' cells of identical genotype*

sequences are synthesized. The behaviour of chromosomes during a mitotic division is shown in Figure 3.3. The distribution of the various organelles throughout the cell prior to division usually ensures that some of each type will be present in each of the two new cells. The rate of cell division varies during the life cycle of an organism, and between different types of cells. In the early stages of an organism's growth and development cells may be dividing almost continuously, but the pace of cell division tends to slow with increasing age. Some cell types, once they have differentiated, undergo no further division.

Meiosis

Meiosis differs in a number of ways from mitosis. First, it involves two successive divisions. Second, it results in a halving of the number of chromosomes. Third, meiosis promotes genetic diversity, a point whose significance will become clear when we discuss evolution in the next chapter.

The behaviour of chromosomes during meiosis is shown in Figure 3.4. The two divisions elegantly combine the need for a reduction in chromosome number with the desirability of reshuffling genes so as to enhance genetic variability. Two processes during meiosis enable new genetic combinations to appear. One of these is associated with the way that chromosomes 'line up' and then separate after duplication (Figure 3.4c). Note that each chromosome unit at this stage comprises four parts, called *chromatids*. These contain the duplicated genetic material of a pair of chromosomes. The chromosome units then separate into two parts, each part comprising a chromatid pair (Figure 3.4d). However, any chromatid can pair with any other chromatid in the unit. Consider a case in which there are just two pairs of chromosomes in a cell which divides meiotically. Chromosomes of one pair are designated *A* and *a*, chromosomes of the other pair are designated *B* and *b*. Duplication prior to the first meiotic division produces two chromosome units. One is designated as *AAaa*, the other as *BBbb*. The two daughter cells from this first meiotic division could be *AA*, *BB* and *aa*, *bb*; or *AA*, *bb* and *aa*, *BB*; or *Aa*, *BB* and *Aa*, *bb*, or *AA*, *Bb* and *aa*, *Bb*.

At the onset of the second division, each chromatid pair comes apart and the two parts migrate in opposite directions. What were formerly called chromatids are now known as chromosomes once again. So what purpose is served by the second division? After all, haploid nuclei are produced by the first division. To appreciate this point we need to recall that during the first meiotic division the homologues comprising a chromosome pair lie alongside each other. At this time genetic material may be exchanged between homologous chromosomes (Figure 3.5). This process, called *crossing-over*, involves two chromatids breaking at the equivalent location, and the corresponding parts exchanging and fusing at the equivalent position on the other chromatid. Equivalent sections of the DNA molecule are consequently exchanged between homologous chromosomes. The result of such genetic recombination is that if the four haploid nuclei survive the second meiotic division they all differ genetically from each other (Figure 3.5).

Very importantly, therefore, meiosis promotes genetic variability. First, chromosomes behave independently when they separate during the first division, so that the same 'versions' do not always migrate together. Second, crossing-over during the first division

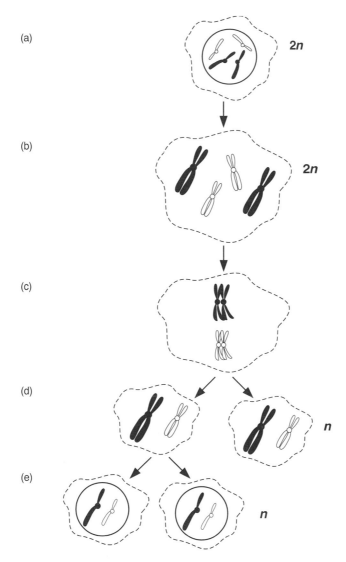

Figure 3.4   *The behaviour of chromosomes during meiosis. Two separate divisions are involved. (a) Prior to duplication, 2n = 4. (b) Chromosomes have duplicated. (c) Homologous chromosomes have come together (unlike mitosis) and 'line up'. (d) The separation of chromosomes gives rise to two haploid (n) cells, each containing one set of chromosomes, but in duplicate form. In this division, the four parts (called chromatids) comprising a chromosome unit separate from each other independently, according to the way they line up initially. The new cells are therefore not genetically identical (unlike mitosis). (e) During the second division, the duplicated chromosomes separate, so each cell has one copy of genetic material. (Both cells from each division do not necessarily survive)*

recombines alleles. The second division therefore capitalizes on any genetic assortment that occurs during the first division. In Figures 3.4 and 3.5 only one or two chromosomes, and just a few genes, are depicted. However, most types of organisms have several pairs of chromosome, all carrying numerous genes. This is why two sexually produced

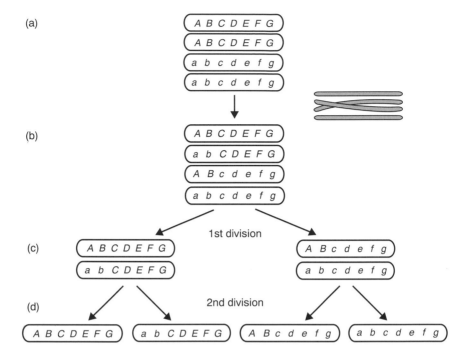

Figure 3.5   *The principle of crossing-over during meiosis. Different letters denote different genes, upper and lower case letters denote different alleles. (a) A pair of duplicated, homologous chromosomes lie together prior to the first meiotic division. Genetic material is exchanged between the chromatids during crossing-over (small diagram). (b) A new sequence of alleles is apparent on the chromatids after crossing-over. (c) New combinations of alleles are evident on chromosomes after the first division; compare with (a). (d) After the second division each of the four haploid cells has a unique combination of alleles. (In the female of many types of organisms, only one nucleus survives each division)*

offspring from the same two parents are never genetically identical (unless the first cell of the new generation splits following fertilization).

Sexual and Asexual Reproduction

Sexual reproduction, involving the combination of genetic material from two haploid nuclei, is confined to eukaryotic organisms. In many types of organisms, e.g. mammals, two parents are required, but for other organisms, many plants for example, fertilization can occur by the union of gametes from the same individual. In contrast, asexual reproduction, which is a widespread phenomenon, involves the production of a new individual without fertilization. Even some animals can multiply asexually: the female gametes of certain insect species can develop into adults without fertilization, which means, of course, they remain haploid.

Clearly, sexual reproduction is an expensive activity in terms of the demands it makes on an organism's resources. Plants invest a lot of energy in producing flowers and pollen, and in rewarding pollinators for their efforts. In most 'higher' animals two separate parents are needed. Because reproduction is possible by asexual means we may well ask 'why did sex evolve?', which is tantamount to asking 'what use is sex?' Traditionally, the simple answer is that sex promotes genetic variability. Sex does not create new genes, but it does ensure that new permutations of genes are being continually thrown up. This is achieved by processes during meiosis, and also by bringing together organisms with different genetic constitutions during fertilization. In contrast, asexual reproduction should produce offspring with an identical genetic constitution to that of the parent. However, the question of the value of sex is much more complex than it seems at face value. A number of theories have appeared to explain the advantages of sexual reproduction, often based on complex mathematical models. One theory with quite a lot of support is that sex confers advantages in combatting the activities of disease-causing agents such as bacteria, fungi and viruses. Sex preserves combinations of genes which may not necessarily have any use at the present time but which may enhance protection against the activities of parasites at some time in the future.

Before leaving this section it is worth commenting briefly on the term 'sexual reproduction', which so far has been used to mean the union of specialized sex cells, the gametes. However, among organisms such as bacteria which do not undergo fertilization, DNA can be exchanged between individuals in other ways. As a result, new genetic combinations continually appear in bacterial populations, and not just when errors are made in the copying of DNA.

Genotype and Phenotype

The term *genotype* refers to the particular combination of genes (strictly alleles) present in a cell or organism. So, if a perfect copy of DNA is made at every cell division, all cells of the same organism will be of identical genotype. The genotype determines the principal structural and functional features of an organism. However, an organism's environment has a modifying effect on growth and development; in other words the environment determines the extent to which the genetic potential is realized. Oak tree seedlings of identical genotype grown in different light environments will show quantitative differences in their morphology, although both are unmistakably oak trees. The environmental influence commences at conception: the offspring of animals that are maintained on a low plane of nutrition during pregnancy may never fully recover from that early check to growth and development.

The genotype therefore provides the ground plan for growth and development while the environment determines exactly how the genotype is expressed. Features differ in the extent to which they may be modified by environmental influence. Some features are genetically fixed, or stable, and are therefore particularly useful for classifying organisms. Also, types of organisms differ in the degree to which their morphology can be modified by the environment. Plants are particularly susceptible to environmental modification: they are said to exhibit *plasticity*.

The form and the functional characteristics of an organism collectively constitute its *phenotype*. The phenotype is determined by the interaction between the genotype and its environment. In examining two organisms of the same type we cannot be sure that any phenotypic differences observed are determined genetically, and not environmentally. However, if phenotypic characteristics of two organisms of the same kind raised in the same environment are compared some conclusions may be drawn about their genetic differences.

4

Evolution

Evolution is one of the key unifying themes in the life sciences. The purpose of this chapter is to introduce the idea of evolution and to consider the processes by which it occurs. The material presented here is essential background for considering the history and geography of the biota later in this book. In an everyday sense, evolution means gradual change; in a biological context, evolution is defined as a directional change in the frequency of genes in a population over time. (Recall that in Chapter 1 a population was defined as a collection of individuals of the same species inhabiting a prescribed area.) In other words, evolution is characterized by a change in the composition of a population's *gene pool* over time. The process primarily responsible for evolution is *natural selection*.

Variation and Natural Selection

Evolution requires genetic variation, i.e. differences in genotype between individuals. Variation is the only raw material on which natural selection can operate. Natural selection cannot create new genes, it can only select from what is available in the gene pool. As a starting point, consider a population of organisms. The performance of individuals in a population always varies: for example, some individuals will grow more quickly than others, some will cope better with adverse weather, some will be less affected than others by disease. One important manifestation of variation in performance between individuals is differential reproductive success. Simply, some individuals leave more offspring than others. In consequence, the genes of some individuals will be better represented than the genes of other individuals in future gene pools.

Now, differences in performance are partly genetic and partly due to environmental factors. Characteristics that are observed and measured are described as phenotypic. However, because an organism's genes have a strong influence on its performance, it is reasonable to assume that *on average* the phenotypically 'superior' individuals are also genetically 'superior' within that particular situation. Differences in reproductive success between phenotypically different individuals will therefore lead to a shift of gene frequency in a population over time, which is the definition of evolution.

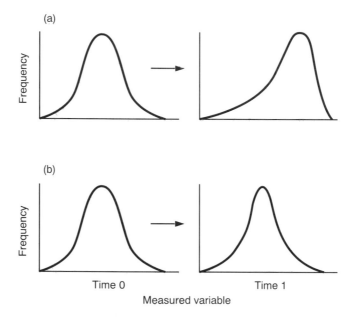

Figure 4.1   *Types of selection. (a) Directional selection. The frequency distribution of the measured trait (e.g. height, length, weight) has changed with time. Selection is evidently for larger individuals. (b) Stabilizing selection. The mean and the mode of the frequency distribution have not changed with time. Selection is for individuals which were most abundant at Time 0. Although it is phenotypic characters that are measured, it is assumed they are correlated with genotype*

The relative intensity with which the environment tends to change the frequency of genes in a population is determined by the **selection pressure**. For example, the widespread use of synthetic organic pesticides after 1945 introduced a powerful new selection agent for insect populations. Variation between insect genotypes in their natural resistance to these pesticides resulted in selection for those traits which enhanced survivability in the presence of insecticides. Thus, many insect populations gradually increased their degree of resistance. It is difficult to quantify selection pressure, but it can be assessed by measuring the survival rates of individuals with different genes.

The term *fitness* is used to refer to the relative success of genotypes in passing on genes to successive generations: the fittest individuals are those that contribute most genes to future gene pools. Any genetically determined characteristic can contribute to fitness. It could be the ability to grow faster, to run more quickly, to withstand drought better, or it could be some behaviourial characteristic. However, a trait can be said to contribute to fitness only if its possession increases the probability that genes will be passed on to future generations.

A change in the characteristics of individuals comprising a population through successive generations can be represented diagrammatically using frequency distributions as in Figure 4.1. Here it is assumed that the measured characteristic varies continuously (body dimensions and weight for example) and measurements are made on individuals at Time 0 and on their descendants at Time 1. In Figure 4.1a population characteristics have clearly shifted over time; mean and mode values have moved to the right. Although there is a possibility that this change is purely phenotypic, it is very likely to have a genetic component. We will assume that selection has been for larger individuals, that size in this environment is correlated with reproductive success. When selection brings about change, as in this example, it is described as *directional*. Selection is not always directional. In Figure 4.1b, means and modal values of the frequency distributions are much the same at Time 0 and at Time 1, so selection has occurred for individuals that are mid-sized. In this case selection would be described as *stabilizing*.

Not all characteristics are continuously variable as are weight and morphological dimensions. Differential reproductive success could be based, for example, on a small difference in a metabolic pathway such that some individuals are more successful than others in breaking down a poisonous chemical released by an invading pathogen. Selection would therefore favour those individuals that possessed the appropriate enzyme, and of course the genes specifying for that enzyme.

Reproductive Potential

Also central to the theory of natural selection is the fact that all types of organisms potentially leave more offspring than is necessary to replace themselves. This is abundantly obvious when we consider the numbers of eggs produced by fish and insects and the seeds produced by plants. Even populations of large mammals, with their characteristically low reproductive output per year, have a high potential for population increase. However, it is also obvious that the potentials for population increase are not realized: in general populations remain more or less stable over fairly long periods of time, although many fluctuate quite violently over comparatively short periods. Clearly then, either most offspring die before reaching reproductive age or else they fail to reproduce. The importance of the potential for population growth in the context of a discussion of evolution is that, on average, those individuals genetically better equipped for their environment are more likely than less well-equipped genotypes to live to reproductive age, and hence leave their genes to succeeding generations.

Adaptations

Genetically determined characteristics that ultimately enhance reproductive success are called **adaptations**. We may say that one type of organism is 'well adapted' to its environment, pointing to particular morphological or physiological characteristics that appear to equip it well for the set of conditions in which it is found. Strictly though, characteristics should be described as adaptive only if their possession demonstrably enhances reproductive success.

An organism's environment comprises all the various factors that impinge upon it throughout its life. Physical factors include temperature, moisture and nutrients, while biotic factors include predation, parasitism, and competition both with other species and other individuals of the same species. The environment can be regarded as a type of filter, or series of filters, which serves to select for some genotypes while discarding others.

Careful studies of a population may suggest which aspects of the environment are important from an evolutionary point of view; in other words, which environmental factors are providing high selection pressure and at what stages of the life cycle they are most critical. It might be fire, it might be salinity or drought, or it could be another type of organism that is important. However, the environment of an organism is multifaceted and complex; weighting the importance of various environmental factors

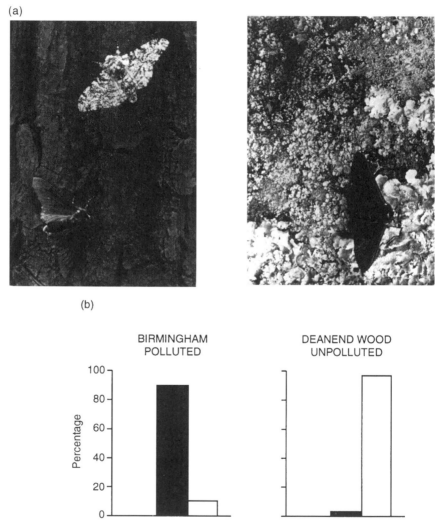

Figure 4.2 *Natural selection at work – the case of the peppered moth in England. (a) Dark and light-winged genetic forms against lichen-free trees and lichen-encrusted trees. (b) Data showing the percentage of moths of the dark form (shaded) and the light form (unshaded) in polluted and unpolluted areas in the 1950s. Differential predation by birds due to the relative conspicuousness of moths was shown to be the principal selection agent in this case. (From Kettlewell, H. 1956 Further selection experiments on industrial melanism in the Lepidoptera. Heredity 10: 287–301. Used with permission of Blackwell Science Ltd, Oxford)*

is usually problematic in practice. Thus the form, function and behaviour of organisms usually represent a compromise response to the total environment. It is usually only in extreme environments that a single factor can be identified as being of overriding significance.

Similar characteristics are frequently seen in two or more quite unrelated organisms, suggesting they have been subject to similar selective forces. So different groups of organisms independently evolve in similar ways in terms of their structure, function and behaviour. This phenomenon is known as ***convergent evolution***. The term ***divergent evolution*** is used when the characteristics of two populations are becoming increasingly different. ***Parallel evolution*** is said to occur when two types of organisms which share a common ancestor appear to be evolving in similar ways.

The characteristics observed today in a population are the net result of past selection pressures. It is important not to forget that the environment changes over time. Genotypes that are well adapted to one set of conditions may be poorly adapted if conditions change. Such changes, in temperature for example, may result in a shift in the geographical range of a species. Some organisms though, particularly plants, can respond to a degree of change in their environment by altering aspects of their physiology or development; they are said to exhibit ***phenotypic flexibility***.

Examples of Natural Selection

There are a number of convincing examples of evolution by natural selection that we could cite. Human agencies are frequently involved because of our unrivalled capacity to change the nature of selective forces very quickly. Probably the most quoted example is that of a moth, commonly known as the peppered moth, in England during the 19th century. Prior to the industrial revolution, trees were typically covered by lichen of generally light colour. However, the deposition of air-borne pollutants resulted in the loss of the lichen cover in and around industrial areas, thus exposing the dark-coloured bark beneath. When trees were covered by lichen, peppered moths were predominantly light in colour, and therefore well camouflaged from predatory birds. Dark-coloured forms of the moth were rare. As the trees lost their lichen cover, light-coloured moths became more conspicuous than dark-winged forms and therefore more vulnerable to predation (Figure 4.2). An increase in dark (melanic) forms occurred at the expense of light-winged forms in polluted areas, but in unpolluted areas the light-winged forms remained predominant. Wing colour is a genetically determined characteristic. Thus, predatory birds selected for genes specifying dark-coloured wings in polluted areas.

Background colour has been shown experimentally to have an effect on the rate of predation within peppered moth populations. However, if predation had not been a major cause of death, the loss of lichen might not have had any effect on the frequency of genes specifying wing colour in the moth populations. It should not be assumed that predation is a major selective force in all populations; as pointed out earlier, populations are subjected to a variety of potentially important selective agents in their environments.

The peppered moth example demonstrates the rate at which evolutionary change can occur in response to powerful selective pressures: as a general rule, the greater the selective force on a particular gene pool, the greater the pace of change in gene frequency. Not surprisingly, the higher the reproductive rate and the shorter the time between generations, then the greater the potential for genetic change.

Mutations

Genetic variation is the only raw material on which natural selection can operate. The variability in the gene pool therefore sets a theoretical limit to the amount of genetic change that can occur. Natural selection cannot add to existing variation by bringing into existence new genes, only new combinations of genes. A permanent change in genetic material, i.e. a change in the DNA of a cell, is referred to as a ***mutation***. A mutation involves a change in the sequence of nucleotide bases along a DNA molecule and hence has implications for the ordering of amino acids and the type of proteins produced. Mutations are usually categorized as either gene mutations, i.e. alterations in a single gene, or chromosome mutations, i.e. those affecting a number of genes. Mutations occur very occasionally under natural conditions, and can also be induced by external agents such as ionizing radiation and certain chemicals. A change in nucleotide sequence, through its effects on protein synthesis, has the potential to alter some aspect of form or function in the cell carrying the 'new' gene. A mutation may be purely ***somatic***, meaning it does not affect the sex cells and hence is not inherited. However, mutations can also be inherited and incorporated into the gene pool. These 'new' genes compensate for those lost from the population because of the failure of some individuals to reproduce.

A mutation may be advantageous or disadvantageous to an organism depending on whether it increases or decreases its chances of passing on its genes to successive generations. In fact, however, most are soon lost from the gene pool. The important point is that genes that have just arisen by mutation are not special in any way; they should just be considered part of the gene pool and therefore part of the raw material for natural selection.

Alternative forms of the same gene, i.e. alleles, arise because of mutations, and all organisms are, by definition, the products of successful mutations in the past. However, mutations do not bring about great changes in genotype within one generation. If large numbers of genes were involved, normal cellular processes would be so disrupted that the cells would cease to function. Furthermore, under natural conditions, the rate at which mutations occur is very low. Nonetheless, mutations are the only source of brand new genetic material and as such play a special role in evolution.

Artificial Selection

Artificial selection is the deliberate selection of individuals for breeding purposes. It has provided us with modern varieties of crops and livestock, ornamental plants and domestic pets. It is, of course, phenotypes that are normally selected, the assumption being that phenotypic differences among individuals will have some genetic component. The products of artificial selection convincingly demonstrate the considerable genetic variation that usually exists within the gene pool of a particular species, and therefore the potential for change which is unrealized under natural conditions. Natural selection did not produce dogs as diverse as the dalmatian, poodle and spaniel; nor did it produce modern wheat and corn varieties: the potential was always there, but has been realized only by deliberate selection and intensive breeding. Plant and animal breeders can utilize the full range of compatible genetic variation that is available, whereas under natural conditions genetic exchange is normally quite local.

Genetic Engineering

We are living at a time of rapid progress in understanding cell processes at the molecular level and in applying this knowledge to manipulate the genome. Such manipulations are often referred to as 'genetic engineering', but *recombinant DNA technology* is the technical term. Genetic modification of an existing genotype may be achieved by identifying strands of DNA specifying for particular characteristics in one organism, isolating the appropriate strands, and transferring them to another type of organism. The universal nature of the genetic code enables quite unrelated organisms to be involved in the exchange of genes. Such techniques, which are central to developments in biotechnology, enable the available gene pool to be expanded much more widely than is possible with conventional breeding.

Transferring genes that specify desired characteristics offers considerable opportunities for the improvement of biotic resources. For example, disease resistance or frost tolerance might be enhanced in crop plants. Genetic manipulations may also be carried out to prevent the development of undesirable characteristics. One such manipulation has resulted in the production in plants of a form of lignin which is more easily digested than the original substance. This advance could be of great importance for the paper industry, in which lignin poses a major problem, and also in agriculture because lignin is poorly digested by livestock. Medical science is another area where genetic manipulation offers considerable opportunities. For example, some human diseases are caused by the possession of a 'faulty' gene. If carriers of this gene can be identified, it might be possible to insert 'correct' copies into the genome.

Not surprisingly, such developments pose a number of ethical and practical problems. For example, should genetic manipulations be made in human sex cells and therefore transmitted to future generations, and can the ecological consequences of releasing genetically modified organisms into the environment be predicted with a high degree of confidence?

Evolution, Complexity and Diversity

Natural selection has been characterized as a process operating on existing genetic variation in such a way as to bring about a progressive change in gene frequencies within a population. Genes are lost from the gene pool through failure of individuals to reproduce, and new genes are very occasionally introduced by mutation. The gradual nature of evolution has been emphasized, notwithstanding the fact that changes in gene frequency can sometimes be observed in nature over relatively short intervals of time. At this stage we may well ask whether known evolutionary processes alone can explain the enormous diversity of life on our planet, all the complexities of structure, function and behaviour displayed by organisms, and the history of life as revealed by the fossil record. The conventional answer is 'yes'. And the reasons that the answer can be given so confidently are that a proven mechanism for evolution exists, the timescales involved are so very long, and anyway the many unifying features of living cells argue strongly for a common ancestry.

Darwin and *The Origin of Species*

The one name above all others that we associate with the theory of evolution by natural selection is that of Charles Darwin (1809–82). Darwin (Figure 4.3) was not the first person to believe in evolution; his special contributions were, first, to provide overwhelming evidence that it occurred and, second, to propose a mechanism, natural selection, by which it could do so. Darwin is widely remembered for his time on HMS *Beagle*, which took him on an expeditionary voyage to the southern hemisphere in the early 1830s, and particularly for his observations on the Galapagos Islands in the eastern Pacific. Here his observations of geographical variation among organisms on the islands contributed towards the development of his ideas on biological change. There were other influences as well. Darwin took with him the first volume of Charles Lyell's classic work, *Principles of Geology*, which had just been published. Lyell's advocacy of slow and gradual change in the natural world and the importance of understanding contemporary processes in explaining past changes provided Darwin with guiding principles. Central also to Darwin's theory of natural selection were the ideas contained in Thomas Malthus's *Essay on the Principles of Population,* which had been published in 1798. Malthus proposed that while human populations tend to increase in a geometric progression from generation to generation (i.e. population number multiplies by a constant), food production increases only arithmetically (i.e. the difference in amounts of food produced during successive intervals remains constant). Therefore, Malthus argued, food resources ultimately set a limit to population size. The potential for an increase in numbers is a characteristic of all plants and animals, so for Darwin an inevitable outcome of a geometric rise in numbers was a 'struggle for existence' between individuals. So Malthus's observation concerning the reproductive potential of organisms is a key feature of the theory of natural selection which requires differential reproduction in a potentially expanding population according to how well organisms are adapted to their environment. In addition, Darwin appreciated the power of artificial selection and breeding to bring about organic change, and in fact devoted the first chapter of *The Origin* to this subject.

The theory of natural selection is associated with another British naturalist, Alfred Russel Wallace. While working in the Malay Archipelago (modern Indonesia) in the 1850s, Wallace sent Darwin his ideas on natural selection. These were essentially similar to Darwin's own, which although by now well developed, had yet to be published. In 1858, papers containing the theories of the two men were read, in their absence, to a small audience at the Linnean Society in London, apparently with little impact. But in 1859, Darwin, spurred by the knowledge that he was not the only person to have discovered natural selection, finally published *The Origin of Species*, unquestionably one of the most influential books ever written. It quickly generated fierce debate among scientists,

Figure 4.3   *Charles Darwin (1809–82), best known as author of* The Origin of Species, *in which he proposed a theory of natural selection (Picture from Darwin, C. 1889* Naturalist's Voyage Round the World. *John Murray, London)*

philosophers and church people, as well as a wider public, and it was to revolutionize scientific thought.

Darwin's theory of natural selection was joined in the early 20th century by laws governing inheritance and a greater understanding of the units of heredity, of which he had no knowledge. The modern, orthodox view of evolution is known as neo-Darwinism.

The Appearance of New Species

The term '*species*' has been used previously in this book but without further comment. However, before we consider how new species arise – which is one of the key manifestations of evolution – it is necessary to discuss the meaning and usage of the term. Because the term species is so common, it is somewhat surprising to learn that it defies close definition. An enormous amount has been written about 'the species concept' and it remains a source of much controversy. The reasons for the controversy lie in the nature of biological variability. So many biological variables are continuous that deciding where to draw boundaries between one species and another is an arbitrary process. Also, what we witness today in any individual population is only a 'snapshot' of a population which is continually changing over time with an alteration of gene frequency. In other words the population is evolving. The fossil record may reveal something of these changes over time, and different species names may be applied at different times in the past. Quite clearly, resemblance must be one of the key criteria for separating one species from another but there are no rules as to how similar two individuals must be before they can be considered the same species. The capacity for individuals to interbreed is usually used as a criterion for their membership of a particular species, although it is difficult to derive a completely satisfactory definition on this basis because two individuals which seem morphologically quite different may be capable of interbreeding. However, just because interbreeding is biologically possible this does not mean that it is a common event, or even ever occurs under normal conditions. The technicalities of the species concept need not provide an obstacle to biogeographical and ecological work, but an awareness of them is important because it is an expression of the nature of biotic variation. A useful working definition of a species has been provided by the distinguished ecologist E.O. Wilson. He has defined a species as a population whose members are able to interbreed freely under natural conditions. Most of the time that definition will serve us well.

It is not normally possible to witness the appearance of a new species, but only to infer what has happened from an understanding of reproductive and evolutionary processes, and a knowledge of life in the past. However, all new species arise from within populations, or gene pools, of existing species. Two different models can be used for the appearance of new species. The first of these, called *vertical evolution*, involves changes in gene frequency throughout the range of an existing species until such time as the populations can no longer be considered members of the same species. The timing of appearance of the new species cannot be known exactly because of the incomplete nature of the historical record, but even if a complete historical record was available, opinions would likely differ concerning its interpretation.

The second model for the appearance of new species is *speciation*, which means the multiplication of species. The key prerequisite for speciation is the erection of breeding barriers between organisms to ensure *reproductive isolation*. Put another way, there must be a cessation of *gene flow*. We will see how breeding barriers can be erected a little later, but the result is that the members of the 'new' and 'old' populations no longer produce fertile offspring. The second prerequisite for speciation is the maintenance of reproductive isolation; a resumption of gene flow between the two populations must not occur. The third prerequisite for speciation is sufficient *evolutionary divergence* between the two populations so that they cannot reasonably be considered the same species. Reproductive isolation in itself does not ensure speciation because the two populations could be evolving along parallel trajectories.

Several mechanisms have been shown to lead to reproductive isolation and speciation, but initially two major patterns can be recognized. The most obvious way is through the geographical separation of two populations. If the distance between two populations is so great that they cannot possibly interbreed naturally, they may become increasingly different over time. This process is known as *allopatric* speciation. If the two populations occupied similar environments, however, and were subject to similar selection pressures,

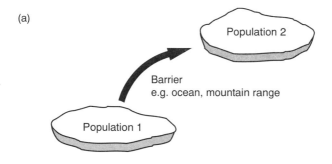

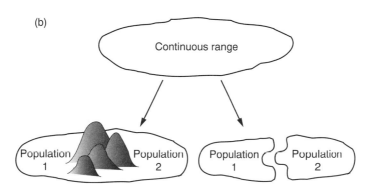

Figure 4.4 *Models of allopatric speciation. Geographical separation of a species range leading to reproductive isolation can be brought about by (a) dispersal across a pre-existent ecological barrier or (b) the fragmentation of a continuous range, e.g. by mountain building (left) or continental drift (right). Speciation requires evolutionary divergence following reproductive isolation*

divergence could be extremely slow. Populations of the same species may occur in different geographical areas for considerable periods of time.

There are basically two models for allopatric speciation (Figure 4.4). One involves dispersal to a new area, the other involves the fragmentation of an existing species range. The process of dispersal, which is discussed further in Chapter 14, involves the movement of organisms (or their propagules) to a new geographical location. This could be achieved by chance dispersal, by swimming or flying or simply by carriage of propagules in air or water currents.

Evolutionary divergence is encouraged by what is known as the ***founder effect***. This phenomenon is based on the probability that the genes present in a population colonizing a new area will be just a tiny and non-random sample of those in the original population. (We can think of it as just a small part of the frequency distributions shown in Figure 4.1.) Consequently, there is a high probability that the evolutionary trajectories of the two populations will be different immediately after colonization.

The second model of allopatric speciation involves the fragmentation of an existing range. This could be brought about by geological events, such as continental movements or mountain building, which leave populations reproductively isolated either side of ecological barriers. It could also be caused by the movements of species in response to climatic changes and the subsequent failure to occupy the whole of the previous range. Knowledge of such events relies heavily on an understanding of geological and climatic events in the past. It is worth noting here that fierce controversies have surrounded the relative importance of dispersal and range fragmentation as factors in speciation.

A new species may also arise from another species within the latter's geographical range. This is referred to as *sympatric* speciation. While there is considerable consensus concerning the importance of allopatric speciation, there has been more debate about the reality of sympatric speciation. If it is to occur then reproductive isolation must be maintained over quite small distances. A variety of possible scenarios have been proposed for this process, of which just two are mentioned here. Consider a case in which there is a close relationship between two species, for example an insect species and its host plant. A chance event may cause some insects of the species to colonize a new species of plant, which subsequently evolves in response to the insect's feeding activities. The 'original' and the 'new' insect populations in turn diverge until they can no longer be considered to be the same species. Second, sympatric speciation may occur where two populations of plants occupy different microclimates in the same general vicinity. The result is a difference in the timing of flower production, thus preventing gene flow between the two populations.

The processes leading to the formation of new species described so far are relatively slow by ecological timescales. Among plants, however, there is a mechanism for reproductive isolation that occurs in one generation. The mechanism involves an increase in chromosome number, giving rise to plants which have three or more chromosome sets. It is caused by the fusion of gametes which contain more than one set of chromosomes as a result of the failure of chromosomes to separate during meiosis (Pages 24–6). The resulting plant is unlikely to be able to interbreed with either of its parents; in other words it is reproductively isolated. The condition of such individuals is appropriately termed *polyploidy*, and the plant is called a polyploid. The terms triploid, tetraploid, etc. indicate how many multiples of the basic (haploid) number of chromosomes are present. Around a half of all known flowering plants are polyploids, so polyploidy is an extremely important process.

5

The Classification of Organisms

While other chapters in Part One emphasize the unifying features of the biota, the purpose of this chapter is to consider the immense variety of life on Earth, and particularly how this variety can be organized by classification schemes. The diversity of life is most obvious when we consider the variety of shapes, sizes and life history patterns that exist among organisms. Considering size alone, the range extends from tiny bacteria that are measured in micrometres to some whales which are 30 metres or more in length and weigh several tonnes. The study of relationships among organisms is called *systematics*, and it includes the important subject of *taxonomy* which deals with the classification of organisms. In this chapter the basic principles of taxonomy are introduced together with some related issues.

Basic Taxonomic Principles

First, it is important to appreciate that classification schemes are the product of human interpretation of biological variation. Organisms are classified scientifically according to features which are chosen by the taxonomist. These features are known formally as *characters*. Characters are used therefore to distinguish one organism from another, and for assigning individual organisms to particular taxonomic groups. The choice of characters is critical, because different characters are likely to generate different classification schemes among the same group of organisms.

As a general rule, characters which are *stable* are chosen. These are features that are genetically determined and not susceptible to environmental modification (Page 27). Morphological characters are very important, but other characters are used as well, including the number of chromosomes, the types of chemicals produced, and metabolic pathways. Obviously, the characters that are chosen vary according to the type of organisms being considered. For the flowering plants, floral structure provides a satisfactory basis for classification as the number and form of the various floral organs is not altered by the environment. Characters can be continuous or discontinuous. An example of the former would be the dimension of a certain organ, while an example of the latter could be the presence or absence of a certain feature. One major consideration in choosing characters for classification is practicality. This is because one of the chief uses of classification is the identification and naming of organisms.

Although the characters chosen for classification purposes vary between different types of organisms, certain substances, notably proteins and nucleic acids, are universal. Molecular variation therefore provides an opportunity to classify organisms independently of morphology and anatomy.

Approaches to Classification

There are two major approaches to modern scientific taxonomy. One is described as *phenetic*, the other as *phylogenetic*. The phenetic approach (Figure 5.1a) is based solely

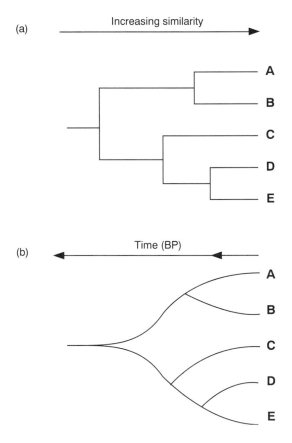

Figure 5.1 *Approaches to classification. Assume agreement that A,B,C,D,E are different species. (a) A hypothetical phenetic classification. The scale indicates overall similarity. Classification above the rank of species could be subject to various interpretations. Thus, one genus could contain species A and B and another genus could contain species C, D and E. Alternatively, species C could be placed in a third genus.*
(b) A hypothetical phylogenetic classification. The scale is time before present (BP). The presumed evolutionary history of the five species is indicated by the branching pattern. As with the phenetic scheme (a) opinions may differ concerning the treatment of these species at genus level and above

on the degree of resemblance between organisms. As indicated earlier, the characters chosen differ between major groups of organisms. Classification schemes based on one, or just a few, arbitrarily chosen characters are termed *artificial*. *Natural* systems of classification, in contrast, are based on the simultaneous use of many characters, an approach known as *numerical taxonomy*. For groups of organisms that are difficult to classify in any other way, the bacteria for example, numerical taxonomy is particularly useful. For most types of organisms, however, use of this approach has been rather limited.

Phylogenetic (or *phyletic*) classifications (Figure 5.1b) are based on evolutionary history, i.e. the *phylogeny* of the relevant organisms. This approach recognizes that groups of organisms shared a common ancestry at some time in the past, but have subsequently diverged. Phylogenetic relationships are usually represented by 'evolutionary trees' which suggest the timings of divergence events (Figure 5.1b). The phylogenetic approach to classification arose logically from an acceptance of evolution. However, its use is constrained by the extent to which the evolutionary history of the group of organisms under consideration is known. Such classification schemes usually require some informed speculation about the pattern of descent.

Now although the phenetic and phylogenetic approaches to classification are different, they often produce similar schemes. This is because the kind of information likely to be useful in establishing evolutionary relationships, i.e. the overall resemblance of extant organisms, is similar to that used to construct phenetic schemes. Also, phenetic schemes are likely to separate characters that evolved early from those that evolved later, even though no attempt was made deliberately to incorporate evolutionary information.

Species Names

The problems of defining 'species' closely and unambiguously were discussed earlier (Page 37). However, the species is a fundamentally important unit within the biota, and species are the basic units in biological taxonomic schemes. Each organism known to science has a proper, or scientific name. The name comprises two parts, both of which are of Latin or Greek derivation, and both of which should be written in italics, or else underlined. The scientific name for the tree commonly known as the coast redwood in California is *Sequoia sempervirens;* the proper name for the orang-utan of Sumatra and Borneo is *Pongo pygmaeus.* The first word is the *generic* name; it tells us to which *genus* (plural *genera*) the organism belongs. The second part, the *specific epithet*, completes the species name. Note that the generic name begins with a capital letter but the specific epithet does not. As specific epithets are always accompanied by a generic name, the same specific epithet can be used in different genera. The rules of zoological nomenclature allow an animal to have the same name for the specific epithet as the genus, as in *Bison bison*, but this is contrary to the rules governing botanical nomenclature. The names chosen for a species are often either descriptive of the organism, named after a geographical locality, or after the discoverer. The number of species within genera varies very widely, from just one to over a thousand in exceptional cases.

It was the Swedish natural historian Carolus Linnaeus (1707–78) who standardized the use of the *binomial system* for organisms. Previously, scientific names had typically comprised several parts, which despite being descriptive, were too cumbersome for general use. The binomial system has been universally adopted by the scientific world.

When written, a species name will often be followed by a capital letter, or an abbreviated name. This signifies the person, known as the **author**, who first described the species. Many species names are followed by L., which stands for Linnaeus himself. Sometimes the species name is followed by more than one author's name, as in *Picea sitchensis* (Bong.) Carr. This denotes a taxonomic revision, the name of the earlier author being bracketed. It is useful to cite the author, particularly when dealing with difficult taxonomic groups, because it removes doubt as to which kind of organism reference is being made.

Sometimes it is possible to recognize **subspecies** or **varieties** of a species. A typical situation involves two populations which have been separated geographically. Each subsequently develops distinguishing characteristics but their divergence is insufficient to warrant separate species status. If the study of a third population showed it to be intermediate between the other two such that variation between the three populations is continuous then the two subspecies categories would no longer be justified. Some taxonomic groups are notoriously difficult to classify, and opinions may well differ as to how the variation present should be categorized. (Taxonomists themselves are often classified as either 'lumpers' or 'splitters', depending upon their treatment of difficult groups.) Artificial selection (Page 34) also generates subdivisions within species. Recognized genotypes are known as **cultivars** in the case of plants and **breeds** in the case of animals.

Although common names are frequently employed for organisms, there is no universally recognized scheme for their use. Such names tend to be used locally and inconsistently, and one name frequently covers more than one species. In the United States, 'robin' is usually taken to mean the species *Turdus migratorius,* but in Britain 'robin' generally means the species *Erithacus rubecula.*

How Many Species Exist?

Notwithstanding the fact that taxonomists may not agree on the way biological variation should be classified, the question 'how many species are there?' is an important one. Really there are two questions here: first, the number of species known to science and, second, the number that actually exists on the planet. Surprisingly perhaps, there is no single inventory for named species. The total number described thus far appears to be somewhat less than 2 million. Estimates of the *total* number of species vary enormously, from around 8 million to upwards of 30 million.

A large area of uncertainty is the diversity of invertebrates, particularly insects, in humid tropical forests. Previous estimates of the numbers of species were based on the ratios of mammals and birds to invertebrates in temperate regions, where numbers are relatively well documented. These ratios were then used to estimate the number of invertebrate species in tropical forests, because here the numbers of mammal and bird species are fairly well known. However, closer study of the insect faunas of tropical forests has revealed that the ratios which hold for temperate regions vastly underestimate the number of insect species in the tropics. Sadly, the pressure on these environments from human activities is such that we may never know whether or not these recent estimates are correct. Another habitat which is not yet well known but which may have very high diversity is the soft sediment of the ocean floor. Early work shows very high species diversity, mostly of tiny organisms, but it is not known whether these same species occur elsewhere in this habitat or whether other species will be found. Whatever the true number of species on Earth, it is clear that the number so far scientifically named and described is only a fraction, probably a very small fraction, of the total.

The Taxonomic Hierarchy

Biological classification schemes are hierarchical, meaning they comprise various levels, or taxonomic ranks, as shown in Figure 5.2. Thus, species are grouped into genera, genera are grouped into *families*, families into *orders* and so on. There are other taxonomic ranks between those shown – subclass and suborder, for example – but this scheme will be quite adequate for present purposes. Moving up the hierarchy, the number of groups becomes smaller and smaller and there is less and less overall resemblance between the species comprising a group. Any particular taxonomic group, of whatever rank, can be referred to as a *taxon* (plural *taxa*).

All taxa belonging to a single *phylum* share certain characteristics, a similar 'ground plan', even though superficially they may seem very diverse. Such fundamental characteristics are very useful for determining long-term evolutionary lineages. For organisms other than animals, the term 'division' has traditionally been used rather than phylum, but the latter is becoming increasingly common.

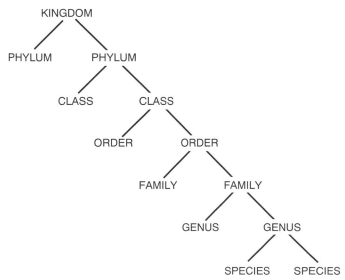

Figure 5.2 *The taxonomic hierarchy. Only the most important ranks are shown. Traditionally, 'division' has been used for plants and 'phylum' for animals, but the trend is to use the latter term for all organisms*

Kingdoms of Organisms

The highest formal taxonomic rank has traditionally been the ***kingdom***. The number of kingdoms recognized has changed over time, reflecting contemporary understanding of structure, life history and function of organisms. Most people faced with the problem of making a primary division of organismic diversity would distinguish between plants and animals, and have no difficulty in assigning most of the organisms around them to one or other of the two groups. The problem with a two-kingdom scheme though is that many organisms do not fit comfortably into either when we try to define the terms 'plant' and 'animal'. Most of these organisms are not visible to the naked eye, so until the first microscopes were used in the 17th century there was no such problem. Even after the discovery of microorganisms, most seemed either more 'plant like' or more 'animal like' and received attention accordingly from either botanists or zoologists. One exceedingly important group of microorganisms, the bacteria, never fitted comfortably into either of the two kingdoms, and bacteriology developed to a large extent as a separate discipline, associated particularly with medicine. As the biology of microorganisms became better understood it was clear that a two-kingdom scheme was unsatisfactory, and a third kingdom was proposed by some biologists.

During the last few decades microorganisms have been shown to differ in such fundamental ways that a further increase in kingdom number has been necessary. Recall that cells (and organisms) are either prokaryotic or eukaryotic (Page 4). The prokaryotes (the bacteria) have been placed in a kingdom of their own, known as the kingdom ***Monera*** or ***Prokaryotae***. All prokaryotes are essentially unicellular, whereas eukaryotic organisms may be unicellular or multicellular. Prokaryotic cells are very much simpler in terms of cellular organization, and also smaller, than eukaryotic cells. The DNA of a prokaryotic cell usually forms a single, circular chromosome, whereas the DNA in a eukaryotic cell is packaged, with associated protein, on several paired chromosomes within a membrane-bound nucleus. Prokaryotic cells do not have the various organelles found in most eukaryotes, although they carry out similar functions. This fundamental difference in cell type is of great significance. The evolution of eukaryotic cells, from prokaryotic cells, perhaps 2 billion years ago was one of the most momentous events in the history of the biosphere. Ideas concerning the treatment of eukaryotic organisms have also changed during the last few decades, particularly with respect to the simpler eukaryotes and the fungi.

A five-kingdom scheme, proposed in the late 1950s by American ecologist Robert Whittaker, has subsequently become very widely used (Figure 5.3a), although the original names are not necessarily retained. The kingdoms are Monera (or Prokaryotae), Protista (or Protoctista), Fungi, Plantae and Animalia. All monerons are prokaryotic, but the other four kingdoms are exclusively eukaryotic. The Protista mainly consists of unicellular organisms (e.g. paramecium and amoeba), but also certain multicellular organisms (e.g. large algae). The fungi are considered sufficiently distinctive to justify a kingdom of their own, although historically they have close botanical associations. The plant kingdom is made up of multicellular, mostly 'green', plants, including mosses and liverworts (bryophytes), clubmosses, horsetails, ferns and the seed plants. The animal kingdom has a greater degree of uniformity than in the former two-kingdom scheme as it no longer contains any unicellular organisms and has lost some of the more 'primitive' multicellular organisms to the Protista.

(a)

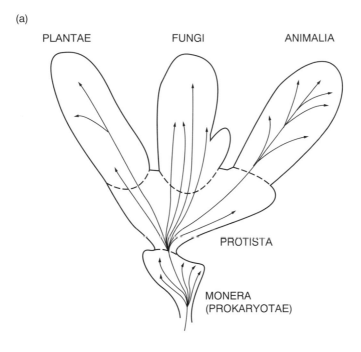

(b)

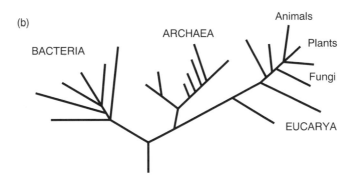

Figure 5.3 *Kingdoms of organisms and the evolutionary 'tree'. (a) A five-kingdom scheme has been in general use for over 30 years. The arrows represent evolutionary lines. (b) A modern scheme based on details of ribosomal RNA which recognizes three kingdoms or domains. The position of plants, animals and fungi in this scheme is shown*

Various modifications have occasionally been proposed to the five-kingdom scheme, but with little impact on the overall structure. More recently, however, a somewhat more radical proposal has been made concerning the primary division of life. This scheme, associated particularly with Carl Woese of the University of Illinois and colleagues elsewhere, is an important development. Unlike other approaches to classification, this scheme is not based upon numerous characters but on just one. Inevitably, it is a molecular character because only such features are common to all organisms. The key character is the sequence of nucleotide bases (or genes) in just one piece of a type of ribosomal RNA. (Ribosomes are the sites where proteins are manufactured from amino acids.) The justification for selecting this feature lies in the claim that the evolutionary history of organisms is revealed best by comparing the degree of divergence in equivalent genes over time. By comparing gene sequences from different organisms the organisms can thus be placed within an evolutionary tree.

Using features of ribosomal RNA, Woese and colleagues have proposed a primary division of all organisms into three major groups, or 'domains'. These are the Archaea, the Bacteria and the Eucarya (Figure 5.3b). So the single prokaryotic kingdom (Monera) of more traditional schemes has been split into two, while all eukaryotic organisms are united in one group. The idea that all eukaryotes, from amoebae to elephants to oak trees, are more closely related to each other than are some bacteria from other bacteria (in the old five-kingdom scheme) certainly challenges our perceptions of life on Earth. Furthermore, this scheme shows the Archaea (or Archaebacteria) to be more closely related to ancestors of the Eucarya than to the Bacteria. Others have emphasized the fact that the Archaebacteria are particularly associated with environments which were probably common close to the time of life's origins. Not everyone agrees with Woese's scheme, or its underlying assumptions. However, it is now widely acknowledged that if all prokaryotes are placed in one kingdom, then two subkingdoms should be recognized, the Archaebacteria and the Eubacteria.

Taxonomic Revisions

From the discussion so far it should be clear that there is no single, universally agreed taxonomic scheme for all known organisms. In fact, taxonomic revisions are continually being made as new information becomes available and existing variation is reinterpreted. Perhaps a study of previously neglected features argues for a new classification, perhaps new fossil evidence suggests a new phylogenetic scheme.

A taxonomic revision might involve the transfer of a species from one genus to another (necessitating a change in its generic name at least); two or more species may be 'amalgamated' or, conversely, one species may be split into two or more taxa. The coast redwood, *Sequoia sempervirens,* mentioned above, provides an example. This taxon was formerly called *Taxodium sempervirens*, indicating that taxonomists felt its resemblance to other members of the genus *Taxodium* justified its inclusion within this group. However, closer examination of these taxa suggested that the coast redwood was sufficiently distinct to justify its transfer from the genus *Taxodium* to a new genus, *Sequoia*. (Note that the specific epithet was retained.) For a large and taxonomically problematic genus, the number of species frequently varies depending on which authority is consulted.

Viruses

Viruses, of which some 4000 are known, have not been mentioned so far in this chapter because they are not considered to be organisms in the conventional sense.

Nonetheless, they are biotic entities of immense importance. A *virus* consists of a strand of nucleic acid and, usually, a protein coat. Replication of a virus can seemingly occur only within a living cell; the host cell's metabolic machinery being used to carry out the instructions coded for by the viral nucleic acid. Viruses are the cause of many diseases of crops, livestock and humans, including AIDS (acquired immune deficiency syndrome).

6

Energy, Nutrients and Life Processes

Energy is defined as the capacity to do work. Living organisms are working entities, and as such they use energy continuously. Organisms also require chemical raw materials for life, elements such as carbon, nitrogen and phosphorus. There is a close connection between the procurement of energy and nutrients, so the topics are considered together. In this chapter we look at the different ways in which organisms acquire energy and nutrients and how energy is harnessed for useful work by living cells.

Introducing Energy

A few basic principles will aid our understanding of the energetics of individual organisms and also some of the functional aspects of ecological communities considered in Part Two. Whenever work is being done energy, in some form or other, is involved. Many of the different forms of energy are part of everyday vocabulary, as in the case of nuclear energy and solar energy. We shall be concerned with three forms of energy, the energy of sunlight (a type of radiant energy), chemical energy (the energy held within chemical substances) and heat. Within living organisms, the energy available for work occurs in chemical form. Energy may be stored for relatively short periods in fairly small molecules such as those of glucose, but for longer periods, large molecules are usually involved. For example, starch is commonly stored in the underground organs of plants and in seeds. In mammals, energy is generally stored for long periods as fat, which is metabolized when energy demands are high, and for shorter periods as glycogen in the liver.

Chemical reactions that involve the release of energy are termed *exergonic*; by definition an exergonic reaction is one in which the energy content (energy state) of the product(s) is less than the starting material. In contrast, *endergonic* reactions require an input of energy in order to proceed. In general, whenever organic molecules are broken down in living cells, energy is released, but the synthesis of organic molecules requires an input of energy. The standard unit for the measurement of energy (and work) is the *joule*, although in the older literature energy values were often expressed in calories (1 calorie = 4.187 joules).

One of the most fundamental laws of science is that energy may be transformed from one form to another, but it can neither be created nor destroyed. If molecules of glucose are broken down to carbon dioxide and water, the energy formerly held by those glucose molecules must be around somewhere in the universe, and in one form or another. A second general rule is that when energy is used, it is converted to a more dispersed, less useful form; in other words it is degraded. In practice this means that when chemical energy is used within a cell, heat is released. These two laws, one pertaining to energy quantity and one to energy quality, constitute in essence the first two laws of thermodynamics, and it is helpful to keep them in mind.

Categorizing Organisms According to Energy Acquisition

Despite the great diversity of life on Earth there are only a few categories of energy metabolism. As far as energy acquisition is concerned, it is important to distinguish between *autotrophic* and *heterotrophic* modes of nutrition. Practically every type of organism can be categorized as either an *autotroph* or a *heterotroph* depending on the manner in which it meets its energy needs. Autotrophic organisms are those which can utilize an external, non-biotic, source of energy to manufacture energy-rich organic molecules. To provide the raw materials for the manufacture of organic molecules, simple substances, notably carbon dioxide, are acquired from the environment. Heterotrophs cannot harness an external, non-biotic, energy source but instead consume energy-rich organic molecules. The consumed molecules are then broken down (digested) and a proportion of the energy released is captured for useful work. The prefixes 'auto', meaning 'self', and 'hetero', meaning 'other', reveal the essential difference between autotrophs and heterotrophs. While the former are independent in terms of their energy needs, the latter are totally dependent on other organisms. Just a few microorganisms can switch metabolism between autotrophic and heterotrophic modes, but these are comparatively rare.

Photosynthesis and Chemosynthesis

There are two types of autotrophic energy metabolism, *photosynthesis* and *chemosynthesis*. Different sources of energy are used and different types of organisms are involved. Photosynthesis involves the 'trapping' of light energy and its conversion to chemical form. Chemosynthesis, which is confined to certain groups of bacteria, involves the oxidation of certain inorganic chemical substances that are scavenged from the environment.

The conversion of solar energy to chemical energy in photosynthesis underpins all life on the planet. The most familiar photosynthetic organisms are of course the 'green' plants on land and plants and algae in water. Some types of bacteria, including the cyanobacteria (formerly called blue-green algae), are also photosynthetic. The green colour of plants and algae is due to the presence of *chlorophyll*, the pigment which is at the heart of the photosynthetic process.

During photosynthesis, hydrogen combines with carbon dioxide to produce simple organic molecules. With the exception of some types of photosynthetic bacteria, water is the source of hydrogen. Oxygen from the water molecules is released into the environment as a by-product. The process may be expressed simply as:

$$H_2O + CO_2 \rightarrow (CH_2O) + O_2$$

Here, (CH_2O) represents a simple carbohydrate (often a molecule of glucose is shown). It is important to be aware that such shorthand expressions for photosynthesis show only the raw materials and products of the process. In fact, photosynthesis is a highly complex process involving a series of biochemical and biophysical reactions.

Some photosynthetic bacteria use hydrogen sulfide, not water, as a source of hydrogen. The raw materials and end products in this case are:

$$H_2S + CO_2 \rightarrow (CH_2O) + 2S$$

Most such bacteria survive only in the absence of oxygen, i.e. in ***anaerobic***, or ***anoxic*** environments. This is believed to have been the first type of photosynthesis to appear on the planet, at a time when there was no free oxygen.

Photosynthesis is one of the key processes in the biosphere. All life on Earth, directly or indirectly, depends on photosynthesis; the free oxygen in the atmosphere is generated by photosynthesis; and the ozone in the upper atmosphere which shields the Earth's surface from ultraviolet radiation (Page 64) is derived from oxygen generated during photosynthesis. Moreover, an increase in oxygen as a result of photosynthesis permitted the evolution of a more efficient form of energy metabolism about 2 billion years ago.

Plants use much of the energy captured by photosynthesis to power the manufacture of energy-rich organic molecules, initially sugars, but also storage compounds such as starch and structural compounds such as cellulose. Later, molecules can be disassembled and their energy used for work by the plant. This is necessary for a variety of reasons: plants do not stop 'working' at night when no light energy is available; some plant parts, e.g. roots, are non-photosynthetic; and at some times of the year there may be no leaves on the plant.

The process by which organic molecules are disassembled is ***respiration***, and it is the same process as that used by the majority of heterotrophic organisms. However, while photosynthetic organisms can manufacture these energy-rich organic molecules by harnessing light energy, heterotrophs require them 'ready-made' in the diet. (Respiration is discussed in more detail below.)

The other form of autotrophic nutrition, chemosynthesis, harnesses the energy contained within simple inorganic substances which are scavenged from the environment. Chemosynthesis is confined to certain types of bacteria, and these are classified according to the substances they utilize. A variety of simple substances are used, including ammonia, nitrite and hydrogen sulfide. Chemosynthesis is extremely important in the circulation of carbon, nitrogen and sulfur through the biosphere. In addition, in environments where there is no light, chemosynthesis provides energy for the manufacture of organic matter. One such environment is around submarine hot springs on the ocean floor where water is ejected at high temperatures. Dissolved in the water is the gas hydrogen sulfide which is oxidized by chemosynthetic bacteria.

Figure 6.1   *Schematic representation of an ATP molecule emphasizing the three phosphate groups and the high-energy bonds linking them*

The Importance of ATP

All organisms, whether they are autotrophs or heterotrophs, produce a comparatively simple substance called ***adenosine triphosphate*** (known universally as ***ATP***) which figures prominently in energy metabolism. ATP occurs in just about every living cell, regardless of type and regardless of organism, and is nearly always involved when work is being done. For this reason it is sometimes referred to as life's 'universal energy currency'. A molecule of ATP is depicted schematically in Figure 6.1. The three phosphate groups are a key feature of this compound. The bonds linking the outermost and middle phosphates, and the middle and innermost phosphates, are known as 'high-energy' bonds. The formation of a high-energy bond requires a substantial input of energy. However, when the bond is broken, energy is released and made available for 'work' by the organism. In other words, the energy associated with ATP molecules is harnessed (although not with 100 per cent efficiency) for useful work during coupled chemical reactions.

When a molecule of ATP is hydrolysed, adenosine diphosphate (ADP) and inorganic phosphate (Pi) are produced. This reaction is reversible: a molecule of ADP combines with a phosphate group to form a molecule of ATP, a reaction which requires an input of energy of course. These reactions can be expressed as:

$$ATP + H_2O \rightleftharpoons ADP + Pi + energy$$

Most of the processes responsible for ATP formation have been discussed already; these are photosynthesis, chemosynthesis and respiration. An outline scheme showing the major processes by which ATP is generated is shown in Figure 6.2. The process called *fermentation*, which is an anaerobic type of energy metabolism, is discussed below.

Respiration

The process of respiration involves the disassembly of molecules of substances such as sugars in a series of enzymatically controlled reactions. The energy released during these reactions is channelled towards the generation of ATP. For all multicellular organisms, and most types of unicellular organisms, free oxygen is necessary for this process. The process is also known as ***aerobic respiration*** and ***oxidative metabolism.*** Only a proportion of the energy contained within the glucose (or other ***energy substrate***) is harnessed as ATP; the rest is released as heat. The chemical by-products of respiration are carbon dioxide and water, so the process can be simply represented as:

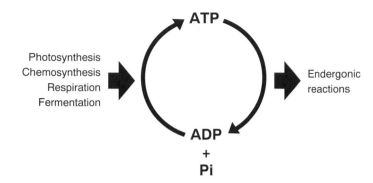

Figure 6.2 *The various biotic processes by which ATP is generated from ADP and inorganic phosphate (Pi). Photosynthetic organisms utilize 'light energy', chemosynthetic organisms oxidize simple inorganic entities. Respiration and fermentation involve the breakdown of energy rich organic molecules and the capture of released energy for ATP generation. The conversion of ATP to ADP, a highly exergonic reaction, is coupled to the many energy-demanding (endergonic) reactions in the cell*

$$CH_2O + O_2 \rightarrow CO_2 + H_2O + energy$$

In terms of chemical raw materials and end products, respiration can be considered the reverse of photosynthesis. In fact, the balance between photosynthesis and respiration has a major influence on the carbon dioxide concentration of the atmosphere (Page 124).

As with photosynthesis, this simple expression for respiration conceals a large number of biochemical reactions: in fact about 20 different enzymes are involved. For simplicity respiration is depicted here as a two-stage process (Figure 6.3). The first stage, which can proceed without oxygen, is called *glycolysis*. If oxygen is present eight molecules of ATP can be formed, but without oxygen only two molecules of ATP are produced per molecule of glucose. From glycolysis *pyruvic acid* is produced (two molecules per molecule of glucose). This is converted to a substance universally known as *acetyl-CoA*. Then the second stage commences. This second stage (Figure 6.3), which does require

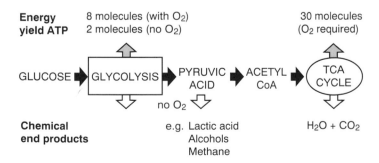

Figure 6.3 *Schematic representation of respiration and fermentation. The scheme involving glycolysis and the TCA cycle applies to most aerobic organisms, although there are differences in detail. Fermentation occurs only in the absence of oxygen. Glucose is shown as the initial substrate but other substances, notably fatty acids, can also serve as energy substrates. Note the by-products from the TCA cycle are the raw materials for photosynthesis*

oxygen, is called the *citric acid cycle*, the *tricarboxylic acid cycle* (*TCA cycle*) or the *Krebs cycle* (after Hans Krebs who contributed so much to its elucidation). The term 'cycle' is used because some intermediate products are made available for the manufacture of other organic molecules. During the TCA cycle, 30 molecules of ATP are generated per molecule of glucose, providing 38 ATP molecules in all during oxidative metabolism. The mechanism by which ATP is generated during oxidative metabolism is somewhat similar to that during photosynthesis. In fact, it seems probable that oxidative metabolism evolved from photosynthesis.

It is not only glucose that can be metabolized during respiration, but substances such as fatty acids (Page 13) and even amino acids (Page 12). In general though, glucose is metabolized preferentially, and fats are broken down only when available carbohydrate is scarce. Long-term energy storage usually involves large molecules, e.g. of starch and triglycerides. Before the energy contained in such substances can be made available to organisms, they must first be converted to much smaller molecules which then enter the various pathways of energy metabolism.

In eukaryotic organisms, oxidative energy metabolism occurs within a special organelle called the *mitochondrion* (plural mitochondria), of which there may be hundreds per cell. In aerobic prokaryotic cells, however, the same processes take place in the cellular cytoplasm.

Energy Metabolism in the Absence of Oxygen

Most organisms require a supply of oxygen and can survive for only short periods in its absence. However, there are some microorganisms, nearly all of them bacteria, which cannot survive in the *presence* of oxygen. They are appropriately referred to as *obligate anaerobes*. The photosynthetic bacteria that use hydrogen sulfide as a source of hydrogen (Page 53) are of this type, and so are certain types of heterotrophic bacteria. Under anaerobic conditions glycolysis proceeds normally. However, the pyruvic acid generated from glycolysis is then converted directly to various by-products. This is the fermentation process mentioned above (Page 54) and it is shown in Figure 6.3. The by-products of fermentation vary according to the organism involved but they include alcohols, fatty acids and carbon dioxide. Fermentation occurs only in the absence of oxygen, and it yields far less ATP than respiration. In practice far less 'work' can be done when oxygen is absent than when it is freely available. A familiar manifestation of this fact is the accumulation of dead organic matter which occurs when soils are starved of oxygen as a result of being permanently waterlogged.

Fermenting microorganisms have been used for thousands of years in certain parts of the world. During fermentation, the yeasts (unicellular fungi) generate ethanol, the principal alcohol in wine and beer, and also carbon dioxide. As carbon dioxide is such an effective rising agent, yeasts are extensively used in baking. The production of silage from grass and other forages is also due to fermentation. The process of ensiling requires the rapid exclusion of oxygen from the forage, usually in a clamp, large bag or silo. Aerobic microorganisms quickly consume the remaining oxygen and the fermenting microorganisms which take over produce a variety of acidic substances. It is the combination of anaerobic and highly acidic conditions which suppresses further biological activity and permits the material to be conserved during times of the year when insufficient fresh plant material is available.

Most organisms are either obligate aerobes (the vast majority) or fermenting obligate anaerobes. However, there are a few exceptions whose importance justifies a mention. Some microorganisms can switch between fermentation and respiration according to whether oxygen is absent or present. They are called *facultative aerobes* or *facultative anaerobes*. The yeasts are one such group of organisms. In addition, there are some types of bacteria that under anaerobic conditions use substances such as nitrate, sulfate or carbonate as a substitute for oxygen. These organisms are said to respire anaerobically, a process which is much more efficient in terms of ATP yield than fermentation.

The Energy Status of Biological Substances

Because chemical energy can be transformed to heat, the energy content of biochemical substances can be determined by measuring the heat generated when a sample of known weight is combusted. The energy content of carbohydrate and protein is similar, about 16.0 and 17.0 kilojoules per gram respectively. Fat, however, has over twice the energy density of carbohydrate and protein, about 38.0 kilojoules per gram. It is important to bear in mind that the *total* energy value of a substance as determined by its combustion is not necessarily the same as its dietary energy value. The example of starch and cellulose as human dietary components will make this point clear. As both these substances are based on glucose molecules they have similar *total* energy values. However, while starch is readily digested, humans do not produce the enzyme (cellulase) necessary to break down cellulose, which is therefore voided. (The so-called fibre component of a diet is largely cellulose.)

Nutrient Acquisition

The nutrition of organisms involves much more than energy supply. It involves the acquisition of the whole range of chemical raw materials required for synthesizing organic molecules and for the metabolic processes necessary to sustain life. Animals meet their energy and nutrient needs from the food they eat. For heterotrophic bacteria and fungi, food energy is acquired from the environment in small molecules such as sugars while nutrients such as phosphorus are absorbed more or less independently. For plants and most other photosynthesizing organisms, carbon and oxygen, supplied as carbon dioxide, are combined with the hydrogen obtained from water. The inorganic nutrients required by such organisms are taken up independently of photosynthesis. In the case of plants these nutrients are taken up through the root system, while algae absorb nutrients from the surrounding water.

Further Reading – Part One

Arthur, W. 1987 *Theories of Life: Darwin, Mendel and Beyond.* Penguin Books, London.
(Although intended as a lay person's guide, this little book provides a sound introduction to evolutionary principles.)

Dawkins, R. 1988 *The Blind Watchmaker.* Penguin Books, London.
(Finely crafted book on Darwinian evolution; accessible and guaranteed to enthuse and enlighten.)

Dawkins, R. 1996 *River Out of Eden: A Darwinian View of Life.* Phoenix, London.
(Persuasive account of Darwinian theory of evolution.)

Margulis, L. and Schwartz, K.V. 1998 *Five Kingdoms – An Illustrated Guide to the Phyla of Life on Earth,* 3rd edition. W.H. Freeman, New York.
(Detailed guide to the diversity of life; strong on functional and morphological aspects.)

O'Neill, P. 1998 *Environmental Chemistry,* 3rd edition. Blackie Academic and Professional, London.
(Very useful introductory guide to the subject with basic principles well explained.)

Postgate, J. 1986 *Microbes and Man*, 2nd edition. Penguin Books, London.

Postgate, J. 1994 *The Outer Reaches of Life.* Cambridge University Press, Cambridge.
(Pair of very readable introductory guides to various aspect of microbial life by a distinguished microbiologist.)

Rose, S. 1979 *The Chemistry of Life,* 3rd edition. Penguin Books, London.
(Accessible, concise introduction to biochemistry.)

Part Two
ECOSYSTEM FUNCTION

The distinction drawn between autotrophs and heterotrophs in Chapter 6 is of great ecological significance. Accordingly, separate chapters are devoted to these two modes of energy metabolism. We consider how organisms acquire and utilize energy, and how this information can be applied to the production of agricultural crops and livestock. The material in these two chapters also underpins an understanding of the functioning of ecosystems, which is the theme of the two chapters that follow. The first of these discusses energy flow, the second considers biogeochemical circulation.

7

Photosynthesis and Primary Production

Autotrophic organisms manufacture energy-rich organic molecules using either sunlight (photosynthesis) or simple inorganic chemicals (chemosynthesis) as an energy source. Autotrophic organisms are thus independent of other organisms for their energy needs. Most of this chapter is concerned with photosynthesis, whose importance to the biosphere was discussed in Chapter 6. The photosynthetic organisms are the 'green' plants, the algae and a few types of bacteria. The photosynthetic bacteria include the cyanobacteria, which are important in aquatic ecosystems, and other types of bacteria which are confined to anaerobic environments and which use hydrogen sulfide rather than water as a source of hydrogen.

In this chapter we consider the rates of organic matter accumulation as a result of photosynthesis and how these are affected by environmental variables. We also consider one of the most important applied aspects of photosynthesis, agricultural yield.

The Earth's Radiation Environment

Before discussing photosynthesis, some elementary principles about radiation are introduced. This will put the source of energy for photosynthesis into context. In Chapter 6 the term 'light' was used without further comment. We have an intuitive feel for what light is, but it will be helpful to elaborate a little, while recognizing that we are dealing with very complex physical phenomena. What we call 'light' occupies just a tiny part of the *electromagnetic spectrum* (Figure 7.1), which refers to the range of wavelengths over which electromagnetic waves are propagated. The wavelength ranges occupied by other forms of radiation, e.g. X-rays and radiowaves, are also shown in Figure 7.1. The term 'wave' is used because the phenomena can be thought of as being emitted as such. Waves are characterized by their length, hence *wavelength*, and also by their *frequency*. The longer the wavelength (and the shorter the frequency) the lower the energy emitted. So radiowaves (comparatively long wavelengths) are lowly energetic, while X-rays are highly energetic.

Our interest is focused on the wavelength range within which the sun's energy reaches the Earth. (The amount of energy which is intercepted at a particular location is referred to as the ***irradiance***.) The irradiance at the upper boundary of the Earth's atmosphere is called the ***solar constant***, and it is about 1360 joules m^{-2} s$^{-1.}$ The wavelength range at this boundary is approximately 200–8000 nm (1 nm = 10^{-9} m). As the radiation passes through the Earth's atmosphere, just over 50 per cent is lost through reflection, absorption or scattering by gases and particles. As a result, the wavelength range, or ***solar spectrum***, at ground level (300–3000 nm) is less than at the outer atmosphere. Irradiance varies considerably over the Earth's surface: it varies from the equator to the poles and it varies according to cloud cover and to altitude.

The part of the spectrum called 'light' extends approximately between 380 and 760 nm. This wavelength range is also called 'visible radiation' because the human eye is sensitive to such wavelengths. The phrase 'white light' is also used. When white light is passed through a prism, a colour spectrum is produced, from violet at one end to red at the other (Figure 7.1).

The range of wavelengths which activate the photosynthetic process (the ***photosynthetically active range***, or ***PAR***) lies just within the wavelength range of visible radiation. The energy within PAR is slightly less than half the irradiance at the Earth's surface. The pigment chlorophyll, which is necessary for the photosynthetic reactions, strongly absorbs blue and, particularly, red light but transmits green light.

Solar radiation of shorter wavelengths than PAR is called ***ultraviolet*** (***UV***) radiation. (The human eye sees hardly any UV radiation, so strictly we should not speak of UV light.) Ultraviolet radiation is categorized as UV-C (<280 nm), UV-B (280–320 nm) and UV-A (320–400 nm). The amount of UV radiation reaching the Earth's surface is dependent primarily upon the concentration of atmospheric ozone. UV-C is almost entirely screened out by ozone, together with most of the UV-B, whereas UV-A is hardly influenced by ozone. UV-C is also responsible for ozone production. This is because molecular oxygen (O_2), when exposed to UV-C, is split into two oxygen atoms, which in turn combine with oxygen molecules to form ozone.

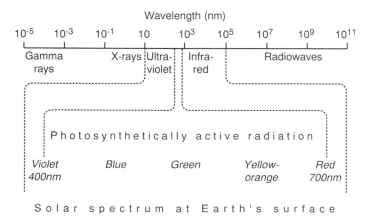

Figure 7.1   *The electromagnetic spectrum. The wavelength range of photosynthetically active radiation, which approximately coincides with light, occupies a very small part of the complete spectrum*

Although UV wavelengths account for only 7 per cent of the solar radiation received at the Earth's surface, these are strongly absorbed by proteins and nucleic acids and can thus impair cell function. (It is no coincidence that the incidence of skin cancer is highest among fair-skinned people in areas such as Queensland, Australia, and the south-western United States.) Evidence for ozone depletion has resulted in international action to phase out the use of chlorofluorocarbons, a group of chemical substances responsible for ozone destruction.

At wavelengths longer than the visible range lie *far-red* and *infrared* radiation. Plants contain pigments which are sensitive to the amount of radiation in the far-red range, and the ratio of red to far-red radiation is important in some developmental processes in plants. Infrared radiation, which is 'invisible' to the human eye, is also called heat.

Light has been characterized as a form of electromagnetic radiation which travels as waves. There is an alternative theory which envisages light as a stream of energy-carrying particles called *photons*. The energy associated with each photon is inversely proportional to the wavelength. Irradiance values are often expressed as *photon flux density*.

Over two-thirds of the Earth's surface is covered by water. As electromagnetic waves pass through water, they are absorbed and scattered differentially. The 'visible' red, together with the infrared wavebands, are absorbed by the water itself in the first half metre or so, reducing the energy by about one-half. In clear water the blue–green wavebands extend much deeper than the red and yellow wavebands. However, the presence of substances in the water, including living algae, has a considerable effect on the rate at which the different wavebands are reduced.

In a water body photosynthesis is confined to the upper, illuminated layer, called the *euphotic*, or *photic zone* (Figure 7.2). The depth of the euphotic zone varies considerably. It varies at each location in response to changes in irradiance and the turbidity of the water, and it varies spatially. In some tropical oceanic water, photosynthesis may occur to depths in excess of 150 metres, but elsewhere the euphotic zone is much less deep. In estuarine waters, which typically contain a considerable amount of material in suspension and in solution, the euphotic zone may not extend beyond a few metres. In shallow water, sufficient light may be available to permit photosynthesis by bottom-dwelling organisms such as sea-grasses. The community of organisms which lives on the sea- or lake-floor is called the *benthos*, and the area they inhabit is termed the *benthic zone*, while the main part of the water body forms the *pelagic zone* (Figure 7.2).

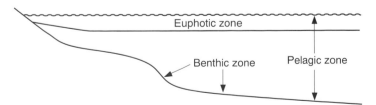

Figure 7.2 *Zones in a body of water. The euphotic zone extends to the depth at which light is adequate for photosynthesis. The depth of the euphotic zone varies both spatially and temporally*

Chlorophyll and Chloroplasts

In the photosynthetic process, radiant energy of particular wavelengths is absorbed by molecules of chlorophyll. There is more than one type of chlorophyll: plants typically contain two forms, known as chlorophyll$_a$ and chlorophyll$_b$, both of which differ from the chlorophyll found in photosynthetic bacteria. When otherwise healthy plant leaves are tinged with colours other than green, it usually means that other sorts of pigments are masking the chlorophyll. The chlorophyll of plants and algae is located within organelles called ***chloroplasts***, but in the photosynthetic bacteria, which have no organelles, the chlorophyll is associated with the outer membranes of cells.

The carbon dioxide used by plants in photosynthesis diffuses from the atmosphere into the intercellular spaces of the leaf via tiny pores (***stoma***) in the leaf surface (Figure 7.3). These pores are surrounded by ***guard cells*** whose water status determines the size of the pore; the whole apparatus is termed a ***stomate*** (plural ***stomata***). The carbon dioxide then goes into solution before passing into cells where it is assimilated as organic molecules.

Gross and Net Photosynthesis

All work carried out within a cell involves an expenditure of energy. So while green plants are photosynthesizing they are also respiring, i.e. breaking down the chemical products of photosynthesis (Page 54). ***Gross photosynthesis*** refers to the total amount of energy captured in chemical form, or the carbon assimilated, before an allowance is made

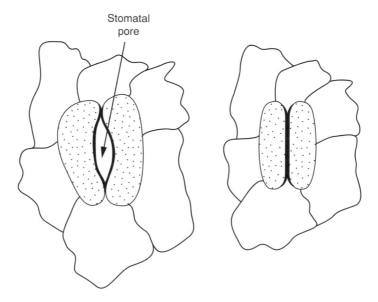

Stomatal
pore

Figure 7.3   *A stomatal apparatus viewed from above a leaf surface. The size of stomatal pores alters in response to changes in the water content of the surrounding guard cells (shaded), thereby altering the conductivity of carbon dioxide and water vapour*

for respiration. ***Net photosynthesis*** refers to the amount of photosynthesis after respiratory losses are taken into account. If a plant uses up more energy in respiration than it gains in photosynthesis during a particular period then it will contain less energy, and effectively weigh less, at the end of the period than at the beginning.

The amount of photosynthetic tissue (which is usually the total area of leaves) relative to the amount of living, but non-photosynthetic tissue, therefore has an important influence on the rate at which a plant grows. A plant from which most of the leaves have been removed may not assimilate carbon rapidly enough to balance the inevitable respiratory losses from its non-photosynthetic parts such as roots and stems. The carbon economy of a plant is clearly crucial to its performance.

Environmental Effects on Photosynthesis

Some Background

The rate at which a leaf, or a plant, assimilates carbon during photosynthesis varies according to the prevailing environmental conditions. The relationship between photosynthetic rate and some key environmental variables is discussed in this section. This will provide essential reference material for some very important ecological concepts, including how the biosphere may respond to global climatic change. It will also facilitate understanding of some of the factors determining the yield of agricultural crops.

Before looking at the environmental variables in turn, we need to introduce the idea that plants can be categorized into two major groups according to their photosynthetic characteristics. These are referred to respectively as C_3 and C_4 plants. (C_3 and C_4 also refer to the types of photosynthesis.) The expressions C_3 and C_4 are used because the first stable product of photosynthesis is, respectively, a 3-carbon compound (phosphoglyceric acid) or a 4-carbon compound (aspartic acid or malic acid depending on type of plant). C_3 and C_4 plants differ in their biochemical and anatomical details, but our interest is based on their different responses to environmental variables.

The sequence of biochemical reactions by which carbon dioxide is 'fixed' was worked out in the 1940s by a research team led by the late Melvin Calvin at the University of California. (For his major contribution to understanding this key life process Calvin was awarded a Nobel prize.) This series of reactions became known as the ***Calvin cycle***, and it was assumed that carbon dioxide was 'fixed' in more or less the same way in all plants. In the 1960s, however, it became clear that this was not the case. Some plants were shown to fix carbon dioxide initially using an alternative pathway, which became known as the C_4 pathway. The cells which fix carbon in this way later pass carbon dioxide on to other cells where it is fixed by the Calvin cycle.

Of the plants examined so far only about 5 per cent have the C_4 mode of photosynthesis. They are mainly confined to parts of the tropics, subtropics and warm temperate zones where there is a prolonged hot dry season. However, even in these zones C_3 plants are usually predominant. Among important food plants, wheat, barley, rice, soy(a)bean and potato are C_3 species, whereas sugar cane and maize (corn) are C_4 species.

Photosynthesis and Light

The effect of different light levels on photosynthesis in leaves of typical C_3 and C_4 plants is shown in Figure 7.4a. (In the laboratory, and in the field, the *apparent* rate of photosynthesis can be determined by measuring the loss of carbon dioxide from an air

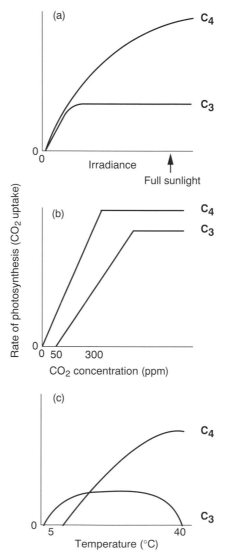

Figure 7.4 *Relationships between the rate of net photosynthesis and (a) light, (b) carbon dioxide, and (c) temperature for leaves of plants with the C_3 and C_4 modes of photosynthesis. No values for carbon dioxide uptake are shown but the scale is an arithmetic one. There is considerable variation between species within each of the two major groups*

stream passed over an enclosed leaf or plant.) It should be understood that these graphs are shown to illustrate the principal differences between the two major types of photosynthesis although in practice there is considerable variation within each group. First, note the response of the C_3 plant. As the light level increases above the minimum necessary for photosynthesis, the rate of photosynthesis increases more or less linearly. This suggests that the availability of light energy is limiting the photosynthetic process. As irradiance increases further, the proportional rise in photosynthetic rate becomes less and less. The light level beyond which photosynthesis fails to respond any further is known as the ***light saturation point***: for C_3 leaves it is typically 25–30 per cent of full sunlight. The C_4 leaf shows a broadly similar response to the C_3 leaf at low irradiance, but differs markedly at higher light levels. It does not 'light saturate': the rate of photosynthesis continues to increase, right up to full sunlight. Notice that the photosynthetic rate at all light levels, except for the lowest, is greater for the C_4 leaf than for the C_3 leaf. This difference increases progressively at light levels above the saturation point for the C_3 leaf.

Photosynthesis and Carbon Dioxide

C_3 and C_4 plants also respond differently to changes in ambient carbon dioxide levels (Figure 7.4b). First, while C_4 leaves typically continue to take up carbon dioxide at ambient concentrations close to zero, C_3 leaves do not assimilate carbon dioxide below about 50 parts per million (ppm). Second, C_4 leaves tend not to respond to ambient carbon dioxide in excess of about 300 ppm (which is a little less than the current atmospheric concentration), whereas C_3 leaves respond to carbon dioxide levels considerably in excess of this value. Thus commercial growers can boost photosynthesis by generating carbon dioxide artificially in glasshouses. (Obviously their efforts would be in vain if they were growing C_4 plants and the carbon dioxide level was already around 300 ppm.)

A satisfactory explanation as to why C_3 and C_4 plants respond differently to ambient carbon dioxide concentrations is really beyond the scope of this book. However, it is useful to appreciate that whereas C_3 leaves release carbon dioxide in the light, C_4 leaves do not. This is because of a biochemical pathway in C_3 leaves which breaks down some of the intermediate products of photosynthesis. This process, which is induced by light, is called ***photorespiration***: it does not appear to serve any useful function and is sometimes described as 'wasteful'. In contrast, C_4 leaves do not release carbon dioxide in daylight. Essentially, this is because enzymes in the outer cells of the leaf (called mesophyll cells) are very efficient at assimilating any carbon dioxide present as malic or aspartic acid. Thus, C_4 leaves can continue fixing carbon when ambient carbon dioxide concentrations are very low. In C_3 leaves, however, the amount of carbon fixed in photosynthesis is insufficient to compensate for the carbon lost as a result of photorespiration if carbon dioxide concentrations fall to around 50 ppm.

The photosynthetic response of plants to carbon dioxide is currently of considerable interest because of the upward trend in atmospheric concentration of this gas (Chapter 10). It is sometimes asserted that a rising carbon dioxide concentration is desirable because it will bring about increased crop yields through a higher overall rate of photosynthesis. However, yield is a complex subject: its understanding requires much more than information on the short-term response of leaves to changes in carbon dioxide. Moreover, the continued rise in atmospheric carbon is likely to be associated with shifts in temperature and rainfall patterns, both of which are critical to crop production. So it is not yet possible to make confident predictions about the effects of rising carbon dioxide levels on world agriculture and yield.

Photosynthesis and Temperature

C_3 plants, particularly those from outside the tropics, typically reveal a comparatively low minimum threshold temperature for photosynthesis (Figure 7.4c), although there is considerable variation between species. Also, their photosynthetic rates are near maximum over quite a wide temperature range. In contrast, C_4 plants tend to have a higher minimum temperature for photosynthesis, but the rate of carbon fixation increases rapidly as the temperature rises (Figure 7.4c). The temperature at which photosynthesis is at its maximum is usually higher for C_4 plants than for C_3 plants, and, again, maximum photosynthetic rates are greater for the former group.

The effect of temperature on photosynthesis is of course complicated by the fact that the rate of respiration is strongly temperature dependent. As the temperature increases, the rate of respiration rises. At very high temperatures, therefore, the rate at which carbon is used in respiration could be equal to the gross photosynthetic rate, in which case no growth would occur.

Photosynthesis and Water

Water is another environmental factor whose supply affects the rate of photosynthesis. The availability of water in the soil (or in a cell) is conventionally referred to as the ***water potential***. Essentially, the water potential of pure water is zero, and as more and more solutes (e.g. sugar or salt) are added, the water potential progressively declines, i.e. becomes increasingly negative. The unit of pressure in which water potential is usually expressed is the pascal (Pa), or megapascal, although bars are used in the earlier literature (1 bar is equivalent to 1×10^5 pascals).

As the water potential of the soil falls, i.e. as the soil becomes drier, the photosynthetic rate tends to decline, although the response of species varies very considerably. The mechanisms which cause these responses are even now not completely understood, despite decades of intensive work. It is important to realize, however, that photosynthesis and water loss from a plant are coupled. This is because the stomatal pores (Figure 7.3) serve as the principal route both for the loss of water vapour and the uptake of carbon dioxide. These pores open and close in response to the amount of water in the two surrounding guard cells. The guard cells have a rigid section of cell wall adjacent to the pore. This thickening ensures that as the cells fill with water and expand, they tend to pull apart, and increase the aperture of the pore. Conversely, as water is lost from the guard cells, they decrease in size and rigidity, and the stomate closes. Hormones can also bring about stomata closure, in fact, rather more rapidly than by a loss of guard cell hydrature.

Stomata have been shown to sense, and be responsive to, atmospheric humidity. A lowered humidity (at constant temperature) means increased potential for evaporation and hence greater water loss from the plant leaf. Stomata tend to close in response to lowered humidity, and open when the atmospheric humidity increases, although there is considerable variation between plant species in this respect.

Life for land plants is clearly something of a compromise in terms of water loss and carbon gain. Closed stomata may effectively restrict water loss, but such a state is not conducive to rapid photosynthesis and growth. On the other hand, wide-open stomata may permit a rapid rate of carbon dioxide diffusion and assimilation, but only at the expense of excessive water loss. The water and carbon economies of plants are therefore closely coupled.

In general, C_4 plants tend to be less responsive than C_3 species to a drop in water availability, which might be anticipated from the geographical zones in which they are concentrated. C_4 plants also tend to have higher water use efficiencies than C_3 plants, typically requiring only 250–350 grams of water per gram of dry matter produced compared with the 550–650 grams of water per gram of dry weight required by C_3 plants.

Some plant species found in hot, dry environments possess a special type of photosynthesis, called ***crassulacean acid metabolism (CAM)***. Such plants take up carbon dioxide during the night through open stomata. The carbon is chemically combined (as molecules of malic acid), and released internally during the succeeding daylight period to be fixed in photosynthesis. By opening stomata at night, and keeping stomata closed during the day, when water loss is potentially excessive, these plants conserve moisture. However, the 'cost' of doing so is a slow rate of growth.

Water is obviously a key environmental factor for plants, often determining their rate of growth and their distribution, both locally and globally. (This theme is returned to in Chapter 14.) While photosynthesis tends to decline with decreasing water potentials (decreased water availability), much of the variation between species is based on differences in the capacity to acquire and conserve water. Some plants therefore effectively *avoid* the problem of water stress. No plant can continue photosynthesis at extreme dehydration. Tolerance to such conditions is based on mechanisms that permit tissues to retain their ability to function during periods of dehydration and to photosynthesize again when rehydrated.

The Efficiency of Photosynthesis

The efficiency with which solar energy is converted to chemical energy in photosynthesis is quite low. The maximum theoretical photosynthetic efficiency for an individual leaf under optimum conditions is only about 17 per cent, but under more natural conditions much lower values are normal. Values of around 10 per cent might be maintained for short periods, but averaged over a whole year photosynthetic efficiency is usually less than 2 per cent. For the Earth's biota as a whole, photosynthetic efficiency is only a fraction of a per cent on an annual basis. Part of the explanation for this low efficiency is that the cover of photosynthetic tissue in many regions is incomplete for a whole year, a fact that is evident to anyone who lives in a seasonal environment. Much incident radiation is thus 'wasted' as far as photosynthesis is concerned. Even where a green cover is maintained throughout the year, photosynthesis is severely constrained by low temperatures or inadequate moisture outside the so-called growing season. But even during the growing season, photosynthesis is limited by various environmental factors such as temperature, light, nutrients and water. In addition, as most plants (C_3) light saturate at around 30 per cent of full sunlight, light levels in excess of this value depress the efficiency of light capture. In large measure, though, the very low efficiency with which solar energy is converted to chemical energy is explained by the photosynthetic process itself. Despite the low efficiency of solar energy conversion, the annual amount of chemical energy made available by photosynthesis is enormous, exceeding by far the world's energy consumption.

Primary Production

Because photosynthetic (and chemosynthetic) organisms manufacture the organic building blocks on which all life depends, they are called ***primary producers***. ***Primary productivity*** refers to the *rate* at which organic matter is produced. It is important to appreciate that the amount of plant material (plant ***biomass***) within an area is not the same as the productivity. There could be several hundreds of tonnes of plant dry matter in a hectare of forest, but unless we know the period of time it has taken for that amount of biomass to accumulate, how much plant material has died, and how much has been consumed by herbivores, we can infer very little about the primary productivity of the forest.

Primary productivity values are presented as units of weight (usually grams or tonnes of dry matter or carbon), or in energy terms (joules are now standard, but formerly calories were commonly used). These values are expressed on a unit area basis and, because it is a rate, on a unit time basis as well. If energy values are available for both solar energy input and primary production for a given area and period, the efficiency of energy capture can be determined. Productivity values are commonly presented on a calendar-year basis, enabling comparison between community types, between geographical areas and between years. In cases where interest centres on variation in productivity within a year, and how this variation correlates with particular environmental variables, data for shorter intervals are required.

The distinction drawn earlier between gross and net photosynthesis applies also to primary production. ***Gross primary production*** is the total amount of carbon, or energy, fixed before an allowance is made for respiratory losses: ***net primary production*** is what remains after respiration. In resource terms, then, it is net primary production that is of principal interest. A compilation of annual net primary productivity values is shown for comparative purposes in Table 7.1. In round figures, 4000 g m^{-2} year^{-1} seems to represent a convenient ceiling value. Although most values fall well below this amount there is evidence that productivity in some tropical wetlands is much greater than this value.

In general, primary productivity is lower in aquatic situations than on land. But, as the table shows, there is some overlap: productivity can be very high around coral reefs and in some estuaries, while on land productivity tends to be low at high latitudes, high altitudes and in dry deserts. Notice the wide range of values within each of the specified

Table 7.1 *Suggested range of annual net primary production values for a variety of community types: compiled from various data sets*

Community type	Productivity (g m^{-2} yr^{-1})
Tropical forest	1000–3500
Temperate forest	600–2500
Boreal forest	400–2000
Tropical grassland	500–3000
Temperate grassland	400–1500
Tundra and alpine	50–400
Desert and semi-desert	10–500
Agricultural land	100–5000
Swamps and marshes	800–3500
Lakes and streams	100–1500
Open ocean	50–400
Nutrient-rich ocean	500–4000

community types. Part of this variation may be attributed to real variation. In part it is because production varies from year to year, perhaps because of differences in the weather. Partly, it is due to methodology. This is because it is extremely difficult to measure primary productivity accurately. It is particularly difficult to obtain reliable values for the productivity of underground plant parts.

Differences in annual primary productivity values are explicable mainly in terms of the variation in the availability of resources, notably light, water and nutrients, and differences in other environmental factors, particularly temperature. Table 7.1 shows some geographical trends in productivity. Within humid zones the annual productivity of both lowland forest and grassland tends to increase from higher to lower latitudes, which correlates with the total amount of time during the year when photosynthesis occurs (Figure 7.5a). Within subhumid, semi-arid and arid zones there is a reasonable

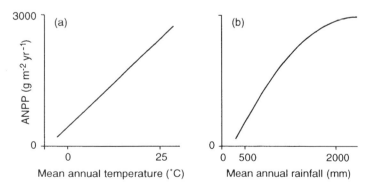

Figure 7.5 *General relationships between annual net primary production (ANPP) and (a) mean annual temperature (assuming moisture is not a major limiting factor) and (b) annual rainfall. The shaded areas indicate that considerable variation in annual productivity occurs at each level of temperature and rainfall*

relationship between annual rainfall and primary productivity (Figure 7.5b), despite the fact that annual rainfall is a fairly crude estimate of moisture availability for plant use. Much of the rain may fall in storm events and be quickly lost by overland flow, or may fall at times of the year when temperatures are too low for plant growth. Nonetheless, moisture is the principal constraint on production over much of the Earth's land area.

In aquatic environments, nutrient availability is usually the critical factor limiting primary productivity on an annual basis. It is of course the nutrient availability in the euphotic zone that is important because it is here that photosynthesis occurs. In freshwater, phosphorus is generally the key limiting nutrient, although there is a tendency for productivity to decline with increasing latitude. In the open oceans annual primary productivity does not decrease with increasing latitude. Rather, it seems that the availability of nitrogen is usually the critical factor. However, this may not be a universal rule because either phosphorus, or the trace element iron, or some other element may be in critically short supply. (Nutrient availability in water is discussed further in Chapter 10.)

This brief overview of the relationship between primary productivity and environment is highly generalized. A satisfactory explanation of what is constraining production in a particular situation requires detailed studies, both of the environment and the organisms within it. When discussing limiting factors, it is useful to distinguish between environmental factors that limit productivity on an annual basis and those that limit productivity at any instant in time. In dry deserts, for example, moisture availability is the key limiting factor for annual production. However, just after a rain storm, water may not be the limiting factor; it could be air temperature, or the availability of some nutrient. Similarly, on an annual basis, key nutrients may be limiting productivity in the oceans surrounding Antarctica, but at any time during the long Antarctic winter it is light that is the critical limiting factor.

Vegetation Components of Primary Production

Environmental factors provide the chief constraint to primary production. However, features of the vegetation also influence the level of primary productivity by interacting with the physical environment. These features are also important to an understanding of agricultural yield, which is discussed in the next section. The key components of plant productivity are:

- the photosynthetic rate per unit area of leaf (*net assimilation rate*, or *NAR*);
- the amount of leaf area per unit area of ground (*leaf area index*, or *LAI*);
- the time that the leaf area index covers the ground (*leaf area duration,* or *LAD*);
- the ratio of photosynthetic to non-photosynthetic tissue (*leaf area ratio*, or *LAR*).

In an earlier discussion of how photosynthesis responds to environmental variables, we focused on individual leaves. Primary productivity, however, requires a consideration of communities of plants. It is not possible simply to extrapolate results from individual leaves to whole communities. In fact, differences in photosynthetic rate per unit area of leaf (NAR) rarely seem to be responsible for differences in production of plants within the same area. Much more important is LAI, because the area of photosynthesizing tissue largely determines the photosynthetic capacity of vegetation. What is required for maximum production is a LAI sufficient to intercept as much incident light energy as possible. This amount varies between vegetation types and depends on the structure of the constituent species. Optimum LAI values for herbaceous plants typically lie within the range of two to eight, but can be much higher. In general, erect leaf angles permit less light saturation (important in C_3 species) and greater light penetration than horizontal leaves. Leaves situated below the light compensation point for photosynthesis tend to die and fall from the plant. Obviously, the period of time that there is leaf cover (LAD) is a key variable. Under natural conditions this period often matches the times of the year when growth is possible. The leaf area ratio is also important. It may seem logical that the productive potential of plants should increase with an increase in ratio of photosynthetic to non-photosynthetic tissue. However, this ignores the fact that plants require nutrients and water: a restricted root system may severely restrict a plant's capacity to procure these resources. Also, plants must get their leaves into the light, which involves extension growth. Moreover, if a plant is to pass on its genes to successive generations it must produce reproductive organs.

Agricultural Yield

The most important 'applied' aspect of photosynthetic research is the production of plants for food and fibre. *Yield*, in an agricultural sense, is not the same as primary production, although the same processes are involved. The key difference is that while annual primary production refers to the *total* amount of organic matter that accumulates, yield refers to specific components of the plant. For cereal crops it is the grain; for sugar cane and sugar beet it is the sugar sucrose; for potatoes it is the tuber; for soy(a)beans and oil-seed rape it is protein and oil; for apples and raspberries it is the fruit. The major exceptions to this generalization are forage crops such as grasses and clover whose total above-ground growth constitutes the yield component. The proportion of production accounted for by the principal yield component is known as the *harvest index*, which is usually expressed on a dry weight basis when the crop is harvested. For cereals, only the above-ground part of the plant is normally used when calculating the harvest index, but for crops grown for their subterranean parts (e.g. potatoes) the ratio must be calculated differently. It is worth noting here that agricultural yields are often expressed on a *fresh* weight basis. Crops with a high water content, such as potatoes, may therefore appear to be very productive. So care is needed when comparing the productivity of natural vegetation with the yield of agricultural crops.

Key factors determining yield in crops are the size and longevity of the leaf canopy, the efficiency with which the leaf canopy captures solar radiation, and the efficiency with which assimilates are allocated to the principal yield component. It is clear that the attainment of a critical minimum leaf area index as early as possible – assuming the environment is suitable for growth – and its maintenance for as long as possible, are very important. Somewhat surprisingly perhaps, differences between genotypes in photosynthetic rate per unit area of leaf have played little part in yield improvement.

The plant characteristic chiefly responsible for the spectacular increases in crop yields during the past few decades has been the harvest index. The total production of wheat and rice, for example, has changed little in the last 50 years, but over this period the proportion of assimilates allocated to the grain has progressively increased. Harvest index values in cereals now commonly exceed 50 per cent in some varieties. This high value has been associated with a shortening in the height of plants by incorporating genes for dwarfing. Plants of shorter stature are, understandably, better able to support the enlarged heads of grain.

The science of agronomy is concerned with identifying the factors which limit crop yield and devising ways of overcoming them. The techniques involve the selection and breeding of plant genotypes that perform well under particular environmental conditions, environmental modification (e.g. drainage, irrigation, fertilization), reducing crop losses caused by pests and diseases and by competition from weeds, and improving husbandry and management.

Until comparatively recently, yields were increased by selecting those individual plants which yielded most, and breeding from them in the hope that their superiority was inherited. Such breeding has become more and more scientific during the 20th century, although it is based on practices which have been in use for many centuries. By empirically selecting for desirable traits such as high yield, the factors responsible for that high yield must also have been unconsciously selected. In the last few decades a lot of attention has been paid to identifying the key factors that contribute to yield, which are the same sorts of factors (NAR, LAI, LAD, LAR) that we discussed earlier.

More recently, advances in biotechnology (Page 35) have permitted genes from other species, and not only plant species, to be incorporated into crop plants. This hugely increases the gene pool available for crop improvement. Introduced genes may change yield components, confer resistance to pesticides, or increase tolerance to salinity or drought.

Modifying the environment of crops, through greater use of fertilizers, irrigation and drainage, and by improved crop protection, has also played a key role in increasing crop yield. In fact, changes in the crop environment have been associated with changes in genotype. For example, modern cereal varieties are more responsive to high levels of nitrogen application than older varieties. High levels of nitrogen, which act primarily by building up photosynthetic area to ensure a high rate of light capture, have been particularly influential. The increased use of irrigation water is another major factor responsible for yield increase. Some 80 per cent of the water used worldwide is applied to crops, and high-yield agriculture in dry zones is absolutely dependent upon artificial water application. Yield losses to pests, pathogenic agents and weeds have been reduced by more effective crop protection, usually involving the application of chemicals.

Although the problem of agricultural surpluses often seems more important than shortages in the West, the issue of global and regional food security is one of continuing concern. Questions are again being asked about how food supplies can be increased significantly in the future against a background of continued population increase, and probable climatic change. There is clearly a limit to the photosynthetic efficiency and to the harvest index. There are also limits to the extent to which crops can be protected from weeds, pests and pathogenic organisms. 'Miracle' crops do not appear to be on the immediate horizon, so the spectacular increases in yield demonstrated by the 'Green

Revolution' wheat and rice varieties in the 1960s and 1970s may not be repeated in the near future. Probably the best hope for the immediate future lies in improved management, for example by matching crop varieties to local conditions, timing more effectively the application of nutrients and water, and better management of weeds, pests and pathogens. Where climate and soil type are essentially uniform, there is usually a big difference between the average yield and the greatest yield. This suggests that opportunities exist for raising yield by changes in management practices.

Of course, agricultural yields do not simply depend on technical and biological factors. Of great importance is the matrix of social, cultural, economic and political conditions in which agriculture is set. The application of nitrogen may well improve yields, but this information is of little use if the farmers cannot afford to purchase fertilizer. In some situations it is war, or social unrest, which is the principal constraint on agricultural output. Local preferences are also important: there is no advantage in introducing a high-yielding crop variety if it is unpalatable.

Another crucial issue is the environmental costs which are incurred in attempting to raise agricultural yield. For example, intensive arable cropping may lead to unacceptable losses of topsoil by erosion; pesticide use may impact upon wildlife and public health; high levels of nitrogen application may raise nitrate to an unacceptable level in water supplies; reliance on a limited genetic base increases the vulnerability to pathogens and insects; irrigation in dry zones tends to raise the concentrations of salts in surface soils and demands effective drainage. Clearly, the intensification of agriculture in an attempt to raise yields has implications, not only for the immediate agricultural ecosystem, but also for public health, for wildlife and for the wider physical environment. Minimizing such costs while progressively increasing yields from the global farm provides one of the greatest challenges for the 21st century.

8

Heterotrophic Organisms and Secondary Production

Heterotrophs are organisms which cannot harness an external source of energy to manufacture organic molecules: they therefore consume 'ready-made' energy-rich molecules. These they obtain either directly from other living organisms, their waste substances or their dead remains. All heterotrophic organisms therefore share a dependence on other organisms. All animals, all fungi, most protists and most bacteria are heterotrophic. Four of the five kingdoms of organisms (Page 46) are therefore exclusively, or mainly, heterotrophic. The energy-rich organic molecules consumed by heterotrophs are broken down in the process of respiration, or fermentation, to generate ATP for useful work (Chapter 6). Another important point is that only a few types of heterotrophs, notably fungi and bacteria, can manufacture amino acids, which are the building blocks of proteins. Other heterotrophs require amino acids or protein in their diet, unless they harbour organisms such as fungi and bacteria within their digestive tracts.

Because heterotrophic organisms rely on preformed organic molecules they are referred to as the *secondary producers* in ecosystems. *Secondary productivity* is defined as the *rate* of organic matter accumulation by heterotrophs and, as for primary productivity, its values are presented in dry weight or energy terms, per unit area per unit time.

The Acquisition of Food

Although feeding mechanisms differ considerably between heterotrophic organisms, as a first approximation we can distinguish between two major groups. One group, represented best by fungi and bacteria, do not have specialized mouth parts. Instead, they release enzymes into their environment and the enzymes bring about the breakdown, or digestion, of complex organic substances (e.g. fats, proteins, starch, cellulose and lignin). The end products of external digestion (e.g. amino acids, sugars) are small enough to be absorbed by bacterial and fungal cells and used in metabolism (Figure 8.1).

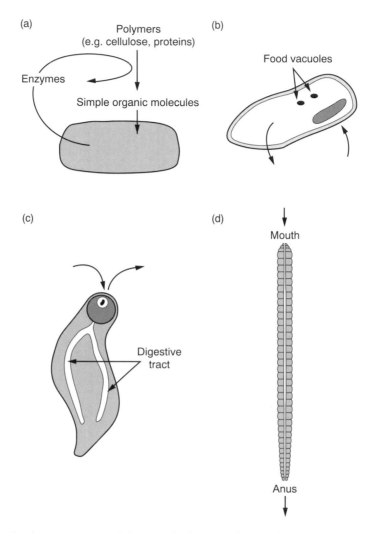

Figure 8.1   *Food procurement and digestion by heterotrophs. (a) Absorption: bacteria and fungi release enzymes which break down polymers to small molecules which are then absorbed. (b) A paramecium: in this unicellular protist digestion takes place within the cell. (c) A fluke, a type of parasitic flatworm: the same orifice is used for ingestion and elimination. (d) An earthworm: with a digestive tract having separate openings for ingestion and elimination of undigested food, this organism provides a model for most larger animals*

Such organisms can be referred to informally as 'absorbers'. They perform vital ecological roles, notably by decomposing organic matter and by releasing inorganic nutrients for subsequent uptake by other organisms.

In contrast to bacteria and fungi, most animals possess an internal space in which digestion occurs, and also a specialized feeding apparatus. Such organisms can be referred to as 'ingesters'. Again, the conversion of large, complex organic molecules to smaller, simpler substances is controlled mainly by enzymes, although enzyme activity is

(a)

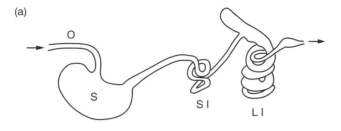

(b)

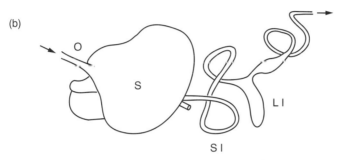

Figure 8.2 *Main features of (a) a simple-stomached mammal, and (b) a ruminant mammal. The stomach of the ruminant is a much enlarged, multichambered space, which functions as a fermentation chamber. O – oesophagus; S – stomach; SI – small intestine; LI – large intestine*

frequently supplemented by physical action. Mobile animals exercise considerable control over the amount and the type of food they eat. By contrast, feeding in most sessile aquatic organism is rather passive: food is simply filtered out of the surrounding water.

For most 'ingesters', the digestive tract can be likened to a tube which extends from the mouth to the anus. Such an animal is represented by the earthworm in Figure 8.1, although in most animals the digestive tract is much more differentiated (Figure 8.2). A key point with all the 'ingesters' is that digestion is external to the animal's cells. Only molecules which are less than a particular size can be absorbed across the wall of the digestive tract, and are therefore available for metabolic activities. (For most animal types, these substances are transported in the bloodstream.) Not all heterotrophs fit comfortably into either of these two major groups. The unicellular paramecium draws food particles into the cell where digestion takes place, which is unusual, while the flatworm uses the same orifice for ingesting food and expelling undigested materials (Figure 8.1).

The Fate of Ingested Food Energy

The fate of the food which is ingested by animals provides important principles for understanding ecosystem function and the exploitation of heterotrophs as a source of food. Again, energy is used as the common currency. However, energy is not the only factor in nutrition. Food also provides the chemical raw materials required by the animal for synthesizing organic molecules, and also the vitamins and minerals essential for normal functioning.

A point to bear in mind when discussing growth in animals is that the energy content of a gram of fat is over twice that of carbohydrate and protein (Page 57). So, if the proportion of fat alters in an animal, the change in weight and the change in total energy content will be different. For example, if fat is broken down and protein is manufactured, total energy content could fall while dry weight remains constant, or even increases. The same principle applies to plants: it is simply that the fat content of most plants is insignificant, while in animals, particularly vertebrates, fat often makes a major contribution to body mass.

A general scheme for the fate of food energy in a typical animal is shown in Figure 8.3. We will follow this scheme, elaborating on points which provide insights to secondary production. First, a variable proportion of ingested food passes out of the digestive tract unused as faeces. Hence, only part of the ingested food energy is absorbed across the wall of the digestive tract. The *digestibility* of a foodstuff is very important because it determines the amount of food energy that is potentially available to the animal. In addition, food which has a low digestibility takes longer to process than food which has a high digestibility. Thus digestibility affects the amount of food which is eaten. Digestibility values vary considerably; they vary between species eating the same type of food and for the same animal on different diets. Information concerning typical digestibility values for particular types of animal is vital in compiling rations for domestic livestock.

For any type of animal, the key factor influencing digestibility is the chemical composition of the food. Plant tissues which are rich in cellulose and lignin are much less digestible than tissues which are low in these substances. For cows, digestibility of young grass and cereal grains may be over 80 per cent, but for old grass and cereal straw digestibility is usually lower than 40 per cent.

Animal species differ considerably in their capacity to utilize cellulose, which is the principal component of plant cell walls. For an animal to make use of a plant's cellular contents, the cell walls must be ruptured, and if the energy potential of the cellulose itself

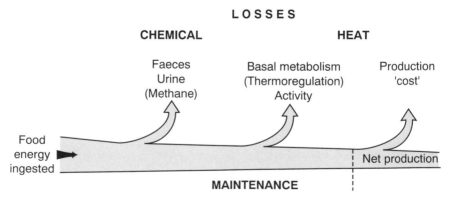

Figure 8.3   *The fate of food energy consumed by an animal. Energy is 'lost' either in chemical form (faeces, urine, methane) or as heat from respiration. A maintenance diet is that at which net production is zero*

is to be used, it must first be digested. Also, cellulose is usually closely associated with lignin, which further reduces its digestibility. The key point is that animal species do not produce the enzyme **cellulase**, which breaks down cellulose to release glucose. However, certain microorganisms, notably some groups of bacteria and fungi, do produce this enzyme, and can therefore use cellulose as an energy source. As some types of animals harbour cellulose-digesting microorganisms in the digestive tract they are able to utilize cellulose-rich diets.

The association between cellulose-digesting microbes and their animal hosts is most highly developed in **ruminant** animals, for example deer, antelope, giraffes, cattle, sheep, goats and camels. Ruminant animals have a multichambered, much enlarged stomach (Figure 8.2b) in which a community of cellulose-digesting bacteria resides, along with protozoans and fungi. Conditions in the rumen are anaerobic, so it functions essentially as a fermentation chamber. Here, the resident bacteria release the enzyme cellulase (just as their free-living counterparts do), which breaks down cellulose to glucose. Other bacteria utilize the glucose molecules and release fatty acids which are then absorbed across the rumen wall. Ruminants also regurgitate partially digested food to the mouth for further physical breakdown (cud-chewing) which further enhances its availability to the animal's microbial residents. Rumen bacteria live a very short life and are continually replaced. On death they are broken down in the digestive tract to provide a significant part of the host animal's energy and protein needs. Some non-ruminant herbivores, e.g. horses and rabbits, have cellulose-digesting bacteria in the large intestine, and it is here that cellulose digestion occurs. Such animals use cellulose-rich diets less efficiently than ruminants because the food passes through the small intestine, where most absorption occurs, before it reaches the large intestine (Figure 8.2a). It is not only in mammals that associations between cellulose-digesting microorganisms and animals occur. One important association is that between bacteria and termites, which are ant-like insects particularly important in tropical and subtropical zones. Some termite species build pillar-like nests of earth which are conspicuous features of the landscape (Figure 8.4). Again, it is the bacteria residing within the hindgut, or pouch, of the termites that produce the key enzyme, and not the termites themselves.

The microbial residents of ruminant animals and termites release methane as a by-product of their metabolism. For cattle, typically 5–10 per cent of the ingested food energy is lost in this form. In fact, the increase in atmospheric methane (a 'greenhouse' gas) witnessed over the last few decades is attributed in part to an increase in the world's population of ruminant livestock.

An ability to digest cellulose is not a prerequisite for being a herbivore. After all, humans are partly, and sometimes exclusively herbivorous. First, many herbivores, including so-called 'simple-stomached' animals such as pigs, possess microbes that carry out a limited amount of cellulose digestion. But, more importantly, many herbivores consume young plants, or plant parts, which contain relatively little cellulose, so cell walls are easily ruptured and the contents released. Humans are of this type. Birds have a special compartment, the gizzard, in which food materials are physically broken down before entering the stomach. Many herbivores, insects in particular, avoid the cellulose problem altogether by sucking the juices of plants or by burrowing inside their cells.

The substances that are absorbed across the wall of the digestive tract are potentially available for use by the animal. A small fraction of the digestible energy is lost as urine

Figure 8.4   A termite mound. Termites can utilize woody materials because of bacterial residents in the hindgut. (Photo, the author)

or as other by-products of metabolism (Figure 8.3). The remainder is termed *metabolizable energy*. A significant proportion of metabolizable energy is used for all those energy-requiring functions (e.g. pumping blood, transmitting nerve impulses, regulating cellular processes) that simply keep an animal alive. The rate at which energy is consumed by such processes is known as the *basal metabolic rate*. Basal metabolism is always an important item in an animal's energy budget, accounting for a significant proportion of metabolizable energy. Although difficult to measure accurately, basal metabolic rate can be approximated by measuring the amount of oxygen consumed, the amount of carbon dioxide released, or the heat generated by an organism while it is at rest in an appropriate 'normal' temperature. In general, the smaller the animal, the greater its metabolic rate per unit of weight. Smaller animals therefore need to eat more food as a proportion of their body weight than larger animals. However, the *total* amount of energy expended in basal metabolism increases more or less linearly with an increase in body weight.

Traditionally, a distinction is made between organisms which can regulate their body temperature and organisms which have little or no capacity for thermoregulation. The former group, represented by the mammals and birds, have body temperatures which are independent of the ambient temperature. They are referred to as *endotherms* (meaning 'internally heated'). Other names are homeotherms (meaning constant temperature), and 'warm-blooded' (because body temperature is generally above that of the surroundings). Other organisms are referred to as *ectothermic* (heat source is external) or poikilothermic (changeable temperature) or, more informally, 'cold-blooded'. Unfortunately, this distinction is far from perfect because there are many exceptions. Some types of invertebrates can raise their body temperatures, e.g. by beating wings vigorously in the case of some insects. The important point though is that some animals, particularly mammals and birds, use a proportion of their food energy to maintain body temperature within a comparatively narrow range. At low temperatures, many ectotherms behave rather sluggishly; endotherms, in contrast, can remain active, which can give them a great advantage. However, ectotherms are not poorly adapted in general; the fact that food energy is not required for temperature regulation may be beneficial when food is in short supply. The body temperature of some endotherms drops at certain times, usually when food is scarce, as is the case with hibernating bears.

Animals also expend energy on voluntary activity. The nature of the activity varies between species, but, for a mobile animal, the greater the amount of movement the greater the energy expended. Activity may account for a significant proportion of an animal's metabolizable energy. Even though animals reveal a variety of behaviour patterns to maximize the nutritional reward from the minimum of energy expenditure, much of an animal's life may be spent in procuring food.

Growth of Animals

An animal can grow only if the food energy ingested exceeds both the energy lost in chemical form and the heat expended in metabolism. Agriculturalists use the useful concept of **maintenance** to refer to a diet which keeps the weight of an animal constant; in other words, food energy intake is equal to the energy lost during a particular interval. Food energy in excess of the maintenance amount is available for growth. However, this energy is not used for growth with 100 per cent efficiency. The rate of growth therefore depends on the efficiency with which food energy in excess of maintenance is used for synthesizing new tissues. Now if the diet of a pregnant or lactating (milk-producing) animal falls below the maintenance requirement, its own body reserves (usually fat) will be broken down to meet the energy demands of the growing foetus or for milk production. But, overall, net production will not be positive for this interval of time. It is quite common for animals to lose body weight during times of the year when food supply is low.

The maintenance costs for staying alive can be regarded as fixed. To maximize production from an animal, whether it be in the form of meat, milk or eggs, the animal should be fed as much food as possible in excess of the maintenance level. A general relationship between energy intake and production is shown in Figure 8.5. At the maintenance level of feeding there is no net change, while below the maintenance level production is negative. But, as the intake of food energy is progressively increased beyond that required for maintenance, the proportion of ingested energy which is used for maintenance becomes less and less. This means that if maximum production is the aim, it is much better to keep fewer animals on a very high plane of nutrition, than a larger number of animals on a maintenance diet. However, animal nutrition is not solely about energy. If maximum use is to be made of ingested energy, other dietary components, particularly protein, minerals and vitamins, must not be limiting.

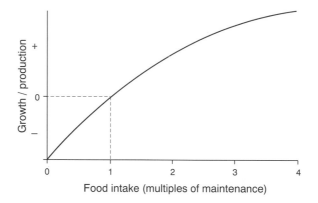

Figure 8.5   *Generalized relationship between food energy intake and production in domesticated livestock. The greater the amount of food consumed, the smaller the proportion that is used for maintenance*

Efficiency of Secondary Production

The effect of different diets on production can be determined by feeding trials. Such work, which involves measurements of food intake, digestibility and growth, is routinely carried out on domesticated livestock. In general, there is much less information on undomesticated animals. However, some years ago W. Humphreys (then of the University of Bath, England) assembled much of the available data. Some of these data are shown in Table 8.1. Here the energy content of new growth (production) is expressed as a proportion of the total energy expended by the animal (respiration). The values therefore refer to metabolizable energy, and not ingested energy, some of which is lost as faeces, urine or other excreted materials. It is clear that the efficiency of food conversion differs enormously between animal types. Notice that the endothermic animals have lower food conversion efficiencies than the ectotherms, presumably because of the energy costs of regulating body temperature. Within the endotherms, four distinct groups emerge – insectivores, birds, small mammals and other mammals. Within the ectotherms, fish and social insects comprise one group, the non-social insects comprise another group, and invertebrates other than insects yet a third group. The herbivorous invertebrates tend to have lower assimilation efficiencies than either carnivorous or detritivorous invertebrates. This suggests that plant material is converted less efficiently than either animal tissue or dead organic matter by consuming animals.

The key point from these data is that the amount of new production is a relatively small, and sometimes tiny, proportion of the food energy assimilated or ingested. In other words, feed conversion efficiencies, although variable, are generally low. For larger animals, it is only with domesticated livestock fed on very high energy and protein diets that production rises to 20–30 per cent of the ingested energy. Such animals have more or less continuous access to high-quality feed, and the objective of the feeding regime is to maximize intake so as to exceed the fixed costs of maintenance by as wide a margin as possible, as long as this is compatible with good health and sound economics.

Table 8.1 *The efficiency with which assimilated food energy is used for productive purposes in several groups of animals. In each case values given are means from a number of studies. (Data from Humphries, W. 1979 Production and respiration in animal populations.* Journal of Animal Ecology *48: 427–454)*

Organism type	Efficiency
Endotherms	
Insectivores	0.9
Birds	1.3
Small mammals	1.5
Other mammals	3.1
Ectotherms	
Fish and social insects	10
Invertebrates other than insects:	
Herbivores	21
Carnivores	28
Detritivores	36
Insects (non-social):	
Herbivores	39
Detritivores	47
Carnivores	56

In some situations, perhaps where future production rather than short-term yield is the aim, it could be advantageous to keep the maximum number of animals on maintenance diets rather than a few animals on a high plane of nutrition. The course pursued will depend on the objectives. Moreover, animals have considerable cultural value in many societies and short-term economic gain may not be the major consideration.

The point was made earlier that fungi and bacteria, but not animals, can manufacture amino acids (the building blocks of proteins). A vital feature of ruminant animals (and some other herbivores) is that their microbial residents manufacture such substances in the rumen, or elsewhere in the digestive tract. This means that such animals are more or less independent of dietary protein, provided that an alternative form of nitrogen (a key component of protein) and sufficient energy are available. The microbial residents of the rumen therefore allow ruminant animals to survive on a diet consisting of poor plant material. They may not thrive on such a diet, but they can produce milk and blood, and reproduce. Nomadic peoples in parts of Africa are still sustained by the products of ruminant animals, such as camels and goats, which feed only on poor quality forage.

So far, the principles of secondary production have been applied mainly to animals, although the role of microbial communities in the digestive tract has been emphasized. Free-living fungi and most bacteria are also classified as secondary producers, and the efficiency of food energy utilization can be measured for these organisms as well. In general, fungi and bacteria have much higher food energy potentials than animals because losses and maintenance costs are much lower. Such organisms have a long history of service to human societies. Some fungi may be consumed directly, as mushrooms are; some are cultured for their enzymes, as in the case of yeasts whose enzymes convert sugar to alcohol. Moreover, the high efficiency of food conversion by these organisms makes them potentially very useful for producing food for both humans and livestock, particularly when waste materials are used as an energy substrate. Fungi and bacteria have particular potential because of their capacity to synthesize amino acids, and hence protein. Microbial biomass is used as a foodstuff for farm animals, while human food based on fungal biomass is becoming more common. Also, the capacity to utilize a huge range of organic substances, including some synthetic ones, means that bacteria and fungi have a great contribution to make in reducing the problems caused by waste materials.

Measuring Secondary Productivity

As with primary productivity, it is very difficult to obtain reliable estimates of secondary productivity. This is particularly so when an estimate of the total secondary productivity of a community is required. Part of the problem lies with the difficulty of determining population abundance for each species present. Many heterotrophic organisms are not amenable to such study in the field on account of their very small size or the habitats they occupy. Indeed, for some organisms, such as bacteria and fungi, the notion of number of individuals is rather meaningless and an alternative approach is necessary. The task is simplified, although still a formidable one, if data on a single species are required. In such a case, field studies of abundance and age and size distributions can be complemented by laboratory studies in order to obtain an estimate of annual production.

Measurements of secondary productivity provide insights to the way energy is transferred through ecological systems (a theme explored further in the next chapter), and they are vital for the management of animals. For example, productivity data for fish could be used to estimate the size of catches possible without jeopardizing future yields.

Livestock Production

Livestock Yield

The concept of yield, introduced earlier for plants (Page 75), can also be applied to animals. Again, the key point is that animals are reared for one or more components, and these constitute the economic yield. It might be meat, milk, eggs, wool or hide, or combinations of these. In the case of an animal kept primarily for breeding, the principal yield component is its offspring. However, while most crop plants are grown for a single yield component, e.g. grain or sugar, there is normally a greater number of useful outputs from animals. In addition to its milk, for example, a cow's production will be represented by one or more offspring a year, a variety of meat products, a hide for leather production and a skeleton which may be used for fertilizer or glue manufacture. Moreover, within the edible component of animal yield there is variation in terms of economic value. In beef cattle the highest premiums are paid for meat from the rear and middle parts of the animal rather than shoulder cuts, while 'muscle meat' is more valuable than meat from the liver and kidneys.

Ecological Efficiency and Yield Improvement in Livestock

Despite the diversity of output from animals, it is still possible to calculate the efficiency of feed use for individual products such as meat, milk and eggs, and also for total secondary production. It is also interesting to express animal yield as a proportion of primary productivity (either total or above-ground productivity). For a situation in which sheep are grazing on pastures it should be relatively easy to determine primary and secondary productivity, but other situations are more complex. Consider an intensive pig or poultry enterprise in which several hundred, possibly several thousand, animals are kept in confined conditions. In this case the output of animals per unit area per year may be very impressive, but what is more important is the area of land, and water, that has been used to provide the high energy and protein diet necessary to sustain these high levels of production.

It is rather more difficult to relate livestock yield to secondary production in an ecological sense than is the case with crop yield and primary productivity. This is partly because of the variety of outputs just referred to, and partly because so often animals are fed partly or entirely on 'imported' food. Hence, livestock output is frequently expressed on a per animal basis, rather than on an area basis as is customary with crops. The advantage of this approach is that it focuses attention on the animal itself. If animal output, for example meat or milk, is expressed on a unit area basis, we could not be sure whether any increase over time in livestock production was due to the animals themselves, or simply due to an increase in forage production which has enabled higher stocking densities. In fact, impressive gains in animal yield have been achieved during the past few decades, particularly in Western agriculture, but to a lesser extent elsewhere. The main contributory factors are analogous to those responsible for increasing crop yield (Page 76), and, again, these factors have interacted.

First, breeding has made a major contribution to increased animal yield. This involves selecting individuals which appear to possess the genes which confer desirable traits. Such traits include greater numbers of offspring, higher milk and egg yield, and more efficient food use. Very importantly, animals are selected because they utilize their dietary energy in particular ways, for example to produce milk rather than to lay down body fat, or to produce muscle rather than fat.

Progress in animal breeding has been accompanied by, and has interacted with, improved nutrition. Particularly important is the use of diets which are highly concentrated in terms of energy and protein. This has enabled the maintenance requirement of animals to be exceeded by increasingly wide margins. Foodstuffs which have a high nutrient density include cereal grains, soy(a)beans and fish meal. Concentrate feedstuffs usually form the basis of a diet for pigs and poultry, while for ruminant animals such as cattle and sheep they are used to supplement forage materials.

The third major factor contributing to higher livestock yields is improved animal health. Better veterinary care, higher standards of hygiene, and the use of drugs and antibiotics have reduced losses caused by metabolic disorders and a variety of biotic agents, including viruses, bacteria, parasitic worms, insects and protozoans.

9

The Transfer of Energy and Matter through Ecosystems

In the two previous chapters, autotrophic and heterotrophic organisms were dealt with separately. Now we consider entire ecosystems, specifically the way that organisms are linked by the transfer of energy and chemical substances between them. This provides an organizing framework for analysing functional aspects of ecological systems. It also provides a way of describing, characterizing and comparing ecosystems. The movement of energy and nutrients between organisms is closely coupled because both are involved when one organism consumes living or dead organic matter. In this chapter the emphasis is on energy flow through ecological systems. In the following chapter the movement of chemical elements is discussed more systematically.

Feeding Relationships

Overview

Feeding relationships are central to the organization and functioning of ecological communities. For any heterotroph (e.g. a bacterium, fungus, animal) the sources of food and the behaviour involved in obtaining food are key features of its ecology. Heterotrophs (or consumers) are categorized according to their feeding habits. Thus herbivores and carnivores feed on plants and animals respectively while omnivores consume both. Terms such as insectivore (insect eating) and frugivore (fruit eating) categorize the diets of consumers even more closely. Detritivores, including fungi and most types of bacteria, consume organic remains, while the term scavenger is used for species (e.g. vultures, jackals, crabs) that feed principally on animals that have recently died. The diet of an individual organism may change as it grows and develops, and it may alter in response to the changing availability of suitable food (Figure 9.1).

The transfer of energy and nutrients between organisms can be quite obvious, as when one animal is killed and devoured by another. However, there are other, much less conspicuous processes involving energy and nutrient transfer. *Parasitism*, which

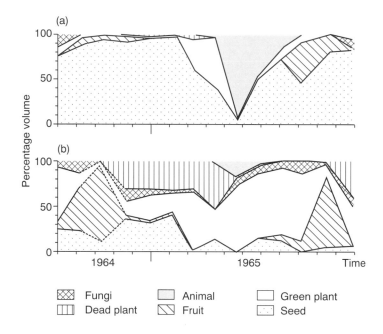

Figure 9.1   *Seasonal dietary variation of (a) wood mice and (b) bank voles in an English wood. Both species are predominantly herbivorous but consume animal tissue in spring when suitable plant material is scarce. (From Watts, C. 1968 The foods eaten by wood mice* (Apodemus sylvaticus) *and bank voles* (Clethrionomys glareolus) *in Whytham Woods, Berkshire. Journal of Animal Ecology 37: 25–41. Redrawn with permission of Blackwell Science Ltd, Oxford)*

practically all organisms have to endure, is one such process. It involves one organism, often of microscopic size, living within or upon another organism (the ***host***). Death of the host may not be a direct result of parasitism (indeed it would not be in the best interests of the parasite), but the host may be seriously weakened by the parasites. Another form of energy transfer is extremely important in insect communities. This involves ***parasitoids***, which are insects that lay their eggs in other insects. The larvae which emerge from the eggs then feed off the host, usually bringing about its death.

Dietary Specialization

The degree to which heterotrophs specialize with respect to their food varies considerably between species; hence the terms 'generalist' and 'specialist' are used for informally characterizing dietary behaviour. Parasitic organisms frequently display a high degree of host specificity; a parasitic species may be found in just one kind of host, and in a particular part of the body. Among herbivores there is considerable variation in dietary specialization. For example, domestic sheep are much more selective than cattle in grazing plants. Herbivores often specialize on particular plant parts: an insect or bird may concentrate on fruit, nectar or seeds, and may be a generalist or a specialist with respect to plant species. To complicate matters, organisms with clear food preferences may switch to other items when the preferred food source becomes scarce. African lions preferentially select large herbivores, but if these are unavailable they consume smaller, insectivorous mammals.

For organisms that hunt and kill prey, relative size and strength of predator and prey influence diet. In cases where carnivore species are smaller than the herbivores used as prey, the predators may work in groups. For passive, filter feeding organisms, size of food particles is important. Differences in lifestyle between two organisms that inhabit the same general area may mean that they never encounter one another: so tree-dwelling animals are unlikely prey for ground-living animals that cannot climb trees. The diet of an animal is not necessarily the same between geographical areas, particularly when prey availability differs. This means that caution is required in extrapolating results gathered in one area more generally.

Potential prey organisms frequently reveal features which reduce the probability that they will be caught and consumed. It could be the production of a chemical to deter feeding, or morphological features such as the spines of some plants. One species may evolve characteristics which make it look or taste like another species that is avoided by certain predators. This phenomenon is known as ***mimicry***.

Determining the Diets of Consumers

A variety of approaches are employed to determine the food used by heterotrophic organisms. Observation is very important for some consumers. We know African lions eat wildebeest and other large herbivores because we can watch them do so. Similarly, observation reveals that herbivorous insects favour certain plant species and particular tissues. In other cases, however, it is very difficult to observe feeding relationships because of the minute size of the organisms and the habitats they occupy. An alternative to observation is the analysis of the gut contents of an animal. A problem with this approach can be that it usually requires sacrifice of the animal. Also, there are problems with interpretation because the various items of food are likely to be digested at different rates. Nonetheless, this method is widely used, particularly for organisms such as fish and other aquatic animals whose feeding habits are difficult to observe. Faeces analysis provides another approach to determining the diet of an animal, although differential digestion rates for food items again present problems.

Feeding habits may be investigated in a more experimental way. After 'labelling' a food source, perhaps a plant, with a small quantity of a radioisotope, organisms in the vicinity can be trapped and their radioactivity levels measured as a guide to what they are eating. Food preferences may also be assessed by providing an organism with a variety of foodstuffs and measuring its consumption of each. In discussing food preferences it is not only animals we are considering, but also the bacteria and fungi. Individual species of such organisms generally show marked preferences for certain types of dead organic matter (faeces perhaps, or certain species of plant), and these can be determined both by field observation and by experiment.

A familiar problem when a variety of species is used to provide energy and nutrients is that it is very difficult to measure the relative contribution of each. And even if accurate data are obtained in one year these may not apply to all years.

Food Webs, Food Chains and Guilds

For an area of landscape, or volume of water, it is theoretically possible to identify all the species present and establish the diet of each of them. Using this information a diagram could be constructed with boxes representing individual species and arrows showing the pathways of energy and nutrient flow between them. Such networks are referred to as *food webs*. Inspection of such a diagram would tell us something of the ecology of the individual species within the community, but also features of the whole community because it is very largely through feeding relationships that organisms are 'connected' to each other. The early development of this approach to studying ecological communities is associated with the work of a British ecologist, Charles Elton, in the 1920s (although he used the term 'food cycle'), but subsequently it has become a central theme in ecology.

Two food webs are shown in Figure 9.2 to illustrate their use and their limitations. First, note that some individual species are shown, but in other cases species are grouped together. Grouping is justified if the species concerned appear to occupy similar positions in the food web. However, there is a more practical reason, which is that there are usually such large numbers of species to be considered that it would take a vast amount of human effort to get all the information required for a complete picture of feeding relationships. Note that the illustrated food webs show only which species are consuming which other species, and not the quantities of energy and nutrients involved. That would require a detailed examination of all the species present over a period of time long enough to be representative. The task may be further complicated by seasonal and yearly changes in diet and with the consumer's stage of development. Furthermore, food webs imply that areas of landscape and volumes of water are discrete, which actually is very unusual. So the picture is complicated by the movements of animals in and out of the area.

Given that the construction of food webs is such an enormous task, it is not surprising that the most satisfactory examples are those for small, comparatively isolated communities supporting relatively few species. Such communities include small ponds and water-filled holes in trees. But even in these cases it is doubtful whether a complete food web has ever been compiled. Nonetheless, for communities that have been intensively studied for a long period of time, the grasslands of North America and East Africa for example, useful general food webs are available, particularly for the above-ground component. Also, the objectives of such studies do not usually require a complete and accurate food web to be constructed, but only the general features. In such cases attention can be focused on the dominant species and the principal pathways of energy and nutrient flow. Often, the purpose of a study is to evaluate the position in the community of an individual species, perhaps because of its economic importance, so the whole community does not have to be closely examined.

Despite the technical obstacles to collecting the appropriate data, food webs provide valuable information about communities. Food webs provide an organizational framework for communities, and a basis for comparing different community types. It is not difficult to appreciate how an understanding of feeding relationships can assist the management of economically important species of fish or mammals. Feeding relationships also enable predictions to be made of the fate of toxic substances released to the environment, especially the likelihood of their incorporation into species consumed by humans.

(a)

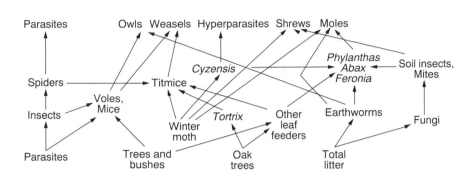

(b)

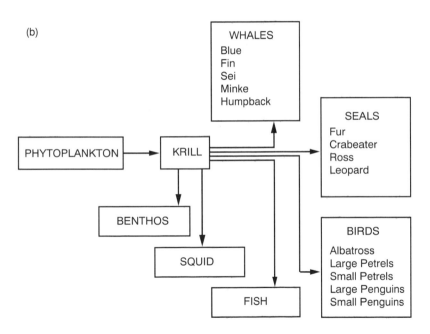

Figure 9.2 *Examples of food webs; arrows indicate the direction of energy and nutrient flow. (a) A wood in southern England. (From Varley, G. 1970 The concept of energy flow applied to a woodland community. In: Watson, A. (ed), Animal Populations in Relation to their Food Sources, pp. 389–404. Redrawn with permission of Blackwell Science Ltd, Oxford.) (b) General scheme for Antarctic waters. Note the grouping of species according to their principal food sources. (From Everson, I. 1984 Marine interactions. In: Laws, R.M. (ed), Antarctic Ecology Vol. 2. pp. 783–819. Redrawn by permission of the publisher, Academic Press Ltd, London, and the author)*

There are other, often more tractable, approaches to feeding relationships than the construction of complete food webs. One approach involves focusing on particular groups of organisms which exploit a common food source in similar ways. Such groups are known as **guilds** (a term proposed by American ecologist Robert Root because of the analogy between such groups of organisms and medieval guilds, of craftsman for example). Ecological guilds could be represented by large herbivores, such as wildebeest, zebra and antelope, all exploiting the grass cover of African savanna environments. Another example is herbivorous insects which are exploiting plant leaves in similar ways.

A second approach was anticipated when we distinguished between herbivores (plant eating) and carnivores (animal eating): it requires assigning species (at different stages in their lives if necessary) to particular feeding, or **trophic levels**. The **trophic structure** approach attempts to reduce what is usually an impossibly complex situation to a number of boxes, as in Figure 9.3. Energy which is made available to the community by the primary producers (plants or algae) passes to other organisms, either in living tissue to the herbivores, or in dead tissue to the detritivores. The proportion of primary production that dies before consumption nearly always exceeds that consumed while still living, particularly in terrestrial communities. Furthermore, the ratio between the two varies in more or less predictable ways between community types. In forests, the proportion of annual net primary production consumed while living is usually less than 10 per cent, while in grasslands it may vary between 10 and 50 per cent. In water, such values typically range between 20 and 80 per cent. The reason for these differences lies chiefly in the chemical composition of the plant material. Woody material (largely cellulose and lignin) is much less palatable and less easily digested than 'softer' leaf tissues, and its breakdown requires specialist consumers with appropriate enzymes. Even in intensively managed livestock systems the proportion of the above-ground production that is consumed is less than 50 per cent, while the proportion of total production, which includes underground plant material, is much less. As might be imagined, it is very difficult to measure accurately the amount of primary production consumed by herbivores, and this applies particularly to below-ground tissue. Just occasionally very large amounts of above-ground tissue are consumed, as when insect outbreaks occur in forests, or when locusts swarm and devour large quantities of vegetation. In aquatic systems, consumption efficiencies tend to be higher than on land, although there is considerable variation. Typically, the principal grazers of the algae are tiny crustaceans or herbivorous fish.

The herbivores provide a source of food for the carnivores, which in Figure 9.3 comprise just one trophic level. It may be, however, that while some carnivores specialize in consuming herbivores, other carnivores consume carnivores, in which case we would need to add another box to represent this additional trophic level. The movement of energy and nutrients from plants through herbivores to carnivores constitutes a **food chain**, so called because of its linked and linear nature. A food chain which originates with living plant material is conventionally referred to as a **grazing food chain**, while a food chain based on dead organic matter is referred to as a **detritus** or **decomposer food chain**. In Figure 9.3 there are just three links in the grazing food chain. However, counting the number of links in a food chain does not require allocating every organism to a box: it is possible to count the number of links in a food chain by identifying individual species which are connected by feeding relationships.

It is not difficult to think of grazing food chains. The variety of herbivores in African savannas and their exploitation by large carnivores is a familiar image. The algae–crustaceans–fish food chain of the oceans provides another example. We often talk of the human food chain to denote the links between food production and its consumption by

Grazing food chain

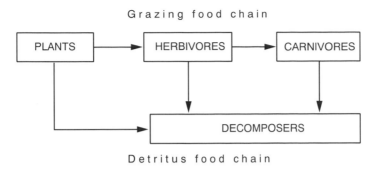

Detritus food chain

Figure 9.3   *The grazing and detritus food chains. A much-used model to represent the transfer of energy and nutrients through ecological communities*

humans. Of critical importance in the human food chain is the possibility of the incorporation of toxic substances by contamination.

While examples of grazing food chains readily come to mind, it should be remembered that a high proportion, usually well over half, of the annual net primary production in a defined area of landscape dies before it is consumed by other organisms. In Figure 9.3 the decomposer food chain is represented by a single box because the feeding relationships involve a large number of species which are very difficult to study on account of their small size, their inaccessibility and their complex interactions. In theory, however, the same approach can be made to the decomposer food chain as to the grazing food chain, with organisms being categorized according to their principal food sources. (Although decomposition refers specifically to the loss of detritus, it should be appreciated that *all* living organisms contribute to the breakdown of organic matter, simply because all organisms transform chemical energy to heat.)

Decomposition is essentially a biochemical process, controlled by enzymes, but supplemented to a greater or lesser extent by physical processes such as leaching, weathering and fire. The biotic processing of detritus in a particular type of habitat is usually fairly predictable, and it involves a variety of organisms. On land, leaf litter is typically colonized by fungi, and also consumed by a variety of invertebrates such as insects (including ants), millipedes, snails and earthworms. Fungi are particularly important for the decomposition of woody material. Many such fungi produce long, filamentous tissues, called **hyphae**, which ramify through the dead tissues, releasing enzymes which break down large, complex molecules to a size which can be absorbed by the fungus (Page 79). 'Bracket' fungi, some of which grow to a considerable size, are often conspicuous features of dead and dying tree trunks. In the tropics, particularly, termites are responsible for the breakdown of woody materials, an ability they owe to the specialized bacteria in the hind gut (Page 83). Heterotrophic bacteria make a major contribution to decomposition in almost all environments and are the chief agents of decomposition in many. Decomposer food chains are at the heart of operations in sewage works. Here, a complex community of invertebrates and microorganisms is responsible for the decomposition of human wastes.

In some situations, organic matter is imported to an area from elsewhere. This is known as the **allochthonous** component, while the organic matter generated within a defined area, by photosynthesis, is known as the **autochthonous** component. This distinction applies particularly to water bodies because the allochthonous material frequently comprises the major part of the organic matter in ponds, streams and estuaries.

Although the detritus food chain is based principally on dead plant material, it should be clear that *all* organisms provide energy and nutrients for the detritivores when they die. Many organisms also release organic matter during their lives, as in the case of undigested food and urine from animals. Detritivores cannot influence the rate at which dead organic matter is made available to them. In contrast, the grazing activities of herbivores can potentially influence their food supply by affecting primary productivity. Extreme levels of grazing reduce the photosynthetic capacity of vegetation, although there is evidence that low levels of grazing can actually stimulate primary production.

The Quantification of Energy Transfer

Several aspects of energy flow through communities can be quantified if the appropriate data are available. Figure 9.4 represents a simple grazing food chain made up of primary

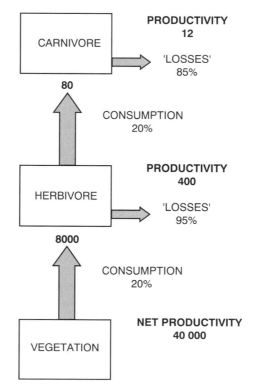

Figure 9.4 *Quantification of energy flow through an idealized food chain. The values (in kilojoules m^{-2} yr^{-1}) are hypothetical but realistic. Consumption efficiency is the proportion of annual production at one trophic level that is consumed by animals at the next trophic level. Energy is lost in chemical form and as heat*

producers, one herbivore and one carnivore. Values are shown for (1) annual net primary production, (2) the proportion of production at one trophic level which is consumed by the animal in the trophic level above and (3) the efficiencies with which the herbivore and the carnivore convert their food to new production. The values chosen here are hypothetical, but realistic. Note the steep decline in productivity with each successive trophic level. The annual production of the herbivore and carnivore populations are only 1.0 per cent and 0.03 per cent respectively of net primary production. A marked drop in production with each successive link in the food chain is a feature of ecological communities, and it has implications for the utilization of biotic resources. This sharp drop in production is due to the low exploitation of food energy by the herbivore and carnivore and also the low conversion efficiency of food to new production. If all secondary production was included in the calculations, however, the decline in production between primary and secondary producers would not be so steep because faecal material and other wastes from animals provide a source of food for other organisms.

There is no satisfactory explanation as to why only a small proportion of available food at one trophic level should normally be consumed by organisms in the next trophic level, and there may be no unifying answer to this intriguing question. The reason for the low conversion efficiency of food energy to new growth was discussed in Chapter 8. It is due primarily to the release of food energy in chemical form (faeces, urine) and to the large respiratory demands of basal metabolism, activity and growth.

Simple arithmetic can be used to calculate various efficiencies and ratios: e.g. the ratio of productivity to biomass at each trophic level; the ratio of biomass and productivity between trophic levels; the efficiency of exploitation of a food source; and the efficiency of energy transfer through the whole food chain. Such values enable food chains to be quantified and different food chains to be compared.

As far as the ratio of productivity between trophic levels is concerned, a positive linear relationship has been found between the logarithm of above-ground primary productivity and the logarithm of herbivore productivity across a variety of community types. However, there is plenty of scatter around the line of best fit. This is partly caused by the higher consumption efficiencies in grassland than in forest. It is also partly caused by differences between organisms in the amount of food energy devoted to thermoregulation (Page 84). The ratio of productivity to biomass also varies. It is much lower in terrestrial communities than in aquatic situations simply because the biomass of the primary producers on land is usually many orders of magnitude greater than in open water.

It should be clear that a sharp decline in productivity from one trophic level to the next could theoretically set a limit to the number of trophic levels. This is because food becomes increasingly scarce with each additional trophic level and, at least with the larger animals, population size is likely to become too small to be viable. The maximum number of links found in food chains appears to be about seven, but food chains with between three and five links are much more common. Some food chains, however, appear to have just two links (as long as parasites are excluded). Perhaps surprisingly, however, attempts to relate food chain length to primary productivity have not been very successful overall.

An American ecologist, Raymond Lindeman, is usually credited with laying the theoretical foundations for the quantification of energy flow in communities with his paper 'The trophic–dynamic aspect of ecology', published in 1942. While not the first ecologist to think about the organization of communities in terms of food chains (we have already mentioned Charles Elton), Lindeman's work stimulated a major interest in energy flow studies during the following decades. Sadly, Lindeman died while in his twenties, before his great contribution became widely acknowledged.

A Closer Look at Food Chains

The diagram in Figure 9.3 provides a useful framework with which to organize thoughts about energy and nutrient transfer through any type of ecosystem. However, real-world situations are usually far more complex and we need to be aware of some of the reasons why caution should be applied when using this model. First, the notion of discrete trophic levels is questionable. How would we deal with a carnivore that feeds on other carnivores as well as on herbivores? Also some animals which might be top predators as adults, may be vulnerable prey to other carnivores when they are young. Second, the notion of two distinct pathways for energy and nutrient flow does not stand up to close inspection. Detritus feeders may well be consumed by organisms in the grazing food chain. Insectivorous birds and mammals are unlikely to discriminate between insects on the basis of whether they belong to the grazing or decomposer food chain, and carnivores such as the big cats of Africa, usually associated with the grazing food chain, may well occasionally consume a mammal, such as the aardvark, that lives partly on detritus-eating insects.

In aquatic ecosystems, there are also close links between grazers and decomposers. A typical overview of marine food chains is represented in Figure 9.5. In this example, the photosynthetic algae continually release organic substances which provide a source of energy for heterotrophic bacteria. These bacteria may then be consumed by protozoans, which in turn are a source of food for the tiny crustaceans of the zooplankton. However, since these crustaceans also consume the photosynthetic algae of the phytoplankton, they occupy a distinctly ambiguous position with respect to the grazing and detritus food chains. So, in practice, it may be inappropriate to assign each species to a particular trophic level and an unambiguous position in either the grazing or the detritus food chain. Calculations of the various efficiencies referred to earlier may similarly be misleading.

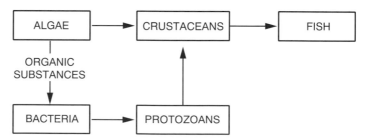

Figure 9.5 *Part of a marine food chain showing a close relationship between the grazing and detritus components. The grazing food chain here is being 'subsidized' by food energy which initially entered the detritus food chain. (Protozoans are single-celled heterotrophic organisms of the kingdom Protista)*

It is important to be aware of the problems inherent in the traditional approach to energy flow studies which recognizes grazing and detritus food chains and a series of trophic levels. The extent to which this approach is valid varies between situations. It certainly provides a reference framework for examining ecological communities, and it considerably facilitates quantification of energy flow. However, the fact is that in attempting to simulate the complexities of the real world it is frequently necessary to make some concessions, and simply acknowledge that the model we construct is not a perfect representation of reality.

Animals or Plants as a Source of Human Food?

The principles governing energy flow have implications for the management of natural resources. The large decline in productivity that occurs between primary and secondary producers has led some to argue for less use of animal products in order to make more food available to the human population. Although this is undisputed in terms of energy, there are situations in which the use of animals as a source of food has several practical advantages. For example, ruminant animals convert plant material of little direct value to high-grade protein. Living animals also effectively store food for long periods, whereas harvested plant products have a limited life unless maintained under special conditions. In addition, animals provide food where crop production would be ill advised because of the risks of erosion. In the case of marine ecosystems it would be an impractical task to harvest the primary producers because of their extremely low biomass. (In fact, most of the aquatic harvest for human consumption is of carnivorous fish.) But, however compelling the arguments for the use of animals as a source of food, there is no escaping the basic rule that energy yields decline markedly with every successive link in the food chain.

'Top-down' or 'Bottom-up' Control in Food Chains?

From the discussion of food chains so far it would seem that the physical environment determines the level of primary production, and that the level of primary production determines the level of secondary production. Such a scenario is referred to as 'bottom-up' control. However, it ignores the possibility that consumers may affect the productivity in the trophic level below them. An example of this type of control was provided on Page 98 when we noted that herbivores can potentially influence their supply of food. Such controls can be described as 'top-down'. The former scenario is the traditional view, but during the past few decades ecologists have been discussing whether 'top-down' controls can operate. This suggestion arose from the general rule that herbivores do not normally exploit their food with anything like 100 per cent efficiency. Thus, it was reasoned, control of heterotrophs must come, not from the quantity of food, but from 'above', by predation. For terrestrial communities there is not a great deal of evidence that 'top-down' controls are generally effective. However, there is more evidence for 'top-down' controls in freshwater communities. A possible scenario is presented in Figure 9.6. Imagine a top predator is added to a food chain which previously had three trophic levels. The effect of this introduction could be significantly to reduce

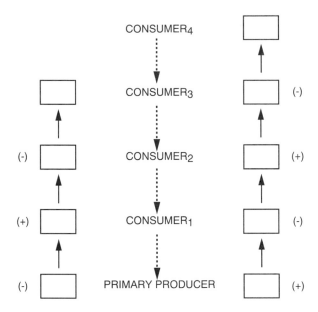

Figure 9.6   *The principle of 'top-down' controls in food chains. The effect of the top consumer is either to increase (+) or decrease (−) the abundance/productivity of organisms in the various trophic levels beneath. In the left-hand diagram, predation by Consumer 3 cascades through the food chain, ultimately constraining primary production. In the right-hand diagram, the effect of Consumer 4 is to reduce grazing pressure on the primary producers*

the productivity of the fish species designated Consumer 2, which reduces predation of Consumer 1. Production of Consumer 1 may therefore increase, which in turn may increase the consumption of the algae to such an extent that primary production declines. Thus the effect of introducing the top predator cascades through the system to the primary producers. Assuming that 'top-down' controls operate at every trophic level, the effect of introducing or removing a top predator will depend on whether the trophic level number it occupies is odd or even. Introducing Consumer 4 could have the effect of increasing primary productivity if it resulted indirectly in a relaxation of grazing pressure on the algae. Although 'top-down' controls have been demonstrated in some freshwater communities, the general view is that primary productivity in lakes in a given climatic zone is principally determined by the level of available phosphorus, i.e. 'bottom-up' controls operate. There appears to be no simple answer as to whether 'top-down' or 'bottom-up' controls are more important in aquatic communities, and it is likely that the nature of the controls on productivity varies considerably from one situation to another. What is important is to allow that both may occur.

Predators and Prey

The above discussion concerning levels of productivity at various trophic levels raises the question as to how effectively predators control the abundance of prey organisms, and, in turn, how the abundance of prey organisms determines the abundance of predators. This is another contentious issue and it has received much attention from ecologists. These problems are central to population ecology and, accordingly, 'abundance' in such studies is usually measured in terms of the number of organisms. However, it is not difficult to appreciate that a general relationship often exists between the number of individuals in a population and its productivity.

Predation does not necessarily bring about the death of the prey organism, but clearly there are examples of predation which do result in prey death; it is this type of predation with which we are primarily concerned here. During earlier discussions of evolution (Page 31) it was pointed out that an intrinsic characteristic of all populations is a potential for growth in numbers. But, in practice, only a fraction, usually only a tiny fraction, of offspring survive to reproduce. So, of the various factors that could contribute to the control of abundance, predation is at least a candidate.

Evidence for the efficacy of predation is provided by certain successful examples of biological control whereby the introduction of a 'natural enemy' has reduced the abundance of an unwanted species. However, it would be unwise to conclude from such rather limited evidence, obtained from somewhat artificial situations, that predation is always a major factor in determining prey abundance. Indeed, many attempts at biological control have been unsuccessful. Predation is *potentially* an important factor in controlling abundance; in some situations it may be very important, but in others it may be of limited significance. To complicate matters, within particular predator–prey systems the influence of predation may vary from year to year. When death is not a direct consequence of predation, it may be that predation contributes to the control of prey abundance by affecting prey organisms in such a way as to increase their vulnerability to other factors, such as adverse weather and disease, and to reduce their capacity to compete with species with similar lifestyles. Generalizations concerning the contribution that predation makes to the control of prey abundance are best avoided: we should note the very complex nature of this subject and the fact that it has long been a source of controversy among ecologists. The truth is probably that its significance varies considerably from situation to situation.

The other question here is how effectively prey availability affects the abundance of predator populations. It is easy to demonstrate experimentally the considerable effect that food quantity and quality have on an organism's performance, including its reproductive performance, but much more difficult to assess the influence of food supply under field conditions. So again, food availability is a potentially important factor in determining abundance of all consumers. Food supply appears to be more critical in determining the abundance of some consumers than others, while for the same species the importance of food supply varies between years and also between stages of the life cycle.

Food Chains Based on Chemosynthesis

Chemosynthetic bacteria are also primary producers because they manufacture organic matter from carbon dioxide using an external energy source. While photosynthetic organisms use light as a source of energy, chemosynthetic organisms use a variety of quite simple chemical entities which they oxidize. Where there is no light, chemosynthesis is the only mechanism for the production of new organic matter. Food chains based on chemosynthesis have been found around hydrothermal vents on the ocean floor. These are situated along submarine mountain chains where new oceanic crust is extruded (Page 144). Here, water is released at temperatures between 300 and 400°C as a dark plume popularly known as a 'black smoker'. These plumes of hot water carry chemical entities in solution, including hydrogen sulfide which is oxidized by chemosynthetic bacteria to provide the energy to manufacture carbon compounds. Hot springs and their associated biotic communities were discovered off South America, in an area known as the Eastern Pacific Rise, in the late 1970s, but further explorations, along the mid-Atlantic Ridge for example, have revealed that such conditions are much more widespread. The chemosynthetic bacteria support a food chain in which there are comparatively large animals, including tube worms and giant clams. Some of the animals appear to have bacteria living within their cells, an association which blurs the distinction between autotroph and heterotroph. Communities based on chemosynthetic bacteria have also been discovered in caves in Romania and elsewhere. Again, these are lightless environments, and the animals, which are blind, have no colour. Some believe that the very first organisms on Earth may have evolved in similar conditions nearly 4 billion years ago (Page 151).

10

Biogeochemical Cycling

Biogeochemical cycling refers to all aspects of the movement of chemical entities between organisms and the physical environment. The term *nutrient cycling* is also frequently used although it is a little more restricted in the sense that it covers just the biotically essential elements. Biogeochemical circulation exerts a huge influence on the functioning of the biosphere, while the biota itself plays a central role in the movement of chemical entities and in their transformation. Biogeochemical studies are also important for evaluating environmental quality, particularly with respect to human impacts on the environment.

This chapter considers general principles relevant to biogeochemical cycling, a basic model for the storage and movement of chemical elements within ecosystems, the inputs and outputs of elements, and some case studies of biogeochemical circulation. Finally, the circulation of two key elements, nitrogen and carbon, is discussed.

The Scope of Biogeochemical Studies

Although the transfer of energy and chemical elements through ecological communities is closely coupled, there is a fundamental difference between them. Energy is made available to the biota in the process of photosynthesis. Once a unit of energy is used by an organism it is transformed to heat. Thus the term 'energy flow' is used rather than 'energy cycling'. In contrast, the various nutrient elements are available in finite supply and are continuously recycled.

The study of biogeochemical cycles encompasses consideration of where chemical elements are stored, the chemical substances in which they are stored, the processes involved in their transfer and their rates of transfer. Although the focus here is on the chemical elements, in general the same principles apply to all chemical substances. Biogeochemical circulation can be studied over a variety of spatial scales. On the one hand, interest may centre on a very small area, a pond perhaps, or part of a forest, while at the other extreme the objective may be to compile a global budget for a certain element. Quite often, nutrient circulation studies focus on a local example of a particular community type, e.g. lowland rain forest, desert, alpine meadow, or cornfield. In such

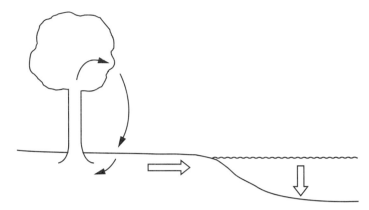

Figure 10.1   *Biogeochemical cycling: the distinction between rapid, local movements (closed arrows), and long-term movements (open arrows) when atoms of the various elements are removed from biotic circulation*

studies measurements will be taken at a number of sample locations. Mean data will then be presented together with the variation between sample points. If the area is representative, and the sampling satisfactory, general features of nutrient circulation in that type of community may be established.

It is useful to distinguish between short-term, local movements of chemical elements and those that operate over very much longer timescales, during which individual atoms may be removed from circulation for millions of years. This distinction is illustrated by the simple diagram in Figure 10.1. In this case a single atom, of potassium for example, is taken up by tree roots in the spring, incorporated into leaf tissue and later returned to the soil when the leaf falls and is decomposed. Such movements between plant and soil might continue for several years before the atom is leached from the soil, carried in solution and deposited on the bed of a lake. If accumulating sediment covered this atom it would be removed from circulation, and become available again only over long timescales and after major environmental changes. All nutrient elements alternate between periods of relatively rapid circulation and very long intervals during which they are unavailable to the biota, although the different elements vary considerably in the temporal and spatial scales involved. Our interest here is primarily in the shorter term, local movements, although certain human activities – mining phosphorus for fertilizer and burning fossil fuels for example – can 'short-circuit' the long-term cycles.

Categorizing Nutrient Elements

The three most abundant elements in organic matter (carbon, hydrogen and oxygen) can exist in gaseous forms at 'normal' temperatures and pressures. For example, carbon is combined with oxygen in both carbon dioxide and carbon monoxide, pairs of oxygen atoms combine to form molecular oxygen (O_2), and the hydrogen in the lower atmosphere exists primarily as water vapour. Carbon and oxygen are taken up by the biota principally in gaseous form. Hydrogen is incorporated into the biota during photosynthesis when it is released from water molecules and combined with carbon dioxide. The other elements essential for life are commonly known as the ***mineral*** nutrients. They include nitrogen, sulfur, phosphorus, calcium, potassium, manganese and iron (a more complete list is shown on Page 10). These are taken up by the biota primarily via plant roots on land and by algae in open water. Only two of the mineral nutrients, nitrogen and sulfur, have significant gaseous phases, and, as in the case of carbon, biotic processes play key roles in their circulation. The other mineral nutrients may, however, be released in gaseous forms during fires if temperatures are sufficiently high.

The Biological Availability of Elements

Each element contributes to a variety of chemical entities, and these are differentially available for uptake by plants and microorganisms. In addition, local environmental conditions influence availability. In practice, this means that a measure of the total amount of a particular element, in soil or in water, may not be a reliable guide to its biological availability. A good example is provided by the element phosphorus, whose availability to plants is closely related to soil acidity. In very acid soils (i.e. of low pH), phosphorus tends to be poorly available. This element becomes increasingly available as pH rises, but in very alkaline conditions (high pH) it again becomes insoluble and poorly available for plants.

The biological availability of the element aluminium, which in solution is quite toxic, is also pH related. One of the main problems resulting from soil acidification due to 'acid rain', is the increased solubility, and hence availability, of aluminium. Soluble aluminium may accumulate at concentrations which impair the normal functioning of plants. In addition, soluble aluminium can be leached from soils by percolating rainwater and melting snow. On reaching water bodies, aluminium forms aluminium hydroxide, which clogs up the gills of fish, thereby inhibiting their capacity for oxygen uptake. This is the main reason for the decline in fish populations so frequently associated with the acidification of water bodies.

Spatial location also affects biological availability. We are particularly concerned here with situations in which nutrients are unavailable by virtue of their location, but could become available over comparatively short timescales. Nutrients in soil might be located below the current rooting depth, but by introducing a deeper-rooted plant species it might be possible to bring those nutrients back into circulation. In swidden agriculture, which involves temporary cropping and a longer fallow period, the restoration of soil fertility is often based on such nutrient 'pumping'.

Nutrients in Aquatic Ecosystems

In oceans and lakes, the vertical distribution of nutrients has a major effect on their availability. This is because the algae, which are chiefly responsible for nutrient uptake, can photosynthesize only to a depth at which there is sufficient light. Nutrients situated below the illuminated, or euphotic, zone are therefore unavailable to the algae. Now since the concentration of nutrients appears to be the key factor limiting primary productivity in aquatic communities, it is not surprising that productivity tends to be relatively low in areas of vertical stability, and relatively high where nutrients are retained within, or returned to, the euphotic zone.

Vertical mixing of water can be promoted in a number of ways. Wind activity can stimulate mixing, sometimes to the bottom in relatively shallow lakes. But wind activity can indirectly promote the upward movement of water through the process known as *upwelling* (Figure 10.2a). Upwelling can occur where surface currents, driven by prevailing off-shore winds, move water away from continental land masses. These surface waters are then replaced by nutrient-rich water from below. Upwelling is particularly associated with seas off western continental margins in the subtropics, notably off West Africa and South America, but also occurs locally off the Antarctic continent. Upwelling zones support some of the most productive fisheries in the oceans.

Gradients of water density (i.e. weight per unit volume) also have a major influence on the degree of vertical mixing. The density of freshwater is determined by temperature: the physical properties of freshwater are such that maximum density occurs at around 4°C. The density of seawater, however, is determined by salinity and temperature, and both therefore need to be considered simultaneously: the lower the temperature (at a given salinity) the higher the density, and the greater the salinity (at a given temperature) the higher the density. Where currents of different density converge, as in sub-Arctic latitudes in the Atlantic and Pacific Oceans and in Antarctic waters, vertical mixing is promoted.

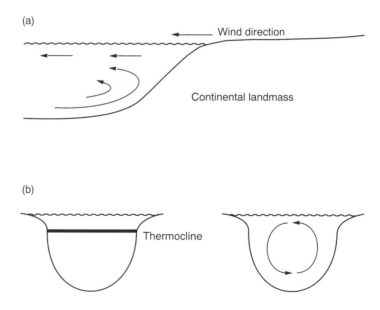

Figure 10.2 *Vertical mixing in water. (a) Upwelling: surface water, moved by off-shore winds, is replaced by nutrient-rich water from depth. (b) Density effects: in the left-hand diagram, warm, low-density water lies above cooler, higher-density water and little vertical mixing occurs. In the right-hand diagram, seasonal cooling has increased surface water density, leading to vertical instability in the water column*

As a first approximation, the oceans exist as three layers. A surface layer, which incorporates the euphotic zone, extends to about 300 metres. It is separated from the deeper layers (which comprise most of the oceanic volume) by a layer called the ***thermocline***, in which the temperature gradient, and therefore the density gradient, is relatively steep. In tropical zones, where seasonal temperature changes are small and the radiation input is relatively high, the layered structure is well maintained. The water body is said to be ***stratified***. In such conditions the movement of nutrients into the euphotic zone is inhibited. As a consequence primary production is very low over vast expanses of open ocean. In pronounced seasonal environments, however, stratification tends to break down during autumnal cooling, and this encourages vertical mixing.

Stratification is often evident during the summer in lakes in seasonal environments, unless prevented by wind activity. The upper (warmer and less dense) layer, is called the ***epilimnion***. It is separated from the deeper (colder and more dense) layer, the ***hypolimnion***, by a relatively narrow thermocline. During autumn, as surface waters cool to the temperature of the water beneath, an 'overturn' of water occurs (Figure 10.2b). Lakes in seasonal climates typically undergo a second overturn in the spring when the temperature of the warming surface water is closer to 4°C (the temperature of maximum density) than the water of the hypolimnion beneath. Seasonal overturns are important for transferring nutrients into the euphotic zone, and also for transferring oxygen to deeper waters. Oxygen replenishment is required for the bacteria and other organisms which make up the decomposer community. Where there are high levels of organic matter, for example from sewage disposal or excessive algal growth, oxygen demand is high. If oxygen is not replenished in sufficient amounts, the bottom of the lake may become anoxic, i.e. devoid of oxygen, either seasonally or permanently.

Studying Chemical Budgets

In carrying out biogeochemical studies it is usual first to delimit a physical area for the investigation. Certain environments, a pond, a river catchment, or a cornfield, for example, have fairly obvious boundaries, but in other cases drawing boundaries is a more subjective process. By delimiting an area of study, however arbitrary, it is possible to address questions concerning the relative 'openness' of ecological systems with respect to chemical circulation. In this context, 'open' ecosystems are those which import and export large amounts of nutrients relative to the amounts stored within them, while 'closed' systems are those characterized by the small throughput of nutrients. A stretch of stream is a very open system due to the continuous throughput of nutrients, while undisturbed tropical forest is generally considered to be a relatively closed system.

The nutrient elements differ between themselves in the extent to which they are mobile. Nitrogen is a relatively mobile element. This is partly because it can be released from soil in gaseous form and partly because it is readily lost by leaching. Phosphorus, in contrast, is a relatively immobile element. It is not normally lost in gaseous form and is not easily leached.

Stores of Chemical Elements

An important feature of an ecosystem is the location and magnitude of nutrient stores. The simple three-compartment model (living biota, dead organic matter and abiotic environment) in Figure 10.3 provides a framework for discussion. In this scheme the boundaries of the physical environment are delimited rather arbitrarily: as an example, the rooting depth could be used to delimit the physical environment on land.

The physical environment usually accounts for a high proportion of each mineral element stored within the system. However, this proportion varies between ecosystem types and between elements. For example, the proportion of the total nutrient amount contained within living biomass is frequently lower for temperate forest than for tropical forest. The distribution of nutrients between the living and dead organic compartments also varies. In temperate and high-latitude forests, a greater proportion of the nutrient capital is held in the litter at the soil surface than is normally the case in tropical forests where nutrients are rapidly returned to the living biota.

A number of subcompartments can be identified within the living biota. In terrestrial ecosystems, the primary producers usually account for most of the biotic nutrient capital. Within aquatic ecosystems, however, the primary producers are tiny, short-lived organisms, so the animals may account for a much greater proportion of the nutrients held in the biota than is the case on land. Vegetation can be subdivided into various components, by growth form perhaps (trees, shrubs, herbs, etc.), by species, and also by tissue types (leaves, stems, roots, etc.). Chemical analyses of such components reveal how elements are distributed at a specific point in time, but reveal little about the dynamics of element circulation. For example, in non-seasonal environments the distribution of mineral elements among plant tissues may not appear to change very much over a year. Such a finding should not be taken as evidence that no nutrient movement has occurred. It is likely that the atoms of the various elements, present in leaves when the vegetation was first sampled, have since been translocated elsewhere and replaced. In seasonal environments, a combination of chemical analyses and growth measurements may well reveal pronounced nutrient uptake at certain times of the year. In general though, a detailed understanding of the dynamics of element circulation requires special procedures, such as the use of radioisotopes whose movement through the system can be followed.

Chemical Movements Within Ecosystems

The arrows in Figure 10.3 indicate the principal directions of movement for mineral elements in ecosystems. On land, uptake by plants is the major routeway for chemical transfer from the physical environment to the biota. Some qualification is necessary here though, because fungi associated with plant roots seemingly nearly always account for a significant amount of mineral nutrient transfer from soil to vegetation. Such associations between plant roots and fungi are called *mycorrhizae*, and they are a feature of most plant species. There are different types of mycorrhizal association and they involve different fungal species. In the most common type, called *vesicular–arbuscular mycorrhizae* (usually abbreviated to *VAM*), strands of fungal tissue (filaments) penetrate the root cells

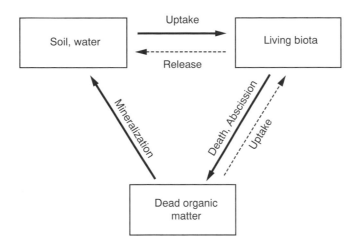

Figure 10.3   *A simple compartment model showing the main stores of mineral nutrients and the direction of flows between them. Note that nutrients in the physical environment and in dead organic matter are not necessarily in a form that can be utilized by organisms. The thicker arrows represent the major routes of transfer*

of the host plant. The other major type of association is referred to as ***ectomycorrhizal***, because the fungal hyphae are concentrated around the exterior of the root. Ectomycorrhizae are largely restricted to trees and other woody plants. Mycorrhizal fungi enhance the ability of the host plant to obtain nutrients, and may be necessary for the plant's survival. In return, the heterotrophic fungus receives a supply of energy-rich organic matter from the host plant. Mycorrhizal fungi in moist tropical environments have been shown to transfer nutrient elements directly from decaying organic matter to plant roots. Such an adaptation enhances nutrient conservation in the wet tropics where the potential for leaching is high. Nutrient uptake in aquatic ecosystems is brought about principally by unicellular algae, although larger algae ('seaweeds'), and rooted and floating plants also make a contribution in near-shore environments.

The rate at which nutrients are transferred between the physical environment and the biota is strongly influenced by the growth patterns of the dominant primary producers. During times of the year when little growth occurs, nutrient uptake may be very low or cease altogether, while at other times there is a rapid transfer of nutrients from the environment (soil or water) to the biota.

Nutrients are transferred from the living biota to the dead organic matter compartment by the death of organisms, the shedding of tissues, and the release of organic wastes by animals and other organisms (Figure 10.3). Leaf shedding is especially important in forests. In deciduous forests, most leaf fall occurs at the onset of either the cold or the dry season, but in evergreen forests, it tends to be more evenly distributed throughout the year. It has been shown that prior to leaf shedding nutrients are usually withdrawn to other tissues, thus retaining nutrients in the tree.

Nutrients can also be transferred directly from living organisms to the physical environment, as when plant leaves are leached by rainwater and metabolic by-products are excreted by animals. However, by far the most important way by which mineral nutrients are returned to the physical environment is through the decomposition of dead organic matter and the associated *mineralization* of chemical elements. The rate of mineralization is controlled by decomposer organisms, whose activities are determined largely by environmental conditions. (Decomposition rates are discussed further during discussion of the carbon cycle, Page 126.)

Inputs and Outputs of Mineral Elements

The idea that some types of ecosystems are more 'open' than others with respect to nutrient movement was introduced on Page 109. The purpose of this section is to provide a framework for considering the transfer of mineral elements into and out of particular areas of land or water. During these discussions it is worth bearing in mind the finite nature of chemical elements: gains in one area therefore mean losses elsewhere and vice versa.

A scheme for nutrient inputs and outputs is shown in Figure 10.4. The inclusion of all major routeways within a single diagram does not imply that all would need to be considered in every investigation. Just a glance at Figure 10.4 will confirm this point. Most obviously, aquatic and terrestrial ecosystems differ in fundamental ways. In fact, one of the first tasks during the planning of a nutrient budget study is to identify which inputs and which outputs are likely to be ecologically significant, and which can be safely ignored.

Atmospheric Inputs

The atmosphere is a potentially important source of chemical elements for ecological systems. From the atmosphere elements may be introduced in solution (in rain and snow), in aerosol form, and deposited 'dry' between precipitation events. Nitrogen and sulfur may also be introduced in gaseous form. Certain vegetation types, particularly forests, effectively trap elements held within mist and cloud. Where such conditions are common, as in many mountainous and coastal locations, this input can be significant. The sea can be an important source of aerial inputs for coastal ecosystems, particularly for the cations sodium, potassium, magnesium and calcium, and the anions chloride and sulfate. Where dry deposition and aerosol inputs are deemed to be important, estimates of nutrient inputs based only on rainfall measurements (known as bulk precipitation) may seriously underestimate the true atmospheric input.

The atmosphere is the major source of nutrients for ecological communities isolated from other sources. In particular, peat may accumulate to such a depth that it no longer receives nutrients in surface water and plant roots can no longer exploit the mineral soil beneath. Without atmospheric inputs the nutrients in the system would be gradually lost by leaching. Peat in this situation is referred to as *ombrogenous*, meaning 'supplied from above'. As ombrogenous peat is poor in nutrients, it is also termed *oligotrophic*.

Nitrogen and sulfur are deposited from the atmosphere in gaseous form. Although both are essential for all organisms, they can occur in chemical species and at concentrations which are injurious to the health of humans and other species. Considerable quantities of

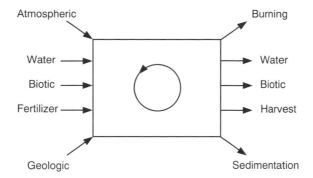

Figure 10.4   *A general scheme for considering inputs and outputs of chemical elements for ecological systems. (Biotic nitrogen fixation and losses are omitted.) In any particular situation only a few of these inputs and outputs will be important*

both elements arc released annually as gaseous oxides during the combustion of fossil fuels. When these substances are removed from the atmosphere in solution, as nitric acid and sulfuric acid, they can acidify soils and water bodies. This is the 'acid rain' phenomenon mentioned earlier (Page 107) when discussing the effects of pH on aluminium solubility. Oxides of sulfur are also directly injurious to plants, and in some areas undoubtedly constrain crop yields. Gaseous nitrogen is also incorporated into the biota by biological processes, a topic dealt with when the nitrogen cycle is discussed (Pages 121–2).

Geologic Inputs and Outputs

Nutrient elements are made available to the biota during the weathering of rocks and minerals. The geologic input varies considerably, depending on the nature of the parent material and prevailing environmental conditions. Soils formed on siliceous (i.e. silica-rich) parent materials, such as granite, tend to have low concentrations of biotically essential elements. Soils formed from calcareous parent materials are potentially more fertile, although in humid climates the nutrients released by weathering can be leached out of the soil. Rates of mineral weathering vary according to climate, tending to be higher in warmer, humid conditions than in colder, dry environments.

The geologic component is often ignored in short-term biogeochemical studies, partly because obtaining reliable values is awkward, but partly because the contribution from this source is usually considered to be negligible. This is in fact one of the least well-quantified aspects of biogeochemical cycling and closer examination could show that its importance has been underestimated. It is also complicated by short-term changes in the biological availability of individual elements.

In some ways analogous to the parent materials of soils are the sediments of the sea- and lake-floor. Sedimentation is usually considered to occur continuously, although the balance between sedimentation and release of nutrients depends on a number of factors, including the nature of the substrate, local environmental conditions and biotic activity. Minerals are also released by eruptive processes on the ocean floor, as from submarine hot springs associated with mid-oceanic ridges. Again, the decision on whether to include sedimentary sources will depend on the nature of the investigation and the local situation. If the focus of the study is the chemistry of seawater over geological timescales, then clearly the balance between the sedimentation and the release of elements would be vital to the study.

Element Transfer in Water

Flowing water always carries chemical elements which may be in solution or associated with particulate matter. This is best demonstrated by the vast quantities of nutrients transferred annually by rivers from land surfaces to the oceans, where most is deposited on the sea-floor. More locally, however, the chemical characteristics of flowing waters have a major influence on the nutrient status of receiving water bodies such as lakes and estuaries. Under natural conditions the chemistry of a river depends a great deal on the geology of its drainage basin. Thus, waters passing over much-weathered, siliceous parent materials (as in the Canadian Shield) carry low concentrations of elements. In contrast, rivers passing over softer, base-rich materials can carry considerable chemical loads. The chemistry of river water is also much affected by human activities within the drainage basin. Nitrogenous fertilizer leached from agricultural land, phosphorus-containing detergents, and sewage, which is rich in both nitrogen and phosphorus, pose particular problems for water bodies because of the close relationship between nutrient availability and aquatic productivity. Human activities can also reduce nutrient transfer along waterways. For example, the Aswan High Dam, constructed in Egypt during the 1960s, trapped sediment so efficiently that the nutrient load of the water reaching the Mediterranean Sea dropped markedly. In consequence, primary productivity declined off-shore with serious consequences for the local fishery.

Movements of water can also affect nutrient budgets on land. Thus, peats that receive nutrients carried in surface and groundwater are often much richer in nutrients than peats which depend entirely on atmospheric inputs. (A nutrient-rich peat is called a *fen* to distinguish it from an acidic, mineral-poor *bog* peat.) Within generally nutrient-poor areas, as occur over much of the British uplands, the emergence of nutrient-carrying spring and stream water may raise nutrient levels locally. This effect is demonstrated by the presence of plant species unable to tolerate the surrounding acidic, nutrient-poor conditions.

In humid climates, nutrients may be transferred downward through soils by leaching. Elements vary considerably in the extent to which they are vulnerable to loss by leaching, while soils vary in their capacity to hold nutrient elements, particularly the cationic elements such as potassium, calcium and magnesium. Cations, which are positively charged, are adsorbed on to negatively charged surfaces of clays and organic matter. Soils which are rich in clay minerals and/or organic matter therefore tend to retain the cationic elements more effectively than sandy soils, which are less chemically active. Nitrogen is relatively vulnerable to leaching losses, but phosphorus is much less mobile. In arid environments, the predominant direction of soil water movement is upwards. This water carries nutrients in solution, giving rise to excessively high concentrations of salts in the rooting zone and thus causing problems for crop production.

Biotic Transfers

In certain situations, mineral elements are transferred in ecologically significant amounts by the movements of living organisms. Examples are provided by gulls and hippopotami. These animals spend part of the day on land, where they feed, and part of the day in water, where they release undigested food and excretions. By this means, large populations of gulls have significantly raised the fertility of at least one of the shallow lakes that make up the Norfolk Broads in eastern England, with a consequent decline in its ecological and amenity value. Inputs of mineral elements in dead plant material, particularly leaves, but sometimes pollen as well, can also make a significant contribution to the nutrient economy of water bodies.

Fire

Fire is an important ecological agent over a considerable proportion of the Earth's land surface. Virtually all natural fires are caused by lightning, with volcanic activity playing a minor, local role. In addition, fire is used widely as a tool in vegetation management, and many large-scale burns are started accidentally. As a general rule, burning of vegetation tends to reduce the nutrient capital in the burnt area. Losses occur during the fire itself as minerals are converted to gaseous form (a process known as *volatilization*), and removed as particulate matter in the smoke. The magnitude of nutrient loss depends largely on the temperature of the burn. Mineral elements differ in their susceptibility to volatilization. Nitrogen and sulfur are lost in gaseous form at relatively low temperatures (a few hundred degrees); phosphorus is lost less readily; while the cationic elements such as potassium, magnesium and calcium are lost in large amounts only at very high temperatures (several hundred degrees).

Fire also increases the vulnerability of nutrients to loss immediately after the fire. This is because during a burn much of the mineral content of the organic matter is deposited as ash. Although this provides a temporary nutrient-rich environment, minerals in the ash are vulnerable to leaching and to wind and water erosion. The extent of such losses depends on the severity of the burn, the rate of vegetation recovery, soil type, local topography and the weather following the burn. However, the loss of vegetation cover inevitably raises the potential for higher rates of rainfall infiltration and higher wind speeds at the ground surface. The losses of nutrients by burning should therefore be taken into account in studies where vegetation is frequently burnt.

Fertilization and Harvest

In agricultural ecosystems, chemical inputs as fertilizers, and outputs as harvested products, can dominate nutrient budgets. The magnitude of such inputs and outputs varies greatly, but is greatest in intensive crop and forage production systems to which large amounts of fertilizer are added and the quantity of harvested biomass is large. Usually, nitrogen is the nutrient applied in the greatest amounts, but phosphorus and potassium are also frequently added. Most nitrogen fertilizer is manufactured following the industrial fixation of atmospheric nitrogen as ammonia, while phosphorus, potassium and calcium are mined.

Agricultural practices also have an indirect effect on nutrient losses. For example, soil that is left with no protective cover of vegetation is inherently vulnerable to erosion and leaching. The magnitudes of such losses depend on a number of factors, most notably topography, climate and soil characteristics.

Examples of Nutrient Circulation Studies

Three very different nutrient circulation studies are used to illustrate the range of work encompassed by this field of enquiry. First, in Figure 10.5 some results are shown from a study of major cations in a sand dune system in north-west England. The location of this study suggested a strong marine influence, so special efforts were made to quantify the inputs in aerosol form from the sea as well as in solution in rainwater. On the output side, the major routeway was considered to be groundwater discharge. Within the dune system the total amount of each cation was partitioned between 'available', 'slowly available' and 'unavailable' components, emphasizing the importance of the concept of biotic availability (Page 107) in studies of biogeochemical circulation.

The second example (Figure 10.6) comes from a long-term study, initiated during the 1960s, in forested catchments in New Hampshire, north-eastern United States. A major aim was to determine the effects of logging on the nutrient budgets in such environments, so cleared watersheds were compared with uncleared, control watersheds. The most important medium for the loss of mineral nutrients was considered to be water, so streams draining the watersheds were dammed, water losses measured, and samples analysed for their nutrient content. Figure 10.6 shows that nutrient losses increased dramatically after clear-felling, and that high rates of loss were maintained as long as vegetation regrowth was suppressed. In contrast, nutrient losses remained low on the forested watershed acting as the control. The enhanced loss of nutrients from the deforested watershed was attributable to three related factors. First, vegetation removal increased the amount of rainfall that reached the soil and percolated through the soil profile, thus increasing leaching losses. Second, the removal of the forest canopy increased both temperature and moisture in the topsoil, which stimulated nutrient mineralization from organic matter. Third, the loss of vegetation severely impaired the capacity of the biota to take up nutrients from the soil, which predisposed nutrients to loss by leaching. Studies of this sort have important lessons for forest management, particularly at the harvesting stage.

The aim in the third example (Figure 10.7) was to compile a national budget for phosphorus. Large amounts of phosphorus are imported annually to Britain, primarily in mineral form for fertilizer manufacture and in feed for livestock. Phosphorus is a valuable resource, but also a potential problem because its discharge into the aquatic environment can have undesirable ecological consequences. Studies of this sort may suggest ways in which phosphorus could be used more efficiently with reduced discharge and waste.

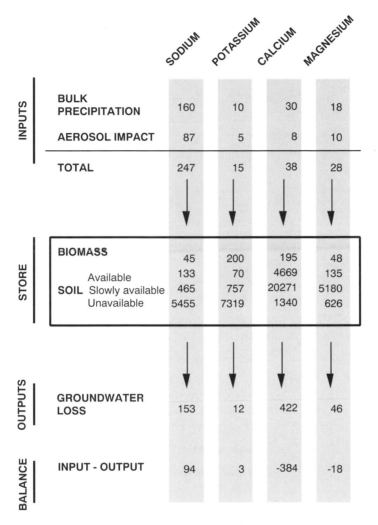

Figure 10.5 *Aerial inputs and groundwater losses (kg ha^{-1} yr^{-1}), and the stores (kg ha^{-1}) of some elements in a sand dune system in north-west England. Note the determination of both bulk precipitation and aerosol impact, and also the partitioning of the soil stores on the basis of nutrient availability. (Data courtesy of Peter James)*

The Biological Nitrogen Cycle

Nitrogen, as a component of proteins, nucleic acids and a number of other biotically important substances, is a major focus of interest in biogeochemical studies. Lack of nitrogen frequently limits plant growth, and as a consequence it is routinely applied as fertilizer. Nitrogen appears to be the key nutrient limiting primary productivity in the marine environment. Nitrogen also plays a major role in several environmental problems, including the loss of stratospheric ozone due to nitrous oxide and the contamination of groundwater by leaching of nitrate.

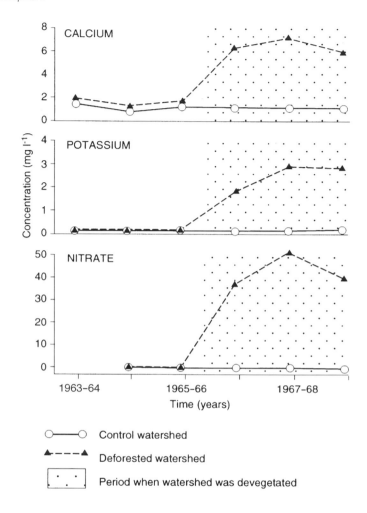

Figure 10.6   *The effect of deforestation and suppression of regrowth on the release of some nutrients in stream-water from a catchment in the north-eastern USA. Note how forest clearing precipitates the rapid and large-scale export of nutrients. (From Bormann, L. and Likens, G. 1979 Pattern and Process in a Deforested Ecosystem, Springer-Verlag, New York)*

The behaviour of nitrogen is unique among the nutrient elements. Nitrogen exists as part of a large number of chemical entities and its circulation at the Earth's surface involves several chemical and biochemical transformations. The complete nitrogen cycle is extremely complex, and many uncertainties exist concerning the quantities involved in the various transformations. An outline scheme for the nitrogen cycle, emphasizing the main biotic phases, is shown in Figure 10.8.

Nitrogen accounts for about 78 per cent by volume of the Earth's atmosphere. Here it exists overwhelmingly (>99.9 per cent) in the form known either as molecular nitrogen, or dinitrogen (N_2). Most of the remainder is held as nitrous oxide (N_2O). In water, also, most of the nitrogen (around 95 per cent) occurs as dinitrogen, with the

INPUTS

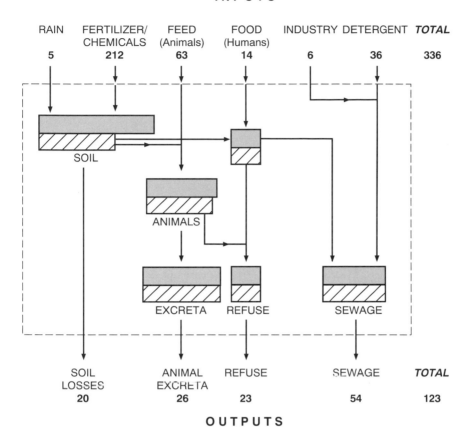

OUTPUTS

Figure 10.7 *Summary phosphorus budget for the United Kingdom. Note the magnitude of the various inputs and outputs and the pathways of phosphorus transfer. Inputs to the various stores within the UK (lightly shaded boxes) and outputs from them (diagonal lines) are more or less in balance except in the case of the soil. From data in Centre for Agricultural Strategy 1978 Phosphorus: A Resource for UK Agriculture, CAS, Reading*

remainder balanced more or less evenly between organic and inorganic forms. All but a tiny fraction of the organic nitrogen is incorporated in dead organic matter. On land, in contrast, nearly 95 per cent of the nitrogen exists in organic form, of which 95 per cent is in dead organic matter. (This excludes the nitrogen held in the rocks of the Earth's crust.) The aggregated distribution of terrestrial nitrogen between living and dead organic components masks considerable variation between different types of ecosystems and geographical areas. For example, the ratio is much lower in peat bogs, where there is a large quantity of dead organic material and a relatively small living biomass, than in tropical forests, which typically have large quantities of nitrogen in the living biomass.

The nitrogen in dead organic matter provides a convenient point of departure for discussing the movements and transformations of this element as it moves through the

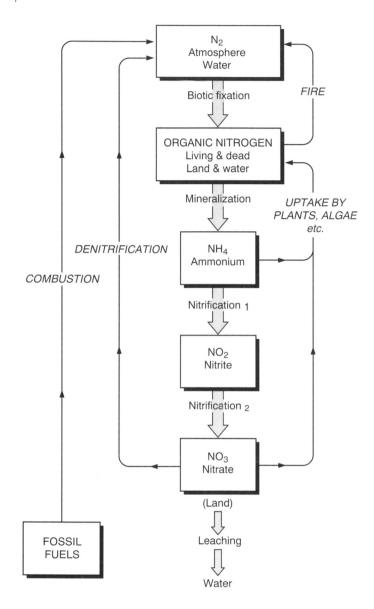

Figure 10.8   *Outline scheme for the biological nitrogen cycle. Only the main stores, routeways and transformations are shown. Further explanation is provided in the text*

biosphere. In organic form, nitrogen is unavailable to most organisms. (This is a good example of the concept of nutrient availability.) However, a few types of bacteria and fungi can utilize organic nitrogen, and in the process they release ammonium. This conversion, from organic to inorganic nitrogen, is the mineralization step shown in Figure 10.8. In aquatic environments, the tiny animals comprising the zooplankton also make a significant contribution to the available nitrogen by excreting ammonia.

Ammonia provides a source of energy for certain chemosynthetic bacteria (usually) of the genus *Nitrosomonas*. (Chemosynthesis is discussed on Page 53.) As a by-product of this process, nitrite ions (NO_2^-) are released. This is the first part of the two-stage *nitrification* process. Nitrite serves as an energy source for other chemosynthetic bacteria, of the genus *Nitrobacter*, which in turn release nitrate ions (NO_3^-). This is the second stage of the nitrification process. Nitrate is the chemical form in which most plants, and algae, preferentially take up nitrogen from their environment. However, nitrate is mobile, which renders it potentially vulnerable to leaching losses. Plants also take up nitrogen as ammonium ions if nitrification is inhibited, for example by waterlogging or low pH.

After being taken up by a plant or a microbe, nitrogen is combined with hydrogen and eventually incorporated into proteins and nucleic acids. Nitrogen can then pass along food chains, from plants to herbivores and so on, just like any other element. Nitrogen returns to the dead organic pool when organisms die, when leaves fall or when urine and faeces are released by animals. Because urine, and other excreted by-products, contain available nitrogen in abundance, grazing animals speed up the movement of nitrogen. Part of this excreted nitrogen is returned to the atmosphere as gaseous ammonia.

One part of the nitrogen cycle can therefore be thought of simply as the mineralization of nitrogen from dead organic matter to forms which can be again taken up by plants, algae and microorganisms. However, there are two other critical components of the nitrogen cycle: one is the biological 'fixation' of nitrogen gas (N_2) and the other is the return of nitrogen to the atmosphere.

Recall that nearly all the nitrogen in the atmosphere, and in water, occurs as dinitrogen (N_2). Only a very few organisms, all of them bacteria, can utilize nitrogen in this form. These bacteria possess the enzyme *nitrogenase*, which enables them to release the individual nitrogen atoms which are strongly combined as nitrogen molecules. Nitrogen atoms are then combined with hydrogen to form ammonium, a much more reactive and biotically useful source of nitrogen. Interestingly, nitrogenase is incapacitated by free oxygen, yet the bacteria themselves are aerobic. Their nitrogen-fixing capacity is attributable to adaptations that prevent oxygen reaching the sites where nitrogen and hydrogen are combined. Biological nitrogen fixation is carried out at 'normal' temperatures and pressures, unlike the industrial fixation process which requires a temperature of 700°C, pressures 100 times greater than atmospheric pressure and a metallic catalyst. Biological nitrogen fixation must have occurred relatively early in the history of life (Page 153). Previously, organisms would have been dependent on the limited amount of combined nitrogen produced during volcanic activity and electrical storms.

Certain types of nitrogen-fixing bacteria form close associations with other organisms, most notably with the roots of some types of flowering plants. (The expression 'nitrogen-fixing plants' is often used, but it is the bacteria that make the nitrogen available.) The most widespread family of such plants is the Leguminosae, which includes many important crop plants such as alfalfa, clover, peas and beans. However, nitrogen-fixing symbionts are certainly not confined to this family, but occur quite widely in the plant kingdom. Nitrogen fixation is also carried out by some types of 'free-living' bacteria, but on land their contribution is usually much less than that of symbiotic bacteria. In open water, the role of nitrogen fixation is brought about principally by cyanobacteria. Rates of nitrogen fixation vary considerably between ecosystem types. This is partly due to the variable contribution of nitrogen-fixing plants to the vegetation, but also to environmental conditions generally, because nitrogen fixation rates are related to primary productivity. Biological nitrogen fixation is widely exploited in agriculture and forestry. Ferns of the genus *Azolla*, which have nitrogen-fixing symbionts, are encouraged in wet-rice cultivation in South-East Asia, and legume species are sometimes sown on nitrogen-poor soils during commercial forest establishment. The practice of rotating crops to maximize the benefit of nitrogen residues was formerly much more widespread than at present in Western agriculture. It may be that the high costs of nitrogen manufacture, together with the environmental problems caused by high nitrate levels in water supplies, will stimulate much greater interest in biological nitrogen fixation in the future.

Compared with biological fixation, the amount of nitrogen made available to the biota during electrical storms and during volcanic activity is tiny. However, the amount fixed industrially, mostly for fertilizer manufacture, is approximately one-third of the amount fixed naturally.

While nitrogen is continuously being made available to the living biota by biotic fixation, it is also being released to the atmosphere, again by certain types of bacteria, in the process of ***denitrification***. Unlike nitrification, which proceeds only if sufficient oxygen is available, denitrification is an anaerobic process. (The bacteria responsible use nitrate ions rather than oxygen in their energy metabolism.) Nitrogen is released in various nitrogenous gases, but principally dinitrogen, thus completing the cycle. Natural denitrification is now supplemented considerably by the release of nitrogenous gases during the combustion of fossil fuels. One such substance, nitrous oxide, is both damaging to the atmospheric ozone and an effective 'greenhouse' gas.

The Carbon Cycle

Overview

Because the chemistry of life is based on compounds of carbon, this element has a unique status in the biosphere. The processes of photosynthesis and respiration play key roles in carbon circulation, but there are physical processes, too, which result in carbon movements. The focus here is on the global circulation of carbon, which is a very active research area. We consider the compartments in which carbon is stored, the routeways and processes of transfer, and the major chemical substances in which carbon is found. The problems inherent in compiling an accurate global budget for carbon, and the 'missing carbon' problem, are also discussed.

More than 99 per cent of the carbon on the planet resides in sediments, particularly in carbonate rocks. Part of the sedimentary compartment consists of the so-called fossil fuels – oil, coal and natural gas. Under natural conditions, sedimentary carbon is relatively immobile and its movements are significant only over very long timescales. Our principal concern here is with the relatively rapid transfers between the other major compartments, that is, the oceans, the atmosphere and terrestrial organic matter. However, the burning of fossil fuels is also included because it has a major impact on the contemporary carbon budget. Peat can also be regarded as a fossil fuel but it is usually categorized as terrestrial organic matter. Another way in which carbon is released to the atmosphere from sediments is in cement manufacture, which is based on carbonate rocks.

Stores of Carbon

Figure 10.9a shows estimated sizes (relative and absolute) of the major carbon stores outside the Earth's crust. The percentage values · give a realistic picture of carbon distribution, but in general there is much less certainty about the absolute quantities involved. (Different studies have generated widely different estimates.) Notice that, in the oceanic compartment, near-surface waters are separated from the waters beneath. The distinction here is between waters that are well mixed by atmospheric influence, which roughly coincides with the euphotic zone, and the rest of the oceanic system which is relatively isolated from the atmosphere.

(a)

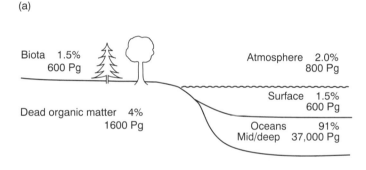

(b)

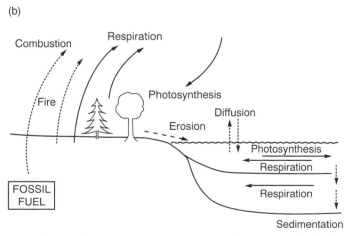

Figure 10.9 *The carbon cycle. (a) Approximate percentage distribution and absolute amounts of carbon in various major compartments. (b) The main processes involved in carbon transfer between compartments*

The major reservoir of carbon is clearly the oceans. However, the carbon concentration in the oceans is very variable, both spatially and temporally, so there is considerable scope for error in determining the total amount. Over 95 per cent of oceanic carbon is in inorganic form, primarily in bicarbonate ions, with a much smaller proportion in carbonate ions, and just a tiny proportion in carbon dioxide. Of the 4 per cent or so of oceanic organic carbon, most is dissolved, a little is present as particulate matter, while only a tiny percentage is contained within the living biota. The *absolute* amounts of carbon tied up with these tiny percentages is enormous, as can readily be seen from the estimates for total carbon in the oceans. (Freshwater is not included because it makes a negligible contribution to the total volume of water on Earth.)

Only a small proportion of the carbon resides in the atmosphere. In contrast to the oceans, the atmosphere is well mixed so there is less spatial variability, and thus more confidence in the recorded values. Most atmospheric carbon is held in gaseous form, principally carbon dioxide, with very much lower concentrations of methane, carbon monoxide and hydrocarbons. Carbon dioxide and methane are 'radiatively active', selectively absorbing infrared radiation, or heat, re-radiated from the Earth's surface. Hence the expression 'greenhouse effect' and the concern over ever increasing levels of these gases.

A historical record for carbon gases in the atmosphere has been established by analysing air bubbles trapped within cores of ice extracted from Greenland and Antarctica (Figure 10.10a). Layers of snow and ice are added annually, permitting air bubbles to be dated. The data show an increase for carbon dioxide and methane over the past few centuries, but particularly since the mid-19th century, which corresponds with the advent of the industrial revolution in Western Europe. An accurate record of recent carbon dioxide concentration, beginning in the mid-1950s has been obtained by analysing the relatively clean air above the Mauna Loa observatory on the Hawaiian Islands (Figure 10.10b). If the present rate of increase is maintained, the carbon dioxide concentration could reach 600 ppm by 2050, compared with about 370 ppm in 2000. The annual oscillations are attributed to the balance between photosynthesis and respiration. The magnitudes of the oscillations are lower in the southern than in the northern hemisphere. This is due to the lower ratio of land to water in the southern hemisphere and the fact that productivity is usually much less in the oceans than on land.

The concentration of methane has also increased in recent decades, principally due to increased bacterial fermentation (Page 56). The reasons for this rise are, first, the extension and intensification of wet-rice (paddy) cultivation; second, an increase in domesticated ruminant livestock; third, an increase in the amount of landfill for waste materials; and, fourth, an increase in seepage from fossil-fuel operations.

On land (Figure 10.9a), much less carbon is held within the living biota than in dead organic matter, although estimates of both values vary a great deal. To estimate a value for the living biota, continents can be divided into major zones based on structural features of the vegetation (discussed in Chapter 15). An average value for biomass per unit area is then allocated to each vegetation type. By multiplying the area of each zone by its average biomass, a total value is arrived at for each zone, and these are summed to provide a global estimate. Total carbon is usually assumed to be 45 per cent of this value. The advent of satellite imagery has offered much greater resolution in determining vegetation types, but even so, the wide range of biomass values within vegetation types

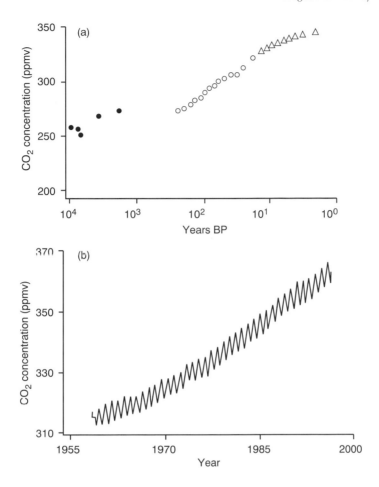

Figure 10.10 (a) Time course of atmospheric carbon dioxide for the past 10 000 years. Circles are ice core data from two locations in Antarctica; Vostock (open circles), Siple (closed circles): triangles show modern record from Mauna Loa, Hawaiian Islands. (b) Modern record of atmospheric carbon dioxide concentration from Mauna Loa. Note the steady increase and the annual oscillations. (Data collected by J. Barnola et al, Vostok; A. Neftel et al, Siple; C. Keeling and T. Whorf, modern record)

gives much scope for error. Clearly, the carbon in the biota is not evenly distributed over the land surface but varies according to vegetation type. Around 70 per cent of carbon in the 'biotic' compartment resides within forest, while tropical forest accounts for nearly 50 per cent of the total.

Dead organic matter comprises material at the soil surface, soil **humus** and peat deposits. (Actually, much of the wood within trees is dead, but it is included within the living biota.) Inspection of a soil profile will usually reveal a gradient in the appearance of organic matter, from the relatively unchanged plant litter at the surface through to the rather amorphous organic material which merges with the mineral layers beneath. Various types of humus characterize different soil types and environments. **Mull** humus is relatively uniform for example, while **mor** humus is characterized by fairly distinct layers of organic matter in various stages of decomposition and transformation. Within the mineral horizons of a soil profile the organic matter is generally dispersed, although the identity of some organic remains may still be evident.

The amount of carbon in dead organic matter varies enormously from place to place, depending upon the balance between the rate of addition of dead material and the rate of its decomposition. In situations where little organic matter is imported, the rate of addition of dead organic matter should be related to primary productivity, although a proportion of the carbon fixed by photosynthesis may accumulate as plant biomass. The quantity of dead organic matter present is not a measure of the amount of material added annually. For example, in tropical forests, where warm wet conditions ensure a high rate of biological activity, the large amount of material added each year is rapidly processed. By contrast, in northern coniferous forests, the relatively small amount of organic matter that drops to the forest floor each year is processed more slowly. In such forests, periodic fires are an important mechanism for removing this accumulated organic matter, and releasing the stored carbon.

There is even more scope for error in estimating a value for dead organic carbon, most of which cannot be 'seen', than for the living biota. Again, average values for different vegetation types and conditions are used, but a major source of error is uncertainty concerning the extent and depth of peat deposits. Whatever the true value for terrestrial organic carbon, it clearly exceeds the atmospheric component by a considerable margin. Changes in carbon storage on land therefore have a major impact on carbon in the atmosphere.

Carbon Movements

Biotic and physical processes bring about the transfer of carbon between compartments (Figure 10.9b). Photosynthesis by land plants removes carbon directly from the atmosphere, while respiration returns carbon to the atmosphere. Carbon is also returned to the atmosphere when vegetation and organic matter is burnt. Fire, in fact, acts in the same way as respiration in that it oxidizes organic matter and releases gaseous carbon compounds. Because large amounts of vegetation are burnt annually, fire plays an important role in carbon circulation. In open water, photosynthesis is confined to the euphotic zone, the carbon dioxide for this process being absorbed from the water. There is considerable uncertainty concerning the amount of oceanic photosynthesis, with estimates ranging from less than 20 Pg to well over 120 Pg annually (1 Pg = 10^{15} g). Respiration, however, occurs wherever there is life in the oceans.

The decomposition of organic matter is primarily brought about by respiration and fermentation, although physical processes such as fire can also contribute. The rate at which decomposition occurs (Figure 10.11) is obviously a major factor in carbon budgets at all spatial scales. In seasonal climates the rate of decomposition varies over the year, and at times may cease altogether, as during cold winters. The rate of decomposition is also strongly influenced by the degree of aeration. When soils are cultivated for the first time, a rapid loss of organic matter usually ensues before a new equilibrium between the rate of organic matter accumulation and its loss is established. Conversely, a reduction in aeration, usually caused by waterlogging, inhibits decomposition. Organic matter accumulates when the rate of decomposition is less than the rate of detritus addition over

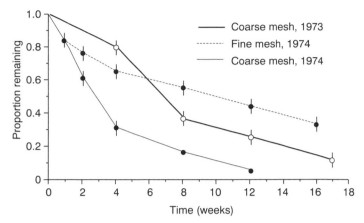

Figure 10.11 *Decomposition. In this example, from an area of shifting cultivation in Nigeria, the rate of decomposition was determined by periodically weighing detritus enclosed in small mesh bags placed at the soil surface. By using mesh of different sizes, the contribution of different types of organisms could be assessed. Note the difference between years. (From Swift, M.J. et al 1981 Decomposition and mineral-nutrient dynamics of plant litter in a regenerating bush-fallow in sub-humid tropical Nigeria. Journal of Ecology 69: 981–995. Redrawn with permission of Blackwell Science Ltd, Oxford)*

a prolonged period. ***Peat*** comprises the accumulated, and physically transformed, remains of plant material. It forms in situations where prolonged waterlogging drastically lowers the oxygen concentration and inhibits decomposition, an effect that is often exacerbated by long, cold winters. Decomposition can still proceed under anaerobic conditions, but at a considerably reduced rate because fermentation is less efficient than respiration (Page 56). The same principles apply to water bodies: if decomposition cannot keep pace with the input of organic matter, organic matter tends to accumulate on the lake- or sea-floor. The discharge of sewage is particularly implicated in such organic matter accumulations, partly because it directly stimulates bacterial activity, which leads in turn to lower oxygen concentrations, and partly because the inorganic nutrients released from the sewage promote primary production, which again leads to enhanced bacterial activity and high oxygen demand.

In addition to photosynthesis and respiration, a number of physical processes are responsible for the movement of carbon between the various compartments (Figure 10.9b). Carbon which is eroded from land surfaces is transferred to the oceans in flowing water. Gaseous carbon is transferred from air to sea at a rate determined by the relative concentration (the partial pressure) of carbon dioxide either side of the air–sea boundary. The flux from atmosphere to oceans is estimated to be about 80 Pg annually. Most of the carbon in the euphotic zone is recycled, but a small proportion is exported downwards in the form of calcium carbonate and organic matter to be deposited on the ocean floor.

Balancing the Carbon Budget

On an annual basis the carbon 'books' can be balanced reasonably well; it is when attempts are made to balance the longer term budget that major discrepancies appear. The biggest problem is that the increased amount of carbon in the atmosphere is much less than the amount of carbon known to have been released by the combustion of fossil fuels. The discrepancy is still greater when this last value is added to the estimated amount of carbon released by human use of the biota. The fossil-fuel data, especially for the last 50 years or so, appears to be quite accurate. Also there is little doubt that most human activities over the last few thousand years have encouraged the release of carbon from terrestrial ecosystems, even though the amounts are not known with any accuracy. For example, deforestation, drainage of wetlands and cultivation of grasslands have all led to the release of gaseous carbon. So, over the last few thousand years, the terrestrial environment should have been a net source, rather than a net 'sink', for carbon.

The problem therefore is to account for the excess carbon. One possible explanation is that it has simply been absorbed by the oceans, which provide the major carbon store. For a long time this was the prevailing view. After all, the oceans are not uniform and compiling accurate data for the total amount of carbon stored is very problematic. However, quite a lot is known about oceanic processes; for example, the rate at which carbon crosses the air–sea boundary and is transported downwards, the rate at which carbon is transferred between carbon dioxide, bicarbonate and carbonates, and so on. Using numerical models based on these types of information, oceanographers have come to the conclusion that the oceans cannot possibly be the sink for all the excess carbon. It is conceded that a proportion of released carbon has been absorbed by the oceans, but certainly not all of it.

It has therefore been necessary to rethink the possible role of the living biota. One suggestion is that the release of nitrogen and sulfur by human activities has had a fertilizing effect on at least some of the world's forests, or that carbon dioxide itself is fertilizing the forests and increasing carbon storage in ecosystems. There is some supporting evidence but it is not really persuasive. But what about the rest of the Earth's land area, particularly the extensive forest areas outside the tropics in the northern hemisphere? In the past there has been a tendency to regard such environments as being in a steady state with respect to carbon balance, i.e. the annual balance between photosynthesis and respiration is about 1:1. However, perhaps this is not the case. It might be that far more carbon is being fixed in photosynthesis than is being released in respiration in these regions. This could be due to the earlier harvesting of timber or a greater rate of natural disturbance, leading to a younger, and more productive, age-class distribution of forest. An alternative possibility is that the oceanographers have underestimated the amount of carbon being absorbed by seawater; perhaps there are areas where carbon is being absorbed at a higher rate than elsewhere because it is being transported away by downward moving currents. Some have suggested that carbon dioxide which is being absorbed by the oceans is being assimilated in photosynthesis at a greater rate than generally thought, and this carbon is falling through the water column to the ocean depths. The fact is no-one knows for sure.

The Carbon Cycle and Climatic Change

The concentration of atmospheric carbon has fluctuated over the last 100 000 years. High levels of carbon dioxide tend to be associated with warmer global conditions, while intervals of relatively low carbon dioxide have been associated with generally lower temperatures. Although these two variables appear to be correlated, the mechanisms involved are not known with any certainty. There is no question that atmospheric concentrations of carbon dioxide and methane have increased significantly since the mid-19th century, and few would dispute that global temperatures are rising. A causal link seems logical because the two gases are radiatively active, and the concentrations of other 'greenhouse' gases, such as nitrous oxide, have also risen. The general view, despite some dissenting voices, is that human activities have contributed significantly to the global temperature rise since 1900 and that greenhouse gas emissions have played a central role.

Further Reading – Part Two

Barnes, R.S.K. and Hughes, R.N. 1999 *An Introduction to Marine Ecology*, 3rd edition. Blackwell Science, Oxford.
(Latest edition of a text providing a good overview of the various zones in the marine environment and more generic themes.)
Begon, M., Harper, J.L. and Townsend, C.R. 1996 *Ecology: Individuals, Population and Communities*, 3rd edition. Blackwell Science, Oxford.
(Many consider this to be the best of the substantive college-level texts on ecology. Very comprehensive, very readable. Note also the CD-ROM version by same authors, 1997.)
Colinvaux, P. 1993 *Ecology 2*. John Wiley & Sons, New York.
(Another fine general ecology text, less bulky than Begon *et al* and Krebs and good on geographical and temporal aspects.)
Krebs, C.J. 1994 *Ecology: The Distribution and Abundance of Organisms*, 4th edition. HarperCollins, New York.
(Another excellent college-level text.)
Moss, B. 1988 *Ecology of Fresh Waters; Man and Medium*, 2nd edition. Blackwell Science, Oxford.
(Highly regarded and well-established textbook covering all aspects of the subject.)
Schlesinger, W.H. 1991 *Biogeochemistry: An Analysis of Global Change*. Academic Press, San Diego.
(Very good coverage of all aspects of biogeochemical circulation.)

Part Three
THE HISTORY OF THE BIOSPHERE

This part of the book is intended to provide a framework for the history of life on Earth. As organisms have been present for the greater part of the Earth's 4.6 billion year history, this would appear to be a very ambitious task. The approach used here is to identify the really important events in the history of life and discuss their evolutionary significance. The first of the three chapters in this part contains important reference material, including the geological timescale, the process of fossilization, and changes in the Earth's environment, particularly those associated with plate tectonics. The second chapter discusses life's origins and also considers the momentous evolutionary innovations that appeared in that long interval of time before organisms were fossilized in abundance about half a billion years ago. The third chapter chronicles key evolutionary events in the most recent half billion years for which there is much more fossil evidence. This chapter ends with a survey of human origins. It is particularly important to be mindful of timescales in this part of the book because these range from events billions of years ago (denoted here as Bya), through events millions of years ago (Mya), to the most recent few thousand years.

11

Understanding the Past

The purpose of this chapter is to provide some background information necessary for studying the history of life. The first theme is the *geological timescale,* which provides a temporal framework for subsequent discussions. The second theme is the preservation and dating of *fossils,* which are defined as the remains of organisms or other tangible evidence of their existence. An important issue here is the biased and incomplete nature of the fossil record. Finally, the Earth's changing environment is discussed, both in terms of continental configuration and climate.

The Geological Timescale

The age of the Earth is usually given as 4.6 billion years. This vast – almost incomprehensible – span of time is subdivided into intervals, whose names are essential vocabulary when discussing the history of life. The primary divisions of geological time are called *aeons,* of which three or four are recognized (Figure 11.1). In the three-aeon scheme, the earliest is the Archaean, meaning 'ancient' or 'beginning'. In the four-aeon scheme, the earliest, known as the Hadaean (from Hades, meaning the 'abode of the dead') precedes the Archaean, which is thus shorter than in the three-aeon scheme. In both schemes the Proterozoic aeon spans the interval from 2.5 Bya to around 0.57 Bya.

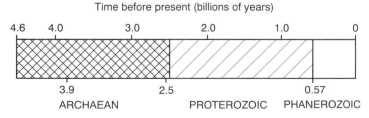

Figure 11.1 *The aeons into which the Earth's history is divided. In the four-aeon scheme, the Hadaean aeon covers the earliest 0.7 billion years of Earth history and the Archaean occupies a shorter interval*

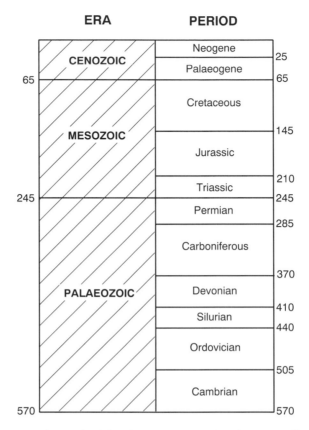

Figure 11.2   *The eras and periods of the Phanerozoic aeon. Numbers are millions of years before present. Boundaries indicate significant changes in fossil assemblages*

This term was chosen (*proto* means earlier) at a time when there was practically no tangible evidence for life before half a billion years ago. The lower boundary of the most recent aeon, the Phanerozoic (meaning 'abundant life'), is variously set between 580 and 540 Bya and it marks the time when organisms began to be fossilized in abundance.

The Phanerozoic aeon is divided into three *eras*, the Palaeozoic, the Mesozoic and the Cenozoic, each of which is subdivided into *periods* (Figure 11.2). Because the Cambrian is the first period of the Phanerozoic aeon, the term Precambrian is commonly used for the 4.0 billion years or so between the formation of the Earth and the beginning of the Phanerozoic aeon. Geological columns tend to emphasize the Phanerozoic aeon, even though the Precambrian interval accounts for 85 per cent of the Earth's history, and it was during the Precambrian that the really fundamental evolutionary events occurred.

The geological timescale is based upon the history of life, the boundaries of named intervals of the Phanerozoic aeon being marked by significant changes in fossil assemblages. Most of these names are derived from the geographical locations in which the geological formations were first described in detail. This system developed during the 19th century in western Europe, at a time when neither the rocks, nor the fossils they contained, could be dated. Absolute dating only became possible with an understanding of radioisotopes in the present century (Page 142). It was possible, however, to infer the *ordering* of events from the relative position of rock strata and from the types of fossils they contained. For example, rocks of the Cambrian period were first described in detail in North Wales in the British Isles. (*Cambria* is the Roman name for Wales.) Thereafter, rock strata containing similar fossil assemblages, wherever they were located, were deemed to be part of the Cambrian system.

The progressive accumulation of fossil evidence in the 19th and early 20th centuries led to a gradual refinement of the geological timescale, while more recently the advent of suitable techniques has permitted the various geological intervals to be dated. As part of this refinement process, the dates of the boundaries are altered, so a selection of texts will likely show differences of a few million years for the same named interval. When dealing with events hundreds of million years ago, such differences are relatively unimportant.

Charting the History of Life

Fossils

The most direct information about life in the past is provided by fossils. Remains of organisms may be preserved unchanged, but much more commonly preservation is associated with chemical alteration. As organisms are dying all the time, it is not easy to define a fossil precisely in terms of its age, but this is not really an issue. Sometimes the term *subfossil* is used to refer to remains younger than a few thousand years.

Conditions for Fossilization

An account of fossilization processes will reveal why fossils provide an incomplete, and highly biased, archive of the history of life. From earlier discussions of ecosystem processes (Pages 126–7) it should be clear that an organism usually decomposes when it dies. As decomposition is essentially a biotic process, its rate is determined by environmental variables, particularly oxygen concentration, temperature and moisture. In the short term, biological decay is normally supplemented to a small extent by diminution and alteration of remains by physical processes. Over much longer timescales, geological processes, involving great increases in heat and pressure, usually alter any organismic remains beyond recognition. Fossilization should thus be thought of as a comparatively rare event.

The fossil record is heavily biased towards organisms with hard body parts such as bones, shells and teeth. These are composed of minerals such as calcium carbonate, calcium phosphate and silica. Not only are mineralized structures relatively resistant to decay, but they may be further mineralized as other chemical substances replace the original structure over time. For plants, the lignin of cell walls and the sporopollenin of spores and pollen grains (Pages 139) are relatively resistant to decay, which may permit their preservation over long time intervals. Soft-bodied organisms usually decay very rapidly. Their preservation requires very special combinations of conditions. The biased nature of the fossil record means that knowledge about evolutionary lineages is quite good for some life forms, but very incomplete for others. It also influences understanding about the functioning of past ecological communities: food web reconstructions, for example, are based primarily on the hard-bodied members of the community.

Hard body parts, unless highly mineralized, eventually disappear if normal decomposition activities are not arrested. Thus the environment in which an organism dies (or to which it is transported after death) is crucial to its preservation. By far the most important environments for fossilization are those in which sediments are rapidly accumulating, thereby burying organic remains. Sedimentation inhibits biological decay by lowering the oxygen concentration and reducing physical weathering. Fossils are therefore associated principally with depositional environments, particularly alluvial lowlands and adjacent shallow waters. Sometimes burial can be very sudden, as in an ash or lava flow, during a desert sand storm, or while a river is in flood. Geographical location is therefore another major source of bias in the fossil record. Fossilized remains of organisms that inhabited upland environments are actually quite rare, and fossilization occurs only in limited situations, such as in some caves.

Diagenesis, defined as the chemical and physical processes that convert soft sediments into hard rock, is another source of bias in the fossil record because organisms vary in the degree to which their remains survive such processes. Metamorphic processes (i.e. changes in rocks due to heat and pressure) and tectonic events (earthquakes) tend to reduce the integrity of organic remains and the probability of their preservation.

Time is a further major source of bias in the fossil record. In general, sediments become increasingly altered with age so that the younger the sediment, the greater the probability that remains will survive. This is reflected in the geological timescale. In the most recent era, the Cenozoic, the periods are very much shorter than in the two preceding eras.

Fossil Types

Preserved impressions of organisms are called *trace fossils*. The size and shape of trace fossils, which may be footprints or burrows, for example, provide clues to the morphology and lifestyle of the organisms that left them (Figure 11.3). Other fossils are moulds or replicas of organisms. A body, or an organ, may disappear some time after it has become buried by sediments, leaving a void which reveals its outline features. Alternatively, after the inner parts of a shelled organism have disappeared, the shell survives long enough for its interior space to fill with minerals. Disappearance of the outer shell then leaves a mineral replica of the organism. The remains of hard body parts may survive virtually intact, or the original mineral structure may be partly or wholly replaced (Figure 11.4). In some fossils the organic structure has been replaced by minerals in solution, thus preserving the organism's original form. This process accounts for the survival for well over 200 million years of the famous petrified logs in northern Arizona, USA (Figure 11.5). Some fossils consist simply of carbon films: fossilized plant leaves are commonly of this type (Figure 11.6).

For reasons discussed earlier, the discovery of preserved soft-bodied remains is a comparatively rare event, and usually of great significance. For the preservation of soft body

Figure 11.3 *Trace fossil. A feeding trace left by the worm* Nereites; *from the Silurian, south Wales. (Photo, Ian Qualtrough; specimen provided by National Museums and Galleries on Merseyside)*

parts, very rapid burial or some other means of excluding decay processes is vital. Some famous fossil finds have been made in bituminous substances such as asphalt, in which organisms were probably trapped and then incarcerated before burial. Amber, a fossilized plant resin, sometimes contains insects or other small organisms which became entrapped in this once viscous substance. Continuous freezing can also preserve soft tissue effectively. In Alaska and Siberia, animal carcasses have been extracted from the frozen silt of the permafrost zone; preservation has been due to rapid freezing and drying on death.

Fossilized pollen grains and spores, which in general are quite durable, are particularly important for studying the evolutionary history of plants and also changes in vegetation during the comparatively recent past. Spores and pollen grains are so useful because their morphology varies between taxa, while their durability is attributable to a decay-resistant outer coat, the ***exine***, which contains a high proportion of the substance called sporopollenin. As pollen grains typically become trapped in depositional environments such as peat and lake sediments, cores extracted from such situations provide information about plant life in the past. Increasing depth is equivalent to increasing age, and various techniques are available for dating the material at different depths in the core. By determining the proportional representation of taxa at different depths, i.e. at different times in the past, a general picture of local vegetation change emerges (Figure 11.7). Furthermore, as the taxa are still present for the most part, the vegetation can be used as a guide to the prevailing environmental conditions and the nature of human activity in the region.

There are certain limitations and drawbacks with pollen analysis. First, typically it is only possible to assign a pollen grain to a genus or family, and not to a species. Second, the pollen may have been transported over a range of distances, so the spatial extent of the vegetation being examined is unclear. Third, the rate at which pollen decays varies considerably between taxa. Fourth, plant species differ in the quantities of pollen they produce, so their representation in pollen samples is not a reliable indicator of their

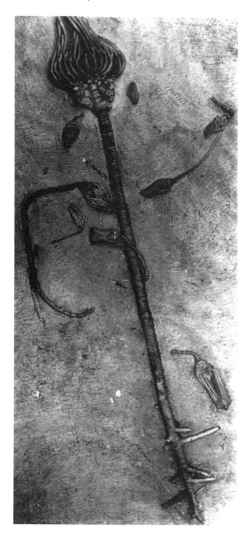 

Figure 11.4   *(a) A crinoid (sea lily); from the Carboniferous, Indiana, USA. The outer calcareous material has been preserved, but further mineral deposition has occurred within the original structure. This organism stood 'upright' on the sea-floor. (b) Tooth of a Miocene shark, Charcarodon, from Florida, USA. The original mineral structure has been preserved virtually unchanged. (Photos, Ian Qualtrough; specimens provided by National Museums and Galleries on Merseyside)*

representation in the vegetation. However, knowledge of the amounts of pollen presently produced by the same taxa allows some accommodation of this source of error. Despite these problems, pollen analysis is the most widely used technique for establishing vegetation change in the comparatively recent past, and for investigating the phylogeny of the flowering plants.

Diatoms, which are unicellular algae, also provide clues to past environments. The durability of diatoms in accumulating sediments is also attributable to a tough outer coat, but one made of silica. As with pollen grains, the structure of this outer coat varies

Figure 11.5   *Petrified logs of Triassic conifers, from northern Arizona, USA. Silica has replaced the original carbonaceous structure. (Photo, Ann Watkin)*

between taxa, permitting their identification following extraction from cores taken from the lake- or sea-bed. A chronology of species change can therefore be assembled. From a knowledge of the ecological conditions (e.g. water chemistry) in which diatoms of various species are presently found, it is possible to infer conditions at times in the past. Such information also provides valuable clues to contemporary ecological processes and

Figure 11.6   *A carbon-film fossil. Fern leaves from Carboniferous coal deposits, north-east England. (Photo, Ian Qualtrough; specimen provided by National Museums and Galleries on Merseyside)*

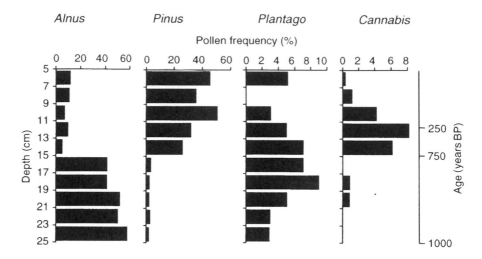

Figure 11.7   *A pollen diagram. The relative abundance of pollen of four taxa, from a bog in north-west England, is shown at different depths which have been dated approximately. Such diagrams are used to reconstruct regional vegetation history and can be used to infer environmental conditions and human activities. (Diagrams provided by Sharon Gedye)*

human activities in the surrounding land area because these often have a determining influence on water characteristics.

Dating Fossils

By looking at the order of sedimentary rock strata in vertical section, and by examining the fossils they contain, it is possible to draw up a *relative* geological column with named intervals. This is as far as the 19th century geologists could go, and any attempt to date the various rocks or geological transitions relied on inferences made on (often dubious) premises. Drawing up a geological column with reasonably accurate dates has been made possible only during the 20th century with the discovery of radioactivity and an understanding of the behaviour of radioisotopes.

To aid appreciation of the use of radioisotopes for dating purposes, a few basic principles are reviewed here. First, chemical elements exist in different forms, called *isotopes*, of which one is usually overwhelmingly predominant. The atomic nuclei of different isotopes of the same element have different numbers of neutrons, but the same number of protons. (The number of protons – the atomic number – characterizes individual elements.) Now some isotopes are inherently unstable: they spontaneously disintegrate, or decay, with the emission of radiation, subatomic particles or both. These are the *radioisotopes*. As atoms of radioisotopes decay, atoms of other isotopes, known as 'daughters', are produced. Because subatomic particles are lost during the decay of radioisotopes, the 'daughter' isotopes belong to other elements. The rates of decay, which vary enormously between isotopes, are expressed as *half-lives*, the half-life of an isotope being defined as the length of time it takes for half the radioactivity to disappear. The ratio of a parent isotope to a daughter isotope in a substance therefore permits the age of formation of that substance to be calculated. This is the basis of radioactive dating.

As half-lives vary so greatly between radioisotopes, a particular 'mother–daughter' system can only be used confidently for a particular timescale. The system rubidium-87 – strontium-87, for example, is used for very long timescales on account of the extremely slow decay rate of the parent isotope (approximately 48.5 billion years) and the inherent stability of the daughter. Potassium-40 – argon-40 is also employed for dating old rocks because potassium-40 has a half-life of around 1.3 billion years.

For organic remains no older than a few tens of thousands of years, radiocarbon dating is used. Age is calculated on the basis of the ratio of two isotopes of carbon; one is carbon-14, a radioisotope with a half-life of 5730 years, the other is the stable isotope carbon-12. Carbon-14 is naturally present as a very tiny, but fixed, proportion of carbon, which is dominated by carbon-12. Carbon dating assumes the two isotopes are assimilated by photosynthesis in this same ratio. Carbon-14 will then decay (to produce an isotope of nitrogen). So by measuring the ratio of the two carbon isotopes it is possible to date the age of the carbonaceous material; the lower the amount of carbon-14 relative to carbon-12, the greater the age of the material because more radioactive carbon will have decayed.

When the time interval occupied by a particular fossil taxon is well known, the fossils themselves can be used to date rock strata. Fossil types which are in regular use for dating purposes are called *index fossils*. Taxa which serve as good index fossils are easily and unambiguously identified; they are abundant and widely distributed; and the taxa lived for clearly defined and comparatively short time intervals. Taxa which are commonly used as index fossils for different time intervals include trilobites (distant relatives of insects), crinoids (sea lilies) and graptolites (primitive chordates).

Changes in the Physical Environment

Continental Movements

A key frame of reference for the history of life is the changing configuration of land masses in the past. The movement of continents has a direct effect on the geographical distribution of organisms (a topic discussed in Chapter 14), but also an indirect effect because of its influence on climate.

The idea that continents could move across the Earth's surface was seriously proposed early in the 20th century by the German scientist Alfred Wegener. Although the theory had its supporters, it was not widely accepted until the 1960s. The revolution in geological thinking that occurred at this time was due to the acceptance of the theory of *plate tectonics*. ('Tectonics' refers to movements in the Earth's crust.) A central feature of this theory is that the *lithosphere*, the rigid outer part of the Earth, is composed of discrete segments, or *plates*. There are eight major plates and several minor ones (Figure 11.8b), although it is believed that their number and configuration has changed during geological time. The plates, which comprise both crust and outer mantle material, 'float' on the denser, but more fluid material of the *asthenosphere* beneath (Figure 11.8a). The

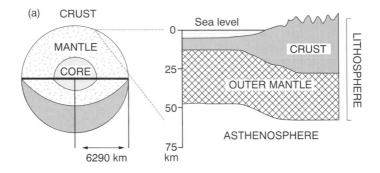

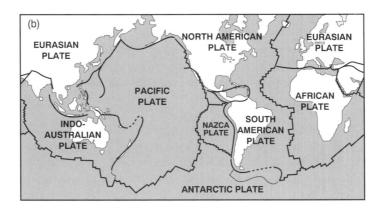

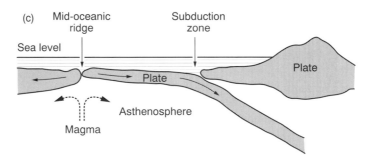

Figure 11.8 (a) The Earth's layered structure: the rigid lithosphere is made up of crust and the thin outer layer of the mantle. (b) The major plates of the Earth. (c) Types of plate margin. New crust is formed at the mid-oceanic ridge as molten material is extruded and cools. At the subduction zone, one section of plate is being forced under the other. The continental plate remains on top due to the relatively low density of continental material. Dashed arrows represent the convective forces believed to be responsible for the extrusion of material and subsequent sea-floor spreading

movement of the plates relative to each other brings about changes in the configuration of the land masses. Plate movement is caused by the extrusion of molten material along narrow, linear zones on the sea-floor, and by the sinking (***subduction***) of plate material elsewhere (Figure 11.8c).

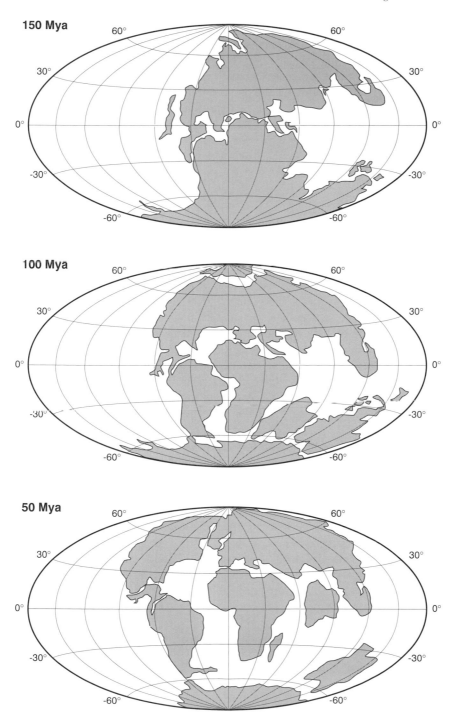

Figure 11.9   *Palaeogeographical reconstructions for various intervals during the Phanerozoic aeon*

It is believed that by late Proterozoic times the Earth's land masses had coalesced, having previously existed as separate 'islands'. During the Palaeozoic era this large land mass fragmented, but by around 250 Mya a 'supercontinent', called ***Pangaea***, had reformed (Figure 11.9). During the Mesozoic era (245–65 Mya), this large land mass separated into two fragments. One of these, ***Laurasia***, consisted essentially of the present northern continents, while the other, ***Gondwana***, comprised the present southern continents plus India. Late in the Mesozoic, Gondwana fragmented and the continental configuration we are familiar with today slowly emerged (Figure 11.9). However, continental movement has continued throughout the Cenozoic, and indeed is still continuing.

Continental Movement and Climatic Change

Every location on the Earth's land masses has experienced marked climatic changes during geological time. This is due partly to global climatic changes, which affect each position on the Earth's surface, and partly to the 'wandering' of continents across climatic zones. It is easy to appreciate that a latitudinal shift in the position of a continent will have direct climatic consequences for each part of the land mass. In addition, however, changes in the size of land masses as a result of their cleavage or coalescence affect rainfall and temperature patterns as the degree of maritime influence alters. Plate movement can also influence climate indirectly, as when mountain ranges which form as a consequence of plate collisions block the passage of moisture-laden air. The direction of ocean currents is affected by the configuration of land masses. This has a major influence on climate because ocean currents transfer heat energy polewards from equatorial regions. The present configuration of the southern continents permits the circumpolar movement of water, which isolates Antarctica from the warming influences of oceanic water from lower latitudes. Around 250 Mya, however, when it seems there was essentially a single continent, currents would have moved relatively unimpeded from the equator to the poles, resulting in much lower latitudinal temperature gradients than is the case today.

In addition to tectonically induced effects, astronomical events may also trigger changes in climate. Such events include slight shifts in the Earth's orbit or in the tilt of its axis, but also catastrophic changes caused by asteroid impacts. However, there is considerable uncertainty concerning the magnitude of such influences.

12

Life in the Archaean and Proterozoic Aeons

It is not known when the first living cells appeared, but it was almost certainly over 3.5 Bya and probably in excess of 3.8 Bya. The record of hard-bodied organisms, which dates to about 0.5 Bya, looks quite recent when set against the entire sweep of life's history. The focus of this chapter is the history of life until the time when organisms were fossilized in abundance. First we consider life's origins and then the major evolutionary events of the following 3 billion years or so. At the end of this chapter it will be apparent that the really fundamental evolutionary innovations can be traced to this interval.

Life's Origins

Prebiotic Evolution

It is very difficult to do justice to this subject within the space of a few paragraphs because it involves hugely complex, and controversial issues. What we can do is to use a fairly basic knowledge of the way cells work to identify key stages and processes in the formation of living, reproducing organisms from the simple chemical entities likely to have been present on the Earth some 4.0 Bya (Figure 12.1).

The Earth's atmosphere, and oceans, arose by *outgassing*, i.e. the release of gases trapped in the Earth's interior. Views about the composition of the Archaean atmosphere have shifted during the last few decades and there is still no consensus which fits an understanding of both physical chemistry and Archaean geology. In the 1920s and 1930s, the British biologist J.B.S. Haldane and the Russian biochemist A.I. Oparin independently proposed that the early atmosphere was strongly reducing (contained no free oxygen) as otherwise simple organic molecules would have been unstable. They suggested that this early atmosphere was composed of hydrogen, methane, ammonia and water vapour. From the point of view of explaining life's origins, it is tempting to envisage such an atmosphere because it contains all the ingredients necessary for the formation of organic molecules. Furthermore, it has been demonstrated that similar gaseous mixtures, when passed over electrical discharges (as a source of energy), can yield a range of organic chemicals, including amino acids. This type of experimental work, pioneered by S.L. Miller and H.C. Urey at the University of Chicago in the early 1950s, thus provided evidence, not only for one step in the formation of life but also for the composition of the early Earth's atmosphere.

In the 1950s, however, American geologist W. Rubey argued that the accepted view of an atmosphere rich in hydrogen, methane and ammonia was not consistent with knowledge of geochemical and atmospheric phenomena, and he proposed a prebiotic atmosphere made up largely of nitrogen, carbon dioxide, water vapour and sulfur compounds. Under laboratory conditions, such a gaseous mixture proved to be less fruitful in terms of organic products than one containing methane and ammonia, although amino acids have been synthesized. There is evidence to support such an atmosphere. First, it is difficult to explain how large quantities of nitrogen could have been added subsequently to the atmosphere. Second, the concentration of atmospheric carbon dioxide was probably higher in the Archaean than today due to the greater amount of volcanic activity. (Much of this carbon is now held within carbonate sediments, having come out of the atmosphere in solution.) Third, methane and ammonia have very short residence times in the atmosphere and so were unlikely to have been present in significant quantities. It is possible that small amounts of ammonia were present locally, perhaps in gas streams emerging from underwater hot springs. It is certainly easier to envisage the synthesis of organic chemicals in the presence of ammonia than in its absence. One lesson from this discussion is that in attempting to explain life's origins, it is important not to conclude that the early atmosphere must have approximated that in which organic synthesis occurs most readily.

The synthesis of organic substances from primarily inorganic chemical species requires a source of energy, first to promote the dissociation (splitting-up) of existing gaseous molecules, and second to stimulate reactions leading to the synthesis of new molecules. The traditional view is that the energy sources were lightning discharges or ultraviolet radiation. The intensity of ultraviolet radiation would have been much greater 4 Bya than now because there was no ozone in the atmosphere, ozone formation being dependent on free oxygen. It has generally been believed that simple organic molecules were initially synthesized in the atmosphere and then deposited in the oceans. An alternative scenario, however, is that such molecules were manufactured in hydrothermal vents (hot springs) associated with volcanic activity.

The next stage to consider in the development of life is how these simple organic chemicals were linked together to form more complex substances such as proteins and nucleic acids. The initial formation of these substances requires a mechanism for the concentration of the chemical building blocks. Clearly, in the open ocean such molecules would be too dispersed to form chemical linkages. Concentration might have occurred in shallow water where evaporative losses greatly exceeded inputs or, possibly, by the freezing of water bodies with the consequent coalescence of organic materials. An alternative proposal is that negatively charged clay surfaces adsorbed small organic molecules and acted as a template for the formation of larger molecules. The selective adsorption of some nucleotides and amino acids has been demonstrated experimentally.

One major source of debate is *which* of the key polymers – DNA, RNA or protein – was the first to be synthesized. If it was protein, there are problems in explaining its replication. If it was DNA there are problems in explaining its synthesis in the absence of

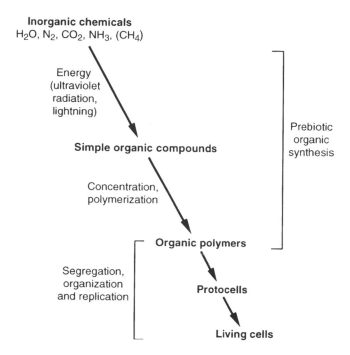

Inorganic chemicals
H_2O, N_2, CO_2, NH_3, (CH_4)

Energy
(ultraviolet
radiation,
lightning)

Simple organic compounds

Concentration,
polymerization

Prebiotic
organic
synthesis

Organic polymers

Segregation,
organization
and replication

Protocells

Living cells

Figure 12.1 *Key stages and processes in the origin of life. There is considerable uncertainty about details such as atmospheric composition, the mechanisms involved in the various phases of prebiotic and protobiotic evolution, and the sequence of some events*

conventional enzymes, which are made of protein. If it was RNA, there are problems again in explaining its replication. At present the RNA theory is favoured, because pieces of RNA have been shown to self-replicate under certain circumstances. However, there is by no means a consensus on this issue, and there are still several conceptual obstacles to be overcome.

In summary, prebiotic chemical synthesis is envisaged as a three-stage process involving, first, the production of quite simple organic chemicals, second, their concentration and, third, their polymerization. It is very unlikely that such a series of processes could occur today. First, ultraviolet radiation – if it was the energy source for initial reactions – is weaker due to the screening effects of ozone; second, any organic chemicals produced abiotically would be unstable in the present oxidizing environment; and, third, as organisms have now colonized even the most inhospitable of environments, any newly synthesized organic substance would be quickly consumed.

The Formation of Cells

The next series of steps involved the isolation of the newly formed polymers from their environment. The isolation process involved the development of a simple type of membrane, indicating the beginnings of cellular formation. Although the ability to reproduce is a key feature of cells, it is thought that the reproduction of chemical molecules preceded cellular formation. Living cells are not simply randomly assembled packages of organic chemicals, however, but reveal a very high degree of biochemical organization. The evolution of even the simplest living cell must have involved a lengthy series of processes and the formation of intermediate stages known as *protocells*. It is not known whether nucleic acids, with their capacity to order biochemical functions through enzyme production, were involved in the earliest energy transformations. Neither is it known how energy, released in the breakdown of organic molecules, was captured and harnessed for use by the earliest cells. It is also difficult to identify at what stage the prebiotic chemical machinery became surrounded by an insulating membrane. However, it is probable that ATP, 'life's universal energy currency', appeared at an early stage, together with the pathway of energy metabolism called glycolysis (Chapter 6).

Despite enormous complexities, experimentation has suggested some possible explanations for a few of the necessary steps, although solutions to other problems remain highly elusive. How, for example, could sequences of nucleotides begin to direct the synthesis of proteins from amino acids, a process that is central to the functioning of living systems?

The possibility of an extraterrestrial contribution to the origin of life should be mentioned. Speculation on this issue has been fostered by claims that rocks of Martian origin found on Earth contain microscopically sized structures resembling cellular features. The general consensus now is that these claims are false, but more compelling evidence of a contribution from space is that some meteorites, known as carbonaceous chondrites, and some comets also, contain carbon compounds not unlike those associated with living processes. The possibility remains then of an extraterrestrial contribution to life's origins on Earth.

Evidence for the Age of the Biosphere

Two major lines of evidence are used to address the problem of when life originated on the planet. One involves fossilized remains, the other depends on geochemical information. As recently as 1950 there was very little fossil evidence for life much before 650 Mya. Currently the fossil record extends back about 3.5 billion years. However, there are considerable difficulties in interpreting remains of such great age. The oldest fossil cells come from rocks of the Pilbara goldfields, near North Pole in Western Australia. These appear as filaments, not unlike those of modern cyanobacteria. Other ancient microfossils, believed to be 3.2 billion years old, come from the Fig Tree formation in South Africa.

Particularly important to an understanding of life during the Archaean and the Proterozoic are structures called *stromatolites*. These are roughly columnar or domed in form, and in vertical section they reveal alternating bands of organic-rich and organic-poor calcareous material. Some of the earliest fossilized cells, in fact, are associated with stromatolites. Although there are several stromatolite locations of Archaean age, these structures are much more abundant in Proterozoic rocks. Even today, localized congregations of 'active' stromatolites occur in warm, shallow, coastal waters, notably in Western Australia, Baja in northern Mexico, and the Bahamas. They increase in size as cyanobacteria and other organisms colonize surfaces and trap sediment. As the bacterial community grows through the sediment to form another microbial mat, more sediment is trapped. Some fossil stromatolites are several metres in height, although most extant examples are much shorter. What seems to be critical to their continued activity is the absence of grazing organisms, due to high salinity. Even without direct evidence of cells, the presence of stromatolites is suggestive of biological activity, although it is true that some stromatolite-like structures are clearly not biogenic.

Further circumstantial evidence for the antiquity of life comes from the chemical signals left in rocks by organisms. The very oldest sedimentary rocks, which belong to the Isua formation in Greenland, have been dated to about 3.8 Bya. These contain graphite, a pure form of carbon that is probably biogenic. Additional evidence comes from very ancient sedimentary rocks in which the ratio of carbon isotopes is characteristic of living organisms.

The Earliest Organisms

Traditionally it has been assumed that the earliest organisms were heterotrophic, meaning they depended on preformed organic molecules for energy. However, a more recent theory is that the first type of energy metabolism to evolve was chemosynthesis (Page 53). In other words, the first organisms may have been autotrophic, meeting their energy needs by oxidizing simple chemical entities obtained from the environment. This idea has been stimulated by the discovery, in the late 1970s, of chemosynthetic bacteria around hydrothermal vents on parts of the ocean floor, but also a general growth of interest in life in extreme environments. Environments with extreme temperatures, such as hot springs, would have been abundant on the early Earth, and possibly it was in such conditions that life arose. Hydrothermal vents, with a continuous stream of raw materials and high temperatures, would seem to be a possible location for life's origins. In addition, the organisms most closely associated with extreme environments today – members of the Archaea, or Archaebacteria (Page 48) – are among the oldest of lineages, although not all of these are chemosynthetic. Speculation will continue concerning the type of environment in which the first living cells originated, and the type of energy metabolism they employed. However, we can accept with confidence that life had originated by 3.8 Bya.

The Origin of Photosynthesis

The first really momentous evolutionary event after the origin of life itself was the 'invention' of photosynthesis. Before photosynthesis appeared, organisms were either heterotrophic or chemosynthetic. Heterotrophic organisms are limited by the supply of energy-rich organic molecules, while chemosynthetic organisms are limited by the availability of suitable inorganic substances for oxidation. Photosynthesis, however, utilizes solar energy which is in continuous supply. So, for the first time, the biota could harness an inexhaustible supply of energy.

It is believed that when photosynthesis first appeared there was no free oxygen. Today, certain types of photosynthetic bacteria are confined to such anaerobic environments. Most such bacteria use hydrogen sulfide to provide the hydrogen which combines with carbon dioxide to form energy-rich organic molecules (Page 53). The first photosynthetic organisms were probably also of this type, and similarly restricted to environments where hydrogen sulfide or another suitable hydrogen donor was available.

Some time during the Archaean a second type of photosynthesis appeared which was destined to transform the planet. Instead of using hydrogen sulfide as a source of hydrogen, this type of photosynthesis used water, which is universally available. The efficiency of energy capture is greater when water rather than hydrogen sulfide is used as a source of hydrogen. The other major consequences of water-splitting photosynthesis are related to the oxygen that is released as a by-product. Ultimately, this oxygen transformed the nature of the atmosphere. It provided the raw material for the generation of ozone, which shields the Earth's surface from biologically damaging ultraviolet radiation, and it enabled oxidative metabolism to evolve.

Evidence for the antiquity of photosynthesis comes from comparing the ratios of the two isotopes, carbon-12 and carbon-13, in fossil remains and in surrounding rocks dated to over 3.0 Bya. Photosynthesis enhances the carbon-13 content, so that organic matter enriched with carbon-13 is likely to be due to photosynthesis. Mineralogical evidence is also vital to dating the origins of water-splitting photosynthesis. At a number of locations around the world, thick deposits of the iron-containing mineral haematite (Fe_3O_2) are found sandwiched between layers of siliceous materials. Most of these deposits, known as **banded iron formations**, date to between 3.0 and 2.5 Bya. Now the only plausible explanation for haematite formation is by the oxidation of iron by free oxygen. So this provides strong evidence for the release of oxygen from at least 3.0 Bya.

Even though oxygen was seemingly being generated by photosynthesis from quite early in the Archaean, it did not immediately accumulate. This is because of the reduced nature of the Archaean oceans, atmosphere and land surfaces. Oxygen released from photosynthesis would have combined with chemical entities in the oceans and would not have diffused to the atmosphere until these 'sinks' were full. Later, oxygen combined with atmospheric gases and minerals on land. One of these minerals is pyrite (FeS_2), which also contains iron. Oxidation of pyrite would have led to the formation of haematite, which would have been transported, by water, from land to the oceans. The deposition of haematite on the ocean-floor produced formations know as 'red beds'. None of these are older than around 2.0 billion years, which indicates that by this time oxygen was probably accumulating in the atmosphere. Note that this is around the same age as the youngest known examples of banded iron formations, which form only under reducing conditions. Both lines of mineralogical evidence therefore point to a date of around 2.0 Bya for the transition from a reducing to an oxidizing environment. Stromatolites, which were mentioned earlier, are also very important for recording the development of photosynthesis. Although some date from earlier than 2.5 Bya, they become much more abundant in rocks of Proterozoic age.

It seems that some 1.5 billion years elapsed between the appearance of water-splitting photosynthesis and the accumulation of oxygen in the atmosphere. This enormous time-lag was due in part to the chemically reduced nature of the Archaean environment. In addition, the oxygen-generating capacity of the Archaean biota, confined as it was to water and therefore probably nutrient-limited, was only a tiny fraction of that of today's biota. The present atmospheric concentration of oxygen (around 20 per cent by volume) would probably double in a few thousand years in the absence of aerobic respiration.

Initially, molecular oxygen posed a threat to anaerobic organisms because to them the 'new' gas was poisonous. Only those organisms that excluded oxygen from their sites of metabolism, or lived in anoxic situations, could survive. Oxygen was therefore a very potent selective force in early Proterozoic times.

Nitrogen Fixation

Nitrogen, one of life's key elements, is biologically 'fixed' by certain types of bacteria. These combine the relatively unreactive gas nitrogen with hydrogen to form ammonia, a much more biologically useful source of nitrogen (Pages 121–2). Prior to biotic nitrogen fixation, the biota would have relied on nitrogen compounds introduced by inorganic processes such as volcanic activity. The appearance of biotic nitrogen fixation meant that the biota could use an inexhaustible supply of nitrogen. Nitrogen-fixing bacteria produce the enzyme nitrogenase, which combines nitrogen and hydrogen. Nitrogenase, however, cannot function in the presence of gaseous oxygen. When oxygen began to accumulate in Proterozoic times, nitrogen-fixing organisms evolved to metabolize aerobically, and this involved excluding oxygen from the sites of nitrogen fixation.

Oxidative Metabolism – Respiration

Oxygen is a highly reactive gas which even today is poisonous for some organisms. As the concentration of oxygen increased in Proterozoic times, organisms survived either by excluding this gas from cellular sites of metabolism or by remaining in anaerobic situations. However, a metabolism appeared which actually made use of this gas. In earlier discussions about energy metabolism (Pages 54–6) it was pointed out that the energy yield per molecule of glucose is much greater during oxidative metabolism than during fermentation, which does not involve oxygen. The appearance of oxidative metabolism facilitated other evolutionary developments which it is difficult to imagine occurring otherwise. In fact, all obligate anaerobic organisms have remained single-celled, and practically all of them are prokaryotes. For the physical environment, too, the appearance and spread of oxygen-using respiration was critical: now the oxygen generated by photosynthesis was being biologically recycled and the balance between the two processes became the principal determinant of the oxygen content of the atmosphere and oceans.

It is worth noting here that by around 2.0 Bya all the types of energy metabolism in evidence today had appeared, i.e. chemosynthesis, anaerobic and aerobic photosynthesis, fermentation and aerobic respiration. The only types of organisms present, however, were the prokaryotes, and life was still confined to water.

The Appearance of the Eukaryotic Cell

The most fundamental division in the classification of organisms is between prokaryotes and eukaryotes (Page 46). Although all the forms of energy metabolism known occur

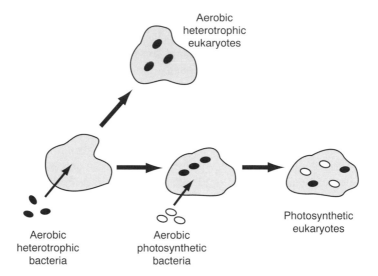

Figure 12.2   *The evolution of eukaryotic cells. Considerable support exists for an endosymbiotic origin involving the consumption of bacteria by other prokaryotes and the subsequent loss of the former's functional independence*

among the prokaryotes, their cellular structure is relatively simple and they are essentially unicellular organisms. Importantly, they contain no true organelles and the chromosome is usually a single looped strand of DNA. Furthermore, cells divide by a comparatively simple process called binary fission (Page 22). In contrast, eukaryotic cells have a membrane-bound nucleus with paired chromosomes and other organelles in which functions such as respiration and photosynthesis are centred. The appearance of the first eukaryotic cells is therefore regarded as one of the most momentous events in the history of life. Every organism other than members of the Archaea or Eubacteria owes its origins to this event.

Evidence for the timing of the appearance of eukaryotic cells is based on the comparative sizes of modern prokaryotic and eukaryotic cells and the structural details of fossil cells. Fossil cells older than about 1.5 billion years are usually much smaller than is typical for eukaryotic cells. However, sediments from about this age have yielded much larger cells, suggesting they are of eukaryotic type. Dimensional clues are supplemented by evidence of organelles within fossilized cells from around 1.5 Bya, although there are the usual difficulties in interpreting the details of cellular structure in remains of such great age.

It is not known whether environmental conditions prevented the evolution of the eukaryotic cell before about 1.5 Bya. Because virtually all eukaryotes are aerobic, it could be that their origin coincided with oxygen levels reaching a critical minimum threshold. The question as to *how* eukaryotic organisms arose from their prokaryotic predecessors is not easily answered. The similarity between the nucleus and some bacteria was noted at the end of the 19th century, leading some to propose that the nucleus had a bacterial origin. This radical view, which was never widely accepted, has now become almost the conventional explanation for the origin of the nucleus, and also other organelles such as the mitochondrion and the chloroplast. The recent development of this ***endosymbiotic*** theory is associated particularly with American biologist Lynn Margulis. Essentially, this theory holds that prokaryotic organisms devoured, but failed to digest, other prokaryotic organisms (Figure 12.2). What resulted, to use Lynn Margulis's own words, was a 'kind of bacterial confederacy'. Somehow the alien cells later evolved into organelles such as mitochondria and chloroplasts. In support of this view is the fact that some DNA is nearly always present in these organelles as well as in the nucleus. Not surprisingly, many conceptual difficulties remain with this theory: for example, there is no really satisfactory explanation for the origin of the multiple, paired chromosomes of the nucleus. The appearance of eukaryotic cells had enormous implications for life on Earth, heralding the evolution of sexual reproduction and the advent of multicellular organisms.

The Appearance of Sex

There are mechanisms by which genetic material can be exchanged between prokaryotic cells and no doubt these appeared early in the history of life. However, sex is normally taken to mean the formation of a new individual by the fusion of haploid gametes. The process therefore involves meiosis, during which chromosomes are duplicated, then sort independently, while genes may be exchanged during crossing-over (Pages 24–6). The chromosome number is halved during meiosis and the full, diploid number is restored during fertilization. Meiosis serves to promote genetic variation: new permutations of genes are continually being thrown up on which natural selection can operate. Meiotic sex, which occurs in the vast majority of eukaryotic organisms, obviously occurred after the evolution of the eukaryotic cell, probably well over a billion years ago.

The evolutionary significance of meiotic sex lies not with reproduction itself but with the opportunities it offers for generating new genotypes as a result of genetic recombination. Superficially, it would seem that sexual reproduction offers the possibility of a faster rate of evolution than asexual reproduction alone, which should be particularly advantageous in a changing environment. Indeed, this was the accepted view until the last few decades. This fairly simple explanation has now been swept away, however, and the evolutionary benefits of sexual reproduction are by no means clear (Page 27). Notwithstanding the arguments concerning the evolutionary benefits of true sexual reproduction, it is a feature of just about all plants, fungi and animals and the majority of protists.

The Emergence of Multicellular Organisms

While there is evidence of chemical communication between unicellular organisms, and some form filaments and mats, they lack the potential of multicellular organisms for growth, differentiation and functional integration. The fossil record does not permit the origin of multicellular life to be dated accurately, and its early development in the three multicellular kingdoms is unclear. Some palaeontologists believe there is evidence for multicellular algae from over 1.3 Bya, but this is not universally agreed. However, the first multicellular organisms were probably algae, not unlike some of the simpler

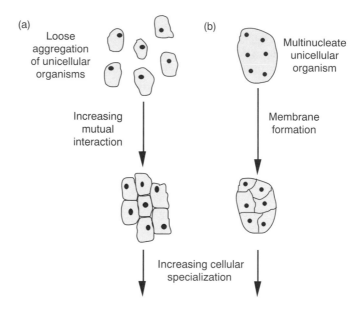

Figure 12.3   *Two models for the origin of multicellular life. One (a) envisages closer intercellular co-ordination and interdependence. The other (b) envisages membrane formation within a multinucleate cell*

seaweeds found today. Accordingly we would classify them as protists, and they are the ancestors of land plants. However, it is the fossils of animals, or at least animal-like organisms, that provide most of the information about early multicellular life. The first evidence for these organisms comes from the tracks they laid and the burrows they dug in the late Proterozoic sea-floor around a billion years ago. Two contrasting models are used to explain the origin of multicellular organisms from their unicellular ancestors (Figure 12.3). One envisages an increasingly close association between separate unicellular organisms, a progressively greater mutual interdependence between cells until they can no longer function as independent entities. The second model envisages nuclear division within a single cell, followed by the formation of membranes which separate the nucleated 'compartments'. Currently, the former of these scenarios is favoured, largely because some of the simplest animals, such as sponges, behave in many ways like a loosely coordinated colony of cells. Evidence for this theory in other animal types is less clear though, and for them a multinuclear origin may be more likely.

Multicellularity offers a range of evolutionary opportunities. A multicellular body provides considerable scope for diversification in design. Multicellularity enables organisms to attain huge increases in size, with much greater control of the internal environment. A multicellular body permits cellular specialization and the formation of tissues and organs with particular functions. Also, as new cells are produced to replace ageing cells, a multicellular organism can live far longer than a unicellular organism. Whatever mechanism was involved, it is believed that plants, animals and fungi arose independently from unicellular eukaryotes (protists) in the later stages of the Proterozoic, and more than once in each kingdom.

Although multicellularity offers numerous evolutionary opportunities not available to unicellular organisms, it is not clear what evolutionary pressures selected for this characteristic. One theory is that predation was the principal selection agent. This theory is based on the premise that larger unicellular algae are less vulnerable to predation by unicellular grazers than smaller unicellular algae. At a time when all organisms were unicellular there could thus have been selection for larger and larger algae, and, in turn, selection for larger and larger unicellular grazers. However, there are limits to the size that individual cells can attain, so those organisms which increased in size by cell division could therefore have been favoured, both as prey and predators. However, multicellular organisms are not necessarily superior to unicellular organisms, as is clear from the huge variety of very successful unicellular organisms on the planet today. Nonetheless, the appearance of multicellular life forms was eventually to bring about a dramatic transformation in the structural and functional characteristics of the biota.

The Late Proterozoic

Until the middle of the 20th century little was known of life before about 600 Mya. By the end of the 1950s, however, a number of fossil finds pushed back the history of life a further 2 billion years, and also provided evidence for the types of multicellular life that existed before the appearance of animals with hard body parts. One of the most important of such discoveries took place in the Ediacara Hills of South Australia. Here, a variety of animal-like, soft-bodied organisms was found dated to nearly 700 Mya. These organisms thus predated by some tens of millions of years the first true hard-bodied organisms. Since this discovery, a number of similar finds from 680 to 580 Mya have been made, for example in Siberia and Newfoundland. Regardless of geographical area, they are all known as Ediacaran, and this term is often applied to this interval of the late Proterozoic. Ediacaran faunas reveal a diversity of body designs which have aroused much interest and controversy. It is claimed that some of the fossils are ancestors of modern phyla, but most appear not to have survived until the Cambrian, the first period of the Phanerozoic aeon. The earliest shelly fossils also come from the later stages of the Proterozoic. Their appearance anticipates a rapid diversification of such animals around the beginning of the Phanerozoic.

Ecological Perspective

In this chapter we have surveyed the momentous evolutionary events of the biosphere's first 3.2 billion years or so. The approximate timings of these events are shown in Figure 12.4. Until the appearance of eukaryotic organisms, ecological communities comprised only primary producers and decomposers. Eukaryotes, specifically those which made their living by grazing on the photosynthetic cyanobacteria, introduced a new functional dimension into these comparatively simple communities around 1.5 Bya. Using an ecological principle that moderate levels of grazing tend to increase species richness (Page 236), the American palaeontologist Steven Stanley has suggested that unicellular eukaryotes, grazing on relatively uniform beds of cyanobacteria, encouraged the

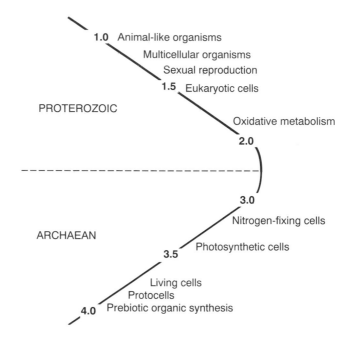

Figure 12.4   *Approximate timings of major evolutionary innovations during the Archaean and Proterozoic aeons. Numbers are billions of years before present*

establishment and survival of novel life forms by suppressing the growth of the most abundant types. Thus, diversification would have been enhanced within the primary producer level, leading to increased evolutionary opportunities among the grazing eukaryotes. This theory is supported by the history and present distribution of stromatolites, those pillar-like formations of shallow marine habitats referred to earlier. Stromatolites underwent a worldwide reduction in range during the late Proterozoic, which might have been due to an increase in grazing pressure by eukaryotes. Certainly, active stromatolites are today confined to shallow waters which are too saline for most types of grazing organisms.

13

Life in the Phanerozoic Aeon

This chapter reviews major evolutionary events of the Phanerozoic aeon. The name Phanerozoic, meaning 'abundant life', was chosen because it is only in rocks of this time span – roughly the last 570 million years – that fossils are widespread. The Palaeozoic, Mesozoic and Cenozoic eras are dealt with in sequence, and, within each, key themes are identified. In order to develop themes when they are introduced, some tracking back and forth in time is necessary, so regular reference to the geological timescale on Page 136 is advised. It will also be useful to consult the palaeogeographical maps on Page 145. Attention focuses on the plants and the vertebrates, but this is not to devalue the continued importance of other organisms.

Extinction and Adaptive Radiation

Despite the incomplete and highly biased nature of the fossil record, it is clear that the appearance and disappearance of taxa has not proceeded at a uniform rate during the Phanerozoic aeon. Periodically, taxonomic diversity has declined very abruptly in geological terms, while at other times taxonomic diversity has rapidly increased. The more or less sudden disappearance of a significant proportion of taxa over a large area is termed a *mass extinction*. Several such extinction events occurred during the Phanerozoic aeon, but five were particularly catastrophic. The most dramatic of these occurred around 250 Mya and marks the close of the Permian period and the Palaeozoic era. Perhaps the most commonly known, however, is the mass extinction at the close of the Cretaceous, around 65 Mya, when the dinosaurs disappeared. The other three major mass extinctions occurred around 440, 370 and 210 Mya, and mark the close of the Ordovician, Devonian and Triassic periods respectively (Figure 11.2).

The Phanerozoic is also marked by intervals of rapid evolutionary diversification, known as *adaptive radiations* or simply *radiations*. Adaptive radiations follow significant extinction events because heavy attrition within a biota offers considerable evolutionary opportunities for the survivors. The pattern of speciation at other times varies, but typically species appear relatively suddenly in the fossil record, remain more or less the same for a few million years and then become extinct. This pattern of relative evolutionary stasis interrupted by quite short intervals of rapid speciation has been referred to as ***punctuated equilibrium***. However, Darwinian evolutionary theory predicts slow, gradual change, explained now in terms of gene-by-gene replacement. In this model, new species arise by progressive modification of existing forms. The failure to observe speciation in the fossil record is conventionally attributed to the fact that it is so incomplete, and also poor temporal resolution. Some palaeontologists, however, have suggested that the alternation of relatively long periods with little morphological change and brief intervals of rapid change may require more than cumulative single gene replacement. Others have strenuously resisted this proposal and the majority view remains that the patterns revealed by the fossil record can be accommodated within neo-Darwinian theory.

The Palaeozoic Era

The Early Palaeozoic

The lower boundary of the Cambrian, the first period of the Palaeozoic era, marks the onset of an interval of very rapid diversification of animals of shallow marine habitats. This phenomenon is commonly referred to as the Cambrian 'explosion'. The basic body plans of all the present-day animal phyla can be traced to a comparatively brief interval in the early Palaeozoic. Other groups appeared which later became extinct. The key feature of the early Cambrian was the appearance of a large variety of organisms with hard body parts, often external skeletons based on calcium or silicon. The earliest such organisms, which belong to a brief interval called the Tommotian stage, were extremely small.

Many well-known groups were present in the Cambrian, including gastropod and bivalve molluscs (respectively snails and clams), brachiopods, corals and sponges. The trilobites (phylum Arthropoda), early relatives of the insects and crustaceans, were abundant from Cambrian to Silurian times (Figure 13.1). The survival of trilobites in the fossil record is due to a tough external skeleton, or carapace. Because individual trilobite taxa occupied comparatively short, well-defined time intervals, they are commonly used for geological dating. Limestone reefs of much greater size than stromatolites formed in Cambrian times. Corals became the principal reef builders and have remained so ever since, even though their activities have been periodically inhibited during mass extinction events.

It is not known what circumstances stimulated the evolution of hard body parts at the lower boundary of the Cambrian. One important factor may have been a change in water chemistry, particularly the concentration of calcium and magnesium. Another factor may have been the increased effectiveness of predation, against which hard outer parts provide some protection. Whatever the factors involved, biotic synthesis of certain minerals (***biomineralization***) on a large scale had important implications for biogeochemical circulation in the oceans.

It was stressed earlier (Page 137) that special circumstances are necessary for the long-term preservation of soft-bodied organisms. The most celebrated find of such fossils of Cambrian age was made around the turn of the 20th century, in a formation known as the Burgess Shale, which is located in the Rocky Mountains in southern Canada. An

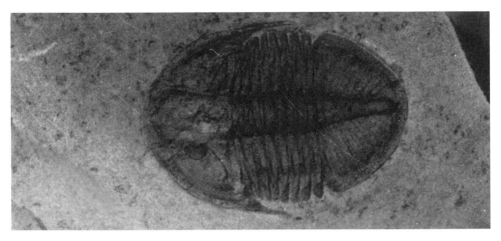

Figure 13.1   *An Ordovician trilobite,* Ogyginus. *Trilobites are well represented in Palaeozoic fossil assemblages. (Photo, Ian Qualtrough; specimen provided by National Museums and Galleries on Merseyside)*

accumulation of muds must have occurred very quickly to provide the combination of physical protection and anaerobic conditions necessary for the survival of such organisms. The Burgess Shale fossils offer a very rare glimpse of the types of organisms that lived in mid-Cambrian seas. However, many of the organisms look very strange to modern eyes and their classification and place in phylogenetic schemes remains a source of controversy. Some have favoured the view that the Burgess Shale fossils provide evidence of previously unknown phyla which have since become extinct. Others, however, have placed such fossils in well-known phyla, particularly the Arthropoda.

The considerable morphological diversification that occurred during the Cambrian, particularly the spread of organisms protected by hard body parts, must have had enormous ecological and evolutionary consequences. No doubt ecological communities became more complex, with longer food chains and more complex food webs.

The Ordovician period, which follows the Cambrian, was a very important interval for diversification of marine organisms: it is often characterized as an interval of consolidation following the 'experimentation' of the Cambrian. The close of the Ordovician, however, is marked by the first of the five big mass extinction events of the Phanerozoic. Many Cambrian taxa failed to survive or became increasingly uncommon. The trilobites, for example, never recovered their former prominence.

Animal Life in Middle and Late Palaeozoic Seas

Swimming animals, most of them predators, can be traced to Cambrian times. Some of these were invertebrates, such as the nautiloids (phylum Mollusca) with their chambered shells, and their descendants, the ammonoids, which appeared later in Devonian times. Other swimming predators of Cambrian age were vertebrates, however. (The vertebrates comprise just one of (usually) four subphyla of the phylum Chordata whose members are characterized by a dorsal nerve chord; in contrast there are many invertebrate phyla.)

Figure 13.2   *A collection of fossilized fish of Devonian age. Note their superficially 'modern' appearance. (Photo, Ian Qualtrough; specimen provided by National Museums and Galleries on Merseyside)*

Notable among the swimming vertebrates were primitive jawless fish, particularly the ostracoderms, which survived until the close of the Devonian period. Jawed fish appeared in mid-Palaeozoic times and gradually replaced fishes possessing primitive characteristics such as heavy armour. In Devonian rocks, a great abundance and diversity of fossil fish have been found, many of them surprisingly modern in appearance: in fact, this period is sometimes characterized as 'the age of fishes' (Figure 13.2). The evolution of fish, with their great capacity for independent movement, was of great ecological significance. Some types of fish, probably from waters subject to seasonal drying, were the first vertebrates to develop lungs, an evolutionary innovation of enormous significance because it preadapted vertebrates for a terrestrial existence.

The late Devonian is marked by the second of the great mass extinction events of the Phanerozoic. Marine organisms were affected much more than those on land, and extinctions were greatest in tropical waters, suggesting that a change in water temperature was a contributory factor. Ammonoids, gastropods, brachiopods, trilobites and corals all experienced heavy losses.

The Colonization of Land

Although it may be difficult for us to envisage extensive areas of landscape which are devoid of life, it seems that terrestrial ecological communities have existed only since late Ordovician times, which is little more than one-eighth of the age of the biosphere. The earliest evidence includes trace fossils of centipede-like animals, plant spores and plant cuticle (waterproof covering). It could be argued that organisms had colonized the land before this time but have left no trace of their existence, or that their remains have yet to be discovered. The fact is, though, that early Palaeozoic strata in which remains of terrestrial life forms might be expected to occur have revealed no signs of life.

The reason why it took so long for land colonization to occur is not known, although it has been suggested that environmental conditions may have prevented land colonization earlier in the Palaeozoic. Life on land certainly requires sufficient atmospheric ozone to absorb much of the sun's ultraviolet radiation (Page 64). Ozone formation depends on free oxygen, which was accumulating as a result of photosynthesis throughout much of the Proterozoic. However, it is generally believed that the amount of atmospheric oxygen by the end of the Proterozoic (about 20 per cent of the present value) would have provided sufficient ozone to make terrestrial surfaces habitable. So, although ozone production was necessary for organisms to move on to land, it does not explain the apparent timing of land colonization.

It is generally agreed that the move from water to land was not a single event. Rather, numerous transitions from aquatic to terrestrial life occurred, involving diverse groups of organisms, at many different times and in many different regions. Land colonization probably occurred where aquatic life forms were exposed to drying conditions. In such conditions, natural selection favoured those characteristics which equipped organisms for a life surrounded by air rather than water. Various evolutionary lineages thus acquired characteristics which gradually lessened their dependency on water. In comparison to a life in air, life in water has several advantages: organisms are immersed in a nutrient medium, water provides mechanical support, movement in water is so much easier than on land, desiccation is not a problem for aquatic organisms, and environmental conditions, particularly temperature, tend to fluctuate less in water than on land. A number of the evolutionary innovations mentioned in the following sections represent adaptations to a terrestrial, rather than an aquatic mode of life. However, the distinction between terrestrial and aquatic organisms is not absolute: many organisms are semi-aquatic, spending part of their life in water and part on land.

Plant Evolution in the Palaeozoic Era

The fossil record is not very revealing about the first photosynthetic land colonists, or their evolutionary history, but they were probably semi-aquatic multicellular algae. Such organisms were the likely immediate ancestors of the true plants. The various phyla that make up the plant kingdom are assembled into two major groups, the bryophytes (notably mosses and liverworts) and the vascular plants, so called because of their specialized tissues for conducting water and nutrients. The general view is that these two major groups both evolved from multicellular algae but did so independently.

Living on land provides a number of challenges for plants. They must restrict water loss but simultaneously take up carbon dioxide from the atmosphere; they need reproductive systems which are independent of standing water; and if they are to grow erect to any size they require both structural rigidity and a system of conducting cells. The suite of evolutionary innovations which arose to solve the problems of life on land included a waxy surface layer (the cuticle), spores with thick walls, stomata (for gas exchange), and conducting cells surrounded by walls strengthened with cellulose and lignin. When, and in what order, these occurred is not known with certainty but it seems that land floras were established by early Silurian times, and perhaps by the late Ordovician.

The earliest true land plants were simply branched stems with terminal spore-bearing tips, anchored to the ground by modified stems (Figure 13.3a). However, from the early Devonian onwards, the types of vascular plants are more familiar because of their living relatives. The lycopods (clubmosses) were present in the early Devonian and may well have been present in the Silurian. Extant clubmosses are fairly small and inconspicuous, but during the Carboniferous some were tree-sized and they contributed to the coal measures that formed in late Carboniferous swamps. The sphenopsids, a group which includes the horsetails, appeared in the late Devonian. Carboniferous sphenopsids (Figure 13.4) were also very much larger than the few living representatives of this group, and they appear to have tolerated rather dry conditions. The ferns probably appeared before the close of the Devonian and were certainly present in the Carboniferous, particularly in humid environments.

None of the plant types mentioned so far produce *seeds*. The seed plants probably appeared in late Devonian times. To appreciate the significance of the appearance of seed plants we need to review a few points made earlier (Page 21) about the life cycles of

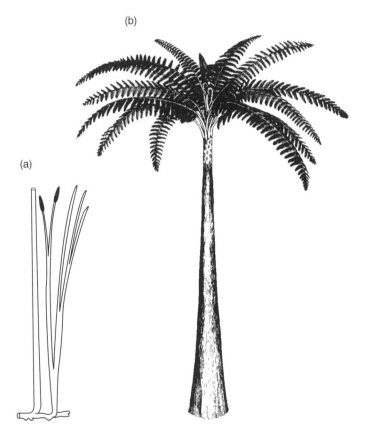

Figure 13.3 *(a) An early land plant,* Rhynia gwynne-vaughani: *note the simple stems terminating in spore cases and the absence of roots and leaves. (b) A seed fern, an extinct order which lived between Devonian times and the late Cretaceous. This specimen was about 8 metres in height, but some species were very small. (From Andrews, H. 1961 Studies in Palaeobotany. Redrawn by permission of John Wiley & Sons, New York)*

Figure 13.4 *Reconstruction of a late Carboniferous swamp forest. The large plants with jointed stems are sphenopsids, a group now represented by horsetails. The large animal is a labyrinthodont amphibian and the insect is the giant dragonfly* Meganeura. *(Photo, Suzanne Yee, diorama in the Liverpool Museum)*

plants in general. Recall that there are two distinct generations in the life cycle of a plant, known respectively as the sporophyte and the gametophyte. The sporophyte generation is diploid whereas the gametophyte is haploid. Which of the two generations is the larger and longer-lived varies between plant types. With bryophytes (mosses and liverworts) it is the gametophyte; for vascular plants (clubmosses, ferns, horsetails and all seed plants) it is the sporophyte. The principle of alternation of generations in plants was shown earlier (Figure 3.1), using a fern as an example. A meiotic division of specialized cells on the sporophyte gives rise to haploid spore cells from which the gametophyte, the sexual generation, develops. From the gametophyte generation male and female gametes are produced. Importantly, the male gametes of seedless plants require water to reach the female gametes.

In contrast to seedless plants, reproduction of seed plants is much less dependent on water. Seed plants produce two types of haploid spores, called ***microspores*** and ***megaspores*** respectively. The microspores are later released as pollen grains. It is from the pollen grain that the male gametophyte develops. The male gametophyte, which carries the male gametes (they are simply nuclei) usually develops as a tube-like structure. The egg nucleus is produced within the gametophyte that develops from the megaspore. A key feature is that development of the megaspore takes place among sporophyte tissue, which provides it with protection. In plants which do not produce seeds, e.g. ferns, the two generations are separate entities, which means that the gametophyte is very vulnerable to desiccation.

Pollen that is shed by flowerless seed plants is carried in air, and if a grain alights in the vicinity of a compatible megagametophyte, the enclosed nuclei are carried towards the egg nucleus. (In the more advanced seed plants the sperm nuclei are carried within a *pollen tube* which extends in response to appropriate stimuli.) A vital point from an evolutionary perspective is that free water is not required for the movement of the male nuclei to the female nuclei for fertilization in seed plants; the only moisture required for this purpose is supplied by the female gametophyte. Successful fusion of male and female nuclei gives rise to a diploid *zygote*, the first cell of the sporophyte generation. Successive cell divisions then occur to produce a seed.

Seeds permit plant development to be arrested at an early stage. Seeds are often quite durable, most survive well in very dry conditions as they tolerate desiccation, many have features that encourage their dispersal, and under suitable conditions some can remain dormant for long periods of time. In summary, seed plants are independent of free water for reproduction, and the seed itself provides a means for preserving an individual plant until such time as conditions are favourable for its growth and development.

The earliest known seed plants are the seed ferns (Figure 13.3b), which produced frond-like leaves resembling those of extant ferns. They appeared first in late Devonian times and are common in Carboniferous fossil assemblages. One group of seed ferns, the genus *Glossopteris*, was particularly abundant throughout the southern hemisphere in late Palaeozoic times. However, this group has no living representatives. The cordaites are an order of tree-sized seed plants which were prominent in late Carboniferous forests. They survived until the Cenozoic era but there are no extant examples of this group.

The conifers, or cone-bearing plants, diversified and expanded during the Permian period, largely at the expense of the tree-sized lycopods, sphenopsids and seed ferns. The rise of the conifers, with their needle-like leaves, is believed to have been associated with climatic changes to drier and warmer conditions. The ginkgoes, a group of seed-bearing trees, originated in the Permian period, but did not become prominent until the Mesozoic era.

Fungi are mentioned here because of their historically close botanical associations, although plants and fungi are usually placed in separate kingdoms. The details of fungal ancestry are not known, but it appears they were present on land at around the same time as the early land plants. The roots of most plant species form very close associations with fungi, known as mycorrhizae (Page 110), which appear to be beneficial to both organisms. The antiquity of this symbiotic association has been revealed by the presence of mycorrhizae on some Silurian plant fossils.

Land Colonization by Animals

Little is known about the early history of land colonization by animals, either in terms of evolutionary relationships or timing. It is assumed that animals colonized the land after plants simply because animals, as heterotrophs, ultimately depend on photosynthesis. The occupation of the terrestrial environment by animals should be regarded as a very gradual process involving transitional phases and a progressive release from dependence on water. Animal groups which colonized the land moved first from marine to freshwater environments and then on to land, although some types of animals have not made the transition from freshwater to a fully terrestrial existence.

The earliest undisputed fossils of land animals come from near the close of the Silurian period, and they include a millipede and some centipedes. It is generally agreed, however, that land animals did exist before this time but either have not fossilized, or their remains have not been found. A rock strata of late Silurian and early Devonian age, referred to as Old Red Sandstone and occurring on both sides of the North Atlantic, is particularly useful for revealing the gradual transition of arthropods, as they moved from open water to terrestrial environments. Within this group are the insects. By late Carboniferous times insects had developed wings and they diversified to occupy a variety of roles, and an ecological importance they have never relinquished.

Although some types of fish can live for extended periods out of water, the first vertebrates to spend most of their lives out of water were the amphibians, which comprise a separate class in the phylum Chordata. Amphibians, which evolved from either marine or freshwater fish, appear first in the fossil record in the late Devonian period. Amphibians are tetrapods (i.e. four-footed), a feature which probably evolved first in water. All amphibians are semi-aquatic: their eggs must be laid in water and they are exclusively swimming organisms during the juvenile stage of the life cycle, only later developing legs for movement on land and lungs for breathing. The amphibians became prominent in terrestrial and semi-aquatic ecosystems at the beginning of the Carboniferous period. Some were essentially herbivorous while others were obviously carnivorous, and some species were much larger than any living today. The position of the amphibians as the dominant land tetrapod group, however, was to be undermined by the ascendancy of the reptiles.

There is some evidence that reptiles appeared early in the Carboniferous period, some 340 Mya, although this date is not generally agreed. Carboniferous reptiles were fairly small, typically growing only to the size of present-day lizards. Reptiles have a number of features that equip them for a terrestrial existence. Particularly significant is the *amniotic egg* which both protects the developing embryo from desiccation and provides it with nourishment. For the first time, therefore, vertebrate animals were independent of standing water for reproduction. In addition, reptiles are covered with dry scales which inhibit moisture loss. They have more efficient lungs than amphibians, more effective dentition, and greater mobility out of water. This suite of features gave them a considerable advantage over the amphibians whose prominence waned in late Palaeozoic times.

Around 300 Mya, in the late Carboniferous, fossils appear which are essentially reptilian, but with some mammalian features. Known appropriately as mammal-like reptiles, these were the likely immediate ancestors of the mammals. The therapsids were a prominent group of advanced mammal-like reptiles in the Permian period; some believe they were endothermic, i.e. able to regulate body temperatures (Page 84) and therefore less dependent on environmental temperature than reptiles. The variety of therapsid types found in late Permian rocks indicates a major adaptive radiation at this time when they may have been the dominant type of land vertebrate.

The Late Permian Mass Extinction

Towards the end of the Permian, the final period of the Palaeozoic, a mass extinction occurred which was more catastrophic than any other extinction event before or since. Extinctions occurred principally in shallow-marine environments, where it is estimated that over 90 per cent of all species, and over half the families, disappeared. Many brachiopods and molluscs, particularly ammonites (Figure 13.5), were lost, while the trilobites, a group in long-term decline, disappeared. Attrition also occurred among land animals, particularly the mammal-like reptiles.

A long-running debate surrounds the factors, or combination of factors, responsible for this drastic change in the Earth's biota. The debate is hindered by the lack of sites which show a continuity in fossil-bearing strata spanning the boundary of the Permian and the Triassic (first period of the Mesozoic era). There is a consensus that the mass extinction was not a 'sudden death' affair, but rather that different groups declined at different rates and succumbed at different times over an interval of several million years. Considerable support exists for the suggestion that a cooling of oceanic water may have been a major contributory factor, because the fossil record shows faunal losses were greatest in tropical zones. Also, it seems that sea levels fell worldwide, and as the seas regressed from the coasts of the 'supercontinent' Pangaea, the extent of shallow marine environments declined. There is a tendency for biological diversity to rise with an increase in the area available for colonization, so it follows that a decline in species richness should be a consequence of habitat reduction. Another suggestion is that it was a reduction in habitat diversity, rather than total area, that led to the extinctions. Species unable to cope with the loss of habitat diversity, it is reasoned, would not have survived. Again, it is modern ecological theory that is invoked to account for biotic changes in the distant past. Other theories cite lowered salinity or oxygen concentration in the marine environment as a causal factor, but neither of these would explain the loss of terrestrial vertebrates.

Figure 13.5   *The ammonite Asteroceras, from the early Jurassic, Humberside, eastern England. Ammonites were prominent marine predators in the Mesozoic but had become extinct by the close of the era. (Photo, Ian Qualtrough; specimen provided by National Museums and Galleries on Merseyside)*

The Mesozoic Era

Life in Mesozoic Seas

The early Triassic can be regarded essentially as an interval of recovery for marine invertebrates, some types undergoing rapid diversification following their decimation at the close of the Permian period. The Permian mass extinction affected invertebrate groups differentially. Bivalve and gastropod molluscs, for example, suffered less attrition than ammonites, although the latter recovered to become important swimming predators in Mesozoic waters. The hexacorals, a group prominent in reef formation today, appeared in the Triassic period to replace older forms which succumbed during the Permian extinctions.

Swimming vertebrates were also prominent in Mesozoic seas. Fish were joined by marine reptiles which had evolved from terrestrial types. This provides an example of organisms returning to the water having previously acquired features which equipped them for a terrestrial existence. Such reptiles included the placodonts and the nothosaurs of Triassic times. The latter were probably the first reptiles to take up a predominantly marine life, although they possessed limbs, which indicates a life spent on both sea and land. Their descendants, the carnivorous plesiosaurs, were more fully aquatic, some species exclusively so. Crocodilians were marine predators from early Jurassic times, having descended from principally terrestrial crocodiles that appeared in the Triassic. The close of the Triassic is marked by another major mass extinction, during which an estimated 20 per cent or so of all animal families in the sea were lost.

Mesozoic Land Faunas

On land, as in the sea, the early Triassic was an interval of recovery from the late Permian extinctions. The mammal-like reptiles suffered a wave of extinctions, although certain types survived, and then radiated to become the dominant vertebrates of the early Triassic. The first animals to be generally regarded as mammals appeared in late Triassic times, and there is good evidence that they evolved from a group of mammal-like reptiles called the cynodonts. Throughout the rest of the Mesozoic era the mammals remained relatively inconspicuous; seemingly no species was much larger than a small dog.

The principal land vertebrates for most of the Mesozoic era were the dinosaurs. The earliest undisputed dinosaur fossils, from Argentina, are about 230 million years old. The early dinosaur species were comparatively small, but by the late Triassic some species were typically 6 metres or more in length. In the early Jurassic, the very large members of this group began to appear, some of which exceeded 40 metres in length. However, while some species did attain such prodigious lengths, others were very small. In fact, the dinosaurs occupied nearly all the ecological niches now filled by mammals. The dinosaurs ranged across all the continents, having appeared at a time when the Earth's land masses essentially formed a single continent. Subsequently, however, their evolutionary history is influenced by the changing configuration of the continents during the Mesozoic era (Figure 11.9, Page 145).

Taxonomically, the dinosaurs form an order – Dinosauria – within which there are two suborders differentiated originally by hip (pelvic) structure. In one group, the ornithischians, the hip anatomy is not unlike a modern bird, while in the other group, the saurischians, the hip structure resembles that of a lizard. In both groups there were species which moved essentially on two legs (bipedal) and species which were principally four-legged. All 'bird-hipped' species were seemingly herbivorous, but the 'lizard-hipped' group contained both herbivores and carnivores.

Although conventionally classified as reptiles, and therefore ectothermic (unable to regulate body temperature internally), it is sometimes argued that dinosaurs could not have been so successful if their activity patterns had been controlled by external temperature, particularly in competition with small mammals. This argument is supported by aspects of their bone and heart anatomy. However, the evidence is by no means conclusive and the conventional view remains that the dinosaurs were ectothermic. Ectothermic animals would not necessarily have been disadvantageous in a world in which global temperatures were higher than they are today. Also, the enormous bulk of the largest dinosaurs would have required prodigious quantities of food to sustain an endothermic metabolism. Furthermore, heat would have been effectively conserved within organisms of such large size. Whatever the truth about their metabolism, the dinosaurs were an extraordinarily successful group as they were the dominant land vertebrates for around 150 million years.

The earliest flying vertebrates, called pterosaurs, were reptiles, and they appeared during late Triassic times. Many were quite small, but later in the Mesozoic era some types had wingspans of over 30 metres, which far exceeds any extant bird. The birds, which comprise a separate class of vertebrate animals, probably originated in late Jurassic times. Their structure indicates a reptilian ancestry, and there is now strong support for the view that they evolved from a group of dinosaurs. However, as feathers do not fossilize well, the early evolutionary history of birds is very sketchy.

Mesozoic Plants and the Origin of the Angiosperms

Land plants were seemingly not greatly affected by the events that caused the catastrophic losses of shallow-marine organisms in the late Permian. Seed ferns and true ferns remained common in Triassic floras, although the former began to decline in abundance. The most prominent seed plants during the Mesozoic era were gymnosperms. These plants do not produce true flowers, and their seeds develop on scales rather than enclosed within an ovary. (Gymnosperm, of Greek origin, means 'naked seed'.) Important gymnosperms of Mesozoic age included the cycadeoids, which are now extinct, the cycads, which have palm-like leaves and still occur in tropical and subtropical zones, and the ginkgoes, of which there is one living representative, *Ginkgo biloba* (maidenhair tree). The most successful of the early gymnosperms, however, were the conifers. They become progressively more abundant in fossil assemblages from Jurassic and early Cretaceous times and of course they still dominate certain types of vegetation.

It seems that the gymnosperms were joined by the flowering plants, the angiosperms, before mid-Cretaceous times. Angiosperms differ from gymnosperms in a number of respects. Most conspicuously, they produce true flowers and their seeds develop within

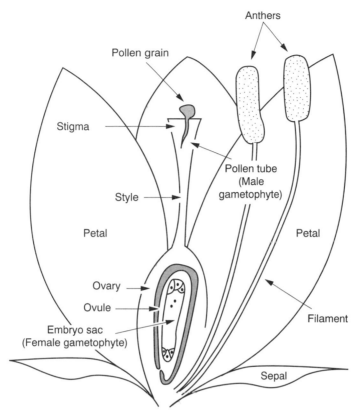

Figure 13.6 *Section through a flower. The basic features in a complete flower are sepals, petals, stamens (anther and filament), and one or more pistils (ovary, style and stigma). Pollen is produced within pollen sacs in the anthers. A pollen grain which lands on a compatible stigma develops a pollen tube which extends inside the style and carries the male gametes to the female gametes. An ovary with one ovule is shown, but there may be several. The seed develops from the ovule, the fruit develops from the ovary. (Drawing, Sandra Mather)*

an ***ovary*** (which offers both nourishment and protection) rather than on cones. Figure 13.6 shows the major parts of a typical flower, although in practice there is considerable modification of this basic structure, particularly regarding the petals.

Angiosperm pollen is received by the ***stigma*** (part of the female organ), which is not adjacent to the female gametophyte as in gymnosperms. If conditions are suitable, and if pollen and stigma are compatible, a tube develops from the pollen and extends inside the ***style***. Within the pollen tube are the male gametes, which are carried to the female gametophyte. (Some advanced gymnosperms also produce pollen tubes, but they are shorter than those of angiosperms.) Unique to the flowering plants is the double fertilization that ensues between sperm and female nuclei. The pollen tube actually carries two sperm nuclei. One of these fertilizes the egg nucleus, giving rise eventually to the seed ***embryo***; the other nucleus unites with a diploid nucleus in the female gametophyte. This second fertilization gives rise to the ***endosperm***, which is a nutrient-storing tissue. Nutrients mobilized from the endosperm can support the development of the embryo and, in some types of plant, seed germination and early growth as well. The seed, with its embryo and endosperm, develops within a *fruit*, which itself develops from the ovary wall. Although fruits are of many different types they can be conveniently categorized as either dry or succulent depending on their degree of 'fleshiness'. The term 'fruit' is also commonly used to refer to any seed-containing structure; it might be several true fruits or it might include other floral parts.

Several aspects of angiosperm origins remain controversial. The conventional view is that the angiosperms appeared fairly early in the Cretaceous, although a minority view advocates a much earlier origin. There is also no consensus concerning the immediate ancestors of the angiosperms, whether the first angiosperms were tree-like or shrub-like, and whether they evolved first in seasonally dry or permanently moist environments. There has been much debate concerning their place of origin, with a number of areas, including Antarctica, having been proposed. There has been strong support for a South-East Asian origin, but now Africa–South America is the favoured region.

Obviously, flowers are not durable structures, and claims made for the antiquity of fossilized flowers have been disputed. Evidence for the evolutionary origins of angiosperms is therefore based largely on other tissues such as leaves, stems, roots and, particularly, pollen grains. Fossilized specimens are compared with known angiosperms in order to judge whether they belonged to flowering plants. A problem here is that such specimens are often poorly preserved, and anyway there is no certainty that the fossilized 'angiosperm-like' plant did actually bear true flowers. However, there is wide agreement that some pollen grains from the early Cretaceous were produced by angiosperms. Similarly, there is strong evidence that the angiosperms diversified rapidly during mid-Cretaceous times and had become the dominant group of land plants by the close of the period. The types of vegetation that existed by the end of the Cretaceous would therefore not seem unfamiliar to us today.

The ascendancy of the angiosperms can be attributed largely to the structural and developmental features referred to earlier. In addition, while the movement of gymnosperm pollen is dependent on its buoyancy in air, many angiosperms use animal pollinators, most notably insects, which are attracted by nutritional rewards or other floral features. Animal pollination is much less uncertain than wind pollination and it greatly assists cross-fertilization between genetically different individuals. The mutual associations that developed between pollinating insects and flowering plants became a potent new evolutionary force and considerable mutual adaptation in terms of behaviour, life cycles and morphology is evident among flowering plants and their pollinators. The term *coevolution* is used to describe such cases of mutual selection between two species, and pollination provides some of the most vivid examples.

Late Cretaceous Extinctions

The most famous mass extinction of all, if not the most catastrophic in terms of lost taxa, occurred around 65 Mya and marks the boundary between the Mesozoic and Cenozoic eras. Some major groups succumbed completely, some experienced considerable attrition, but others, notably the mammals, were given enormous evolutionary opportunities by the extinction event. Conventionally, the expression 'K/T' boundary

(K, from the Greek 'kreta') is used to refer to the interval separating the Cretaceous and the Tertiary. (Tertiary is in common use to refer to all except the most recent 2 million years of the Cenozoic.)

The K/T boundary is known best as the interval when the dinosaurs became extinct. However, several other taxa, particularly marine organisms, also experienced heavy losses. In the oceans, pelagic (open water) organisms suffered much greater losses than benthic (bottom dwelling) organisms: the marine reptiles and the ammonites finally became extinct, and the diversity of planktonic organisms declined markedly. While there is uncertainty as to how suddenly extinction occurred for some groups, in general, extinctions seem to have been more abrupt than at the end of the Permian period.

Of the very large number of theories that have been advanced to explain the K/T mass extinction, many have focused on the dinosaurs, although a satisfactory explanation must take all groups of organisms into account. The comparatively sudden loss of so many planktonic species suggests a sudden change in their physical environment, such as a cooling of oceanic water or a drop in salinity. One theory that has been popular since its proposal in the late 1970s is that an enormous asteroid struck the Earth, creating a dust cloud of sufficient thickness and duration to obscure sunlight, and hence prevent photosynthesis, and also reduce global temperatures. A drastic drop in photosynthesis and primary productivity, it is reasoned, would have affected all organisms to a greater or lesser extent. There is evidence that such an impact occurred. Sediments deposited at the end of the Cretaceous period, from widely separated locations, contain an unusually high concentration of the element iridium. This element is extremely rare on Earth, but is often found in much higher concentrations in meteorites. Furthermore, a number of K/T boundary sections contain fragments of 'shocked quartz', a term used to refer to quartz minerals which have experienced high-pressure impacts, as occurs when meteors hit the Earth. More recently, the theory has been given further encouragement by the discovery in the Yucatan peninsula (eastern Mexico) of a huge sediment-filled impact crater which has been dated to around 65 Mya. However, the impact theory of Cretaceous extinctions is still highly controversial. Even if we accept an extraterrestrial origin for the iridium-enriched deposits at the K/T boundary, it does not automatically follow that the impact was responsible for the extinctions. Furthermore, not all types of organism were affected in the late Cretaceous, and the extinctions that did occur were not necessarily simultaneous. All dinosaur species, for example, did not become extinct at the same time. But, whatever the cause, the consequences of the K/T extinctions were enormous.

The Cenozoic Era

A Note on Intervals

The Cenozoic, from the Greek meaning 'new life', covers the most recent 65 million years. This era is very much shorter than either the Palaeozoic or the Mesozoic and its fossil record is more revealing. Different schemes are in regular use to divide the Cenozoic into intervals, and this can be a little confusing. The most common are shown in Figure 13.7. The epochs are used rather more than the periods in this era because the fossil record permits a greater degree of temporal resolution than in the two earlier eras.

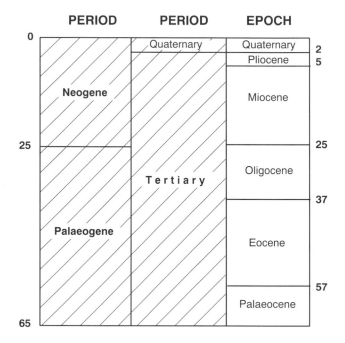

Figure 13.7   *Common schemes in use for subdividing the Cenozoic era. Numbers are millions of years before present. The Pliocene–Quaternary boundary, which is set at various times, is not marked by changes in fossil assemblages. The Quaternary is divided into the Pleistocene and the Holocene (most recent 10 000 years)*

For simplicity, the terms Palaeogene and Neogene are used here unless further refinement is justified. The most recent 2 million years, often known as the Quaternary, can be further subdivided into the Pleistocene and Holocene.

At the beginning of the Cenozoic era, South and North America were not joined. The former southern hemisphere land mass, Gondwana, was fragmenting, while Laurasia in the northern hemisphere remained largely intact. India, which was formerly part of Gondwana, later rafted northward to join the Asian continent.

Ascendancy of the Mammals

The mammals originated at around the same time as the dinosaurs in the late Triassic, but they remained small and inconspicuous throughout the remainder of the Mesozoic era. Although diversification occurred within the mammals in the late Mesozoic, it was the demise of the dinosaurs in the late Cretaceous that provided them with the opportunity to radiate and become the dominant group of land vertebrates.

Mammals are recognized by combinations of features, including glands on maternal parents from which milk is supplied to young offspring, a covering of body hair, a capacity to regulate body temperature, and, particularly important in fossil remains, features of the jaw, dentition and ear. Three extant mammalian groups are recognized: the placentals, the marsupials and the monotremes. The oldest and rarest are the monotreme mammals, represented now only by the duckbilled platypus and echidna and confined to Australia and New Guinea. Although monotremes are mammals, they also lay eggs, as reptiles do. Marsupial mammals, which evolved later, release their young at a relatively early stage of development into a pouch. Marsupials are the most conspicuous mammals in Australia and New Guinea and occur naturally elsewhere only in the Americas. Australia's diverse marsupials include the familiar kangaroos, wallabies and koala. Extant American marsupials include the opossum, but here the marsupial fauna is much reduced compared with just a few million years ago. The placentals are by far the largest of the mammalian groups. The name derives from the ***placenta***, the structure uniting the parent with the foetus developing within its womb. Placental mammals release their young at a later stage of development than is the case with marsupials.

Mammalian size appears not to have increased very much during the first 10 million years or so of the Cenozoic, but diversity greatly increased and many modern mammalian orders can be traced to this relatively brief interval. One such order, the Rodentia (e.g. mice and rats), now contains more species than any other mammalian order. The course of mammalian evolution was influenced by the progressive cooling and increased seasonality of climates that occurred from mid-Palaeogene times. Indeed, it is conjectured that the general cooling of climates gave the mammals, with their temperature-regulating capacity, a selective advantage they did not possess during the Mesozoic when temperatures were generally warmer. In response to climatic changes, the area of closed forest shrank while more open, savanna-like vegetation expanded. One of the most successful plant families, the Gramineae (grasses), appeared over 50 Mya and eventually became a dominant feature of these open landscapes. Grasses are particularly well adapted to withstand grazing because vegetative growth occurs predominantly from around ground level. So, unless severe and prolonged, grazing tends to stimulate regrowth.

The expansion of open landscapes provided new opportunities for the mammals, particularly the hoofed mammals (ungulates), but it also brought new challenges. Grasses usually contain silica, a tough and abrasive mineral. It seems that in response to a largely grass diet, certain features of herbivore dentition evolved, including tough enamel ridges, which maintain an effective grinding surface, and continuously growing teeth. Also associated with a fibrous diet is cud-chewing, i.e. regurgitation of food from the stomach to the mouth for further processing. This process allows the animal to spend less time than would otherwise be necessary in grazing on open grasslands, and digestion is completed when and where the animal is less vulnerable to predation. The danger of predation has doubtless selected for speed of movement: in some types of grazing herbivore the leg bones became progressively better adapted for faster movement during late Palaeogene and Neogene times. A capacity to utilize cellulose, the major chemical component of plant cell walls, is another feature of hoofed herbivores, particularly the ruminants (Page 83). Cellulose can be utilized by such animals only because microbial residents of the digestive tract produce enzymes that break the bonds linking the component sugar units. Although mutualistic associations between animals and cellulose-digesting microbes did not appear first in hoofed herbivores, it is within this group of animals that such associations are most highly developed. During mid-Palaeogene times the dominant ungulates were the odd-toed type (today, rhinoceros, horse and tapir), but in the later stages of the Palaeogene, dominance shifted to the even-toed, or cloven-hoofed, ungulates (now, e.g. sheep, cattle, camels, antelopes and pigs), a position they have held ever since.

Mammalian evolution was not confined to land; the whales appeared, as descendants of land mammals, quite early in Palaeogene times and underwent an adaptive radiation in the Neogene. Other mammals which appeared in the Neogene, the seals, walruses and sealions, are predominantly aquatic, although they reveal their terrestrial ancestry by coming ashore to breed. Mammals also took to the air in the early Palaeogene. Bats are the only flying mammals; they now have an almost worldwide distribution and they comprise one of the largest mammalian orders.

The Late Cenozoic

The global trend towards cooler, drier and more seasonal climates continued during the Neogene and was accompanied by a progressive increase in open vegetation. Against this background the mammals evolved progressively more modern characteristics. Neogene grasslands apparently supported large herds of grazing herbivores together with their predators. Today, a similar community can be witnessed only on the savannas in eastern and southern Africa.

Global cooling became more marked around 3.0 Mya, heralding the onset of the interval commonly referred to as *the* 'ice age'. In fact, it is just the most recent of several ice ages that have occurred during the history of the planet. *Ice ages* are extended intervals of global cooling when snow and ice cover extensive areas. The general direction of ice movement is from high to lower latitudes, although mountain glaciers ahead of the main continental ice sheets also expand. The most recent ice age occupies the interval known as the Pleistocene. Its commencement is usually set at about 2.0 Mya, although this is somewhat arbitrary. Continental ice sheets may have started to form a million years earlier. At its maximum, ice covered about 30 per cent of the Earth's surface (compared with less than 10 per cent today). The ice cover was not continuous throughout the Pleistocene. Rather, expansions were interrupted by several minor retreats (*interstadials*) and some major retreats (*interglacials*). These glacial oscillations provide the basis for subdividing the Pleistocene into named intervals. Pleistocene climatic changes were not confined to glaciated and nearby areas, but were global in extent. Outside the areas of immediate glacial influence, glacial advances were typically associated with cooling, and often increased aridity. For example, the area of tropical rain forest shrank at times to scattered remnants. Simultaneously, however, other areas actually became wetter.

Large accumulations of snow and ice lead to a drop in sea level, which in turn permits the migration of species between previously separated land masses, as, for example, between Alaska and Siberia, and between Australia and New Guinea. In the northern hemisphere, there was a trend for species to migrate more or less south and north in response to alternating cooling and warming, with consequent shifts in the composition of the biota in particular regions. However, we should not think of whole communities shifting more or less intact. Rather, each species would have responded independently to climatic changes, so it is quite probable that species assemblages formed which were rather different from those in existence today. The role of climatic events in biogeography is taken up again in Chapter 14.

The most recent 10 000 year interval is known as the Holocene (or Recent) epoch. Ten thousand years is a convenient date for the onset of much warmer conditions and glacial retreat in the northern hemisphere. The term 'post-glacial', which is sometimes used, is misleading because we are actually living in an interglacial interval.

Late Pleistocene Mammalian Extinctions

In late Pleistocene and early Holocene times, large mammals in several areas of the world suffered significant extinctions, whose possible causes are a continued source of controversy (Figure 13.8). It is tempting to regard climatic change as the primary cause, but it is not easy to explain why extinction was mostly confined to large mammals, and why it did not occur on a similar scale during earlier climatic changes in the Pleistocene. These animals have close living relatives, but our identification with them goes further because they were contemporaries of our own species. Inevitably, then, we must consider to what extent human activity may have contributed to their demise.

For North America in particular there is support for the view that human hunting contributed significantly to mammalian extinctions. This view has been championed by Paul Martin of the University of Arizona whose theory incorporates estimates of the contemporary human population and its impact as a result of hunting. Exactly when peoples from north-eastern Asia first crossed the Bering land bridge during the late Pleistocene is debatable, but human activity was probably widespread over much of North America by the time the first wave of extinctions occurred around 11 000 years ago. Within just a few millennia many of the larger mammals, including ground sloth, camel, peccary, horse, mammoth, mastodon and great plains cat became extinct in North America. In South America, too, extinctions evidently followed human colonization. Large herbivores of South American origin disappeared together with many species of North American ancestry which had migrated south after the two continents coalesced at the Panama Isthmus some 3 million years earlier (Page 207). Extinctions in northern Europe and Asia generally preceded those in the Americas. In just a few millennia, commencing about 25 000 years ago, the woolly mammoth, woolly rhinoceros, musk ox, giant deer, bear, bison, cave lion and cave hyena had become extinct over most of the main Eurasian landmass. Although these extinctions may have coincided with the emergence of hunting peoples in Eurasia, there is less enthusiasm for the hunting explanation than is the case for American extinctions, partly because species likely to be favoured for eating, e.g. the red deer, survived while those less favoured, e.g. woolly rhinoceros, became extinct.

Australian large mammals, which included marsupials of much greater size than extant forms, also experienced considerable attrition during the Pleistocene. This continent was colonized to a limited extent by humans well over 40 000 years ago. The major wave of extinctions seemingly commenced around 30 000 years ago, and again

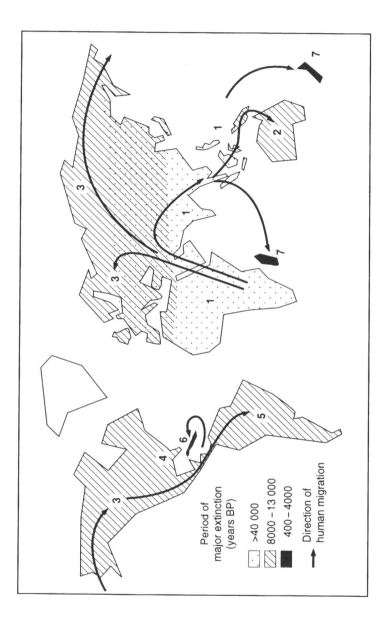

Figure 13.8 *Late Pleistocene extinctions. Intervals of major extinctions are shown, together with the pattern of human diffusion. Numbers denote the sequence in which different regions experienced extinctions. (From Martin, P. and Wright, H. (eds) 1967 Pleistocene Extinctions: The Search for a Cause. Redrawn by permission of Yale University Press, New Haven)*

took just a few millennia. On the islands of New Zealand, the largest animals were flightless birds. Extinction here is much more recent, beginning about 1200 years ago, but humans were responsible. Clearly, there are no easy answers to the problem of late Pleistocene extinctions and different factors may have been responsible in different regions. Nonetheless, the fact that human societies witnessed these extinctions cannot be disregarded, so explanations which do not consider their involvement are not entirely satisfactory.

Human Origins

The subject of human origins is full of uncertainty and controversy because of the poor fossil record. The remains of our recent ancestors are typically fragments of a skeleton or skull and opinions often differ concerning their place in phylogenetic schemes and their taxonomic treatment. All the problems of re-creating evolutionary lineages and classifying groups of organisms discussed in Chapter 5 are much in evidence here. Different books and articles, especially if published over a range of dates, are likely to show different schemes. The objective here is to provide a workable framework for human origins, and to point out major areas of controversy.

We begin with the primates, a mammalian order which probably originated towards the end of the Cretaceous period. In early Palaeogene times, the primates diverged into distinct lineages, including 'Old World' and 'New World' monkeys, and a group called the Hominoidea. The living representatives of this 'superfamily' are the great apes (orang-utan, chimpanzees, gorilla), the gibbons, and ourselves. The general view is that the line leading to the gibbons diverged around 20 Mya and the line to the orang-utan diverged around 15 Mya (Figure 13.9a). Traditionally, the great apes and humans have been placed in separate families (Pongidae and Hominidae respectively), but molecular evidence has argued for a reclassification. Now the African apes and humans are often viewed as one family (Hominidae), while the orang-utan, which occurs naturally only in Borneo and Sumatra, is the sole representative of the family Pongidae.

The fossil record for apes, or at least ape-like animals, extends to around 24 Mya. The oldest specimens come from tropical Africa, but subsequently they moved into southern Africa and, as Africa and Asia became connected, into Eurasia as well. It is from African apes that the line leading to the genus *Homo* emerged (Figure 13.9a). The timing is uncertain but it was probably between 8.0 and 7.0 Mya. Previously it was thought that the lines leading to modern apes and humans had developed independently.

Although the African apes are now often grouped within the family Hominidae, the term 'hominid' is in general use for taxa that are more human-like than ape-like, and this convention is continued here. Included within the hominid group are *Homo* species and also extinct genera, notably *Australopithecus*. The oldest known hominid, from about 4.4 Mya, was discovered in central Ethiopia in 1992 (Figure 13.9b). It has been named *Ardipithecus ramidus*, and from the little fossil evidence it seems to have been able to move both in trees, as apes do, and on two legs. Proposing a new genus for these remains was a big step because previously the australopithecines had formed the oldest hominid genus.

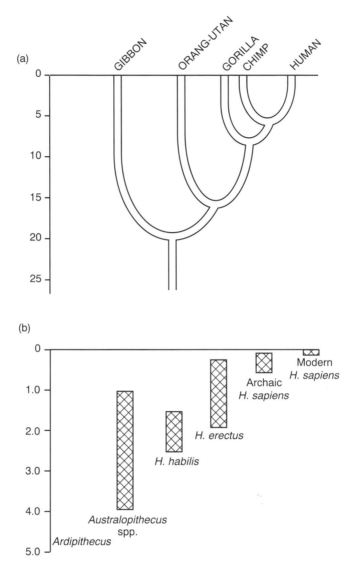

Figure 13.9 *Hominid evolution. (a) Suggested evolutionary relationships among extant members of the 'superfamily' Hominoidea. (b) The approximate time spans of different hominid taxa. H. stands for Homo. Numbers are millions of years before present*

Since the first specimen to be called an australopithecine was found, in South Africa in 1924, much controversy has surrounded this taxon, particularly its boundaries, the taxonomic treatment of its members and its relationship to the genus *Homo*. Importantly, australopithecines were bipedal. The oldest known type, now generally called *Australopithecus afarensis*, has been found in Ethiopia and Tanzania, and probably lived between 4.0 and 3.0 Mya. This taxon was proposed as the ancestor for all other members of the genus *Australopithecus* as well as the genus *Homo*. Others had favoured the view that the two genera evolved independently. It seems that the australopithecines lived between about 4.0 and 1.0 Mya, and only in eastern and southern Africa. It is generally accepted that the genus *Australopithecus* should comprise a handful of species, designated as either 'gracile' or 'robust' types. The heads of the robust type were more heavily constructed, with a more exaggerated dentition believed to have been associated with a coarse plant diet. The more slender gracile types, of which *Australopithecus afarensis* is one, preceded the robust form. The conventional view is that the human lineage arose from a gracile type of australopithecine, and that before the australopithecines disappeared different hominids co-existed.

During the 1970s and 1980s, a degree of consensus emerged that the *Homo* lineage should comprise three main species, *Homo habilis, Homo erectus* and *Homo sapiens.* Finds of *Homo habilis,* the oldest of these, in Tanzania's Olduvai Gorge during the early 1960s, are associated particularly with the Leakey family who have contributed so much to knowledge about human origins. The epithet *habilis,* meaning 'able', was chosen because stone tools were found in the vicinity of some of the remains. *Homo habilis* probably originated about 2.5 Mya and was fairly widely distributed over southern and eastern Africa. Subsequently, other finds of similar age suggest that another species, known as *Homo rudolfensis,* was a contemporary of *Homo habilis.* Others believe these differences are simply differences between the sexes of one species. Although *Homo habilis* has been widely regarded as the earliest *Homo* taxon, some workers suggest it should be transferred to the genus *Australopithecus. Homo habilis* appears to have lived until around 1.7 Mya and therefore overlapped with the larger, bigger-brained taxon called *Homo erectus,* which lived from around 2.0 to 0.25 Mya. Remains of *Homo erectus* (formerly often referred to as *Pithecanthropus)* have been found not only in Africa, but also in south-west Asia, China, Java and, arguably, in Europe. So *Homo erectus* was the first hominid to leave the African continent. *Homo erectus* did not just use stones as tools, as *Homo habilis* had done, but appears to have fashioned them for a variety of uses. From about 1.4 Mya *Homo erectus* appears to have used fire as well, although when and how fire was first used is a contentious issue.

The earliest undisputed remains of modern *Homo sapiens,* again from East Africa, are only a little over 100 000 years old. *Homo sapiens* is distinguished from *Homo erectus* by a number of features (Figure 13.10): average brain size is greater, the lower jaw and mouth project less, the forehead is higher and less browed, and there are differences in leg and pelvic anatomy. The term 'archaic *Homo sapiens*' is used for hominid fossils which are not unequivocally *Homo sapiens* but which are too modern to be called *Homo erectus.* These date back to about 500 000 years ago. (For some such specimens, the name *Homo heidelbergensis* has been applied.) Most of the older European hominid fossils, including those discovered during the 1990s in northern Spain, come into this category. The well-known Neanderthals (discovered in the Neander River valley in Germany in the 19th century) have been variously regarded as a subspecies of *Homo sapiens* and as a separate species. The Neanderthals probably lived from 200 000 to just over 30 000 years ago and occupied much of northern and southern Europe. The fate of the Neanderthals and their relationship to modern *Homo sapiens* (known as Cro-Magnons) are still unresolved.

Figure 13.10   *Some hominid skull casts. From left* Australopithecus africanus, *a gracile type of australopithecine;* Homo erectus; *modern* Homo sapiens. *(Photo, Ian Qualtrough; specimens provided by the Department of Human Anatomy and Cell Biology, University of Liverpool)*

Hominid evolution in Africa was characterized by anatomical changes and occurred against a background of changing climate and vegetation. Crucially important was the shift to bipedalism. One of the best known pieces of evidence for the antiquity of bipedalism is the set of australopithecine footprints from 3.6 Mya at Laetoli (Tanzania). The prints were made in wet volcanic ash which subsequently set hard, and they were then buried. Advantages proposed for an upright gait include relatively low heat absorption, freedom to use the upper limbs (e.g. for gathering food, throwing missiles and using tools), and an enhanced capacity for long-distance movement over land. Brain size also increased greatly, from less than 500 cc (cm^3) for the early australopithecines to around 1000 cc for *Homo erectus*, and typically 1400 cc for modern *Homo sapiens*. So bipedalism preceded the increase in brain size, and presumably provided the circumstances for the selection of increased mental capacity.

As far as changes in climate and vegetation are concerned, it seems the East African tropics became progressively drier from around 5.0 Mya, while western Africa remained predominantly wet. In consequence, the vegetation in eastern Africa became more open, while closed forest remained predominant in the west. As closed forest favours an arboreal way of life, the great apes, with their climbing abilities, continued to flourish. In contrast, a gradual loss of tree cover in the east would have selected for a different set of characteristics, those which promote survival in a hot, dry, largely open landscape. But, despite reproductive isolation and evolutionary divergence for over 5 million years, we still share all but a few per cent of our genes with the African apes.

Not only is there much uncertainty surrounding the evolutionary relationships of the later hominids, but also their pattern and timing of diffusion. One view is that *Homo sapiens* evolved more than once from *Homo erectus* populations in separate geographical areas of the Old World. The majority view, however, favours a single origin, in Africa, and subsequent diffusion throughout the Old World. In this scenario, populations of *Homo erectus* and other *Homo* taxa were gradually replaced by populations of modern *Homo sapiens*.

Postscript

The life-span of our own genus – roughly 2.5 million years – is just a tiny proportion of the 3.8 billion years or so that have elapsed since organisms first left traces of their existence on the planet. Translated into a timescale that we may comprehend, this is equivalent to a little less than the final six hours of a calendar year.

In surveying important events in the history of life, it is hoped that no hint has been given that the appearance of our own species represents an end point in any sense, or that evolution has a purpose and has finally achieved its goal. The concepts of mind, consciousness and culture may not be applied in quite the same way to other living species, and no other shares our mental capacity, but this does not mean that our own species represents an end point to the evolutionary process, or that our origin was predestined. If the dinosaurs had not disappeared 65 Mya, we would not be here today.

Further Reading – Part Three

Delcourt, H.R. and Delcourt, P.A. 1991 *Quaternary Ecology*. Chapman & Hall, London.
(Good overview of ecological and environmental change during the last 2–3 million years with discussion of underlying processes.)

Fortey, R 1998 *Life: An Unauthorized Biography*. HarperCollins, London.
(A survey of life's history interwoven with the author's own experiences as a practitioner. A rare best-seller inside and outside scientific circles; hugely enjoyable.)

Lewin, R. 1993 *Human Evolution*, 3rd edition. Blackwell Science, Oxford.
(Very clear introductory treatment of human origins.)

Margulis, L. and Sagan, D. 1997 *Microcosmos: Four Billion Years of Evolution from our Microbial Ancestors*. University of California Press, Berkeley.
(Lively but authoritative discussion of important evolutionary innovations emphasizing the Precambrian interval.)

McNamara, K. and Long, J. 1998 *The Evolution Revolution*. John Wiley & Sons, Chichester.
(Pleasing and useful guide to the history of life.)

Nisbet, E.G. 1991 *Living Earth: A Short History of Life and its Home*. Chapman & Hall, London.
(Accessible but rigorous treatment of the subject; strong on Precambrian events.)

Stanley, S. 1993 *Exploring Earth and Life Through Time*, 2nd edition. W.H. Freeman, New York.
(Excellent reference for studying the history of life in geological and climatic context – highly recommended.)

Van Andel, T.H. 1994 *New Views on an Old Planet: A History of Global Change*, 2nd edition. Cambridge University Press, Cambridge.
(Stimulating, clear and authoritative introduction to Earth history, including evolutionary events.)

Part Four
SPATIAL ASPECTS OF THE BIOSPHERE

The focus in the final part of the book is large-scale spatial phenomena in the biosphere. The first of the three chapters here is concerned with the geography of individual taxa, particularly species. Some basic principles are introduced, emphasizing the factors controlling the distribution of taxa. The next chapter considers the zonation of the world's biota, first, according to the distribution of taxa and, second, according to structural characteristics of vegetation. In the final chapter the subject of biodiversity is introduced, particularly global patterns in species diversity.

14

The Geography of Taxa

Each taxon, whatever its position in the taxonomic hierarchy (species, genus, family, etc.), has distributional limits over the surface of the Earth. Describing and explaining these distributions is a major objective of biogeography. In the first part of this chapter the focus is on species distributions, but later, when considering longer timescales, higher taxonomic levels are considered.

As discussed in Chapter 5, the species is the fundamental unit in the classification of organisms. Species are also key units within ecological communities. An important aspect of the biology of a species is where it lives, and this question can be considered at a variety of spatial scales. At one extreme we can attempt to define the local conditions in which a certain species is most likely to be found. For a plant it could be the degree of soil wetness, or the amount of available nitrogen that is important; for an animal it could be the type of vegetation that is crucial. The term 'habitat' is used to refer to such local conditions. Characterizing the habitats occupied by particular species is a major objective of ecology, and often combines fieldwork with experimental work under controlled conditions.

An alternative objective is to establish the entire range of a species. In fact, the difference between ecological and geographical approaches to species distributions is really one of emphasis. An ecologist who is working with a certain species may not be concerned with its entire geographical range, or how its range has changed over long periods of time. Biogeographers, on the other hand, are interested in the 'big picture', both spatially and temporally. But biogeography is not simply concerned with mapping distributions: that is just the first stage. The more interesting and challenging task is to explain these distributions. This requires a consideration of the ways in which organisms respond to their environment (a theme central to ecology), but it may also require an understanding of longer term geological and climatic changes. Because such long time periods are involved, biogeographers are also concerned with the evolutionary history of taxa, so the principles of speciation introduced in Chapter 4 are very relevant.

Species Distributions

The geographical range of a species (genus or family, etc.), is frequently shown, either on a world scale or regional scale, as in Figure 14.1. Such maps suggest the type of climate (tropical, temperate, arid, etc.) in which the species is found and, by extrapolation, other geographical areas where the physical environment might be suitable for its colonization. If we are working outside the range indicated on the map we can be reasonably confident that the species will not be encountered. (This last point is worth remembering when attempting to identify species in the field because species can often be excluded on this basis.) However, the map in Figure 14.1 shows only the distributional limits of the species and not the actual range it occupies within this area. Therefore the map provides no information about the probability of finding the species in different parts of its geographical range.

A more informative way of representing species distributions is shown in Figure 14.2. In these examples the British Isles has been divided into grid squares of equal area and within each the presence (or not) of the species is indicated. A further refinement would be to vary the size of dots to denote abundance. Just from the proportion of squares occupied it is usually possible to draw some tentative conclusions about how common and abundant the species is. The map in Figure 14.2b provides both ecological and biogeographical information. Ecologically, *Atriplex portulacoides* is confined to coastal locations (salt-marshes), while geographically this species is only occasionally found to the north of the Scottish border.

The extent of geographical ranges varies enormously between species. At one extreme there are plant species that are confined to a single valley, and fish species restricted to a

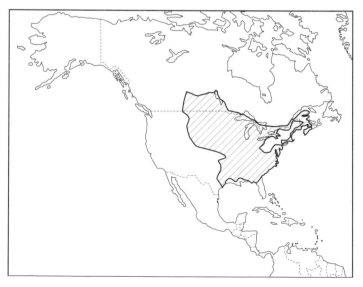

Figure 14.1   *The geographical distribution of the tree species* Fraxinus pennsylvanica *in North America is indicated by shading. (From Ritchie, J. 1987* Postglacial Vegetation in Canada. *Redrawn by permission of Cambridge University Press, Cambridge)*

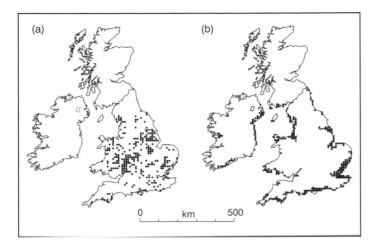

Figure 14.2 *Geographical distribution of two plant species in the British Isles is shown on the basis of presence within 10 km grid squares. (a) The tree species* Tilia cordata *(small-leaved lime) fails to regenerate beyond its northern boundary due to temperature limitations on reproductive processes. (b) The salt-marsh plant* Atriplex portulacoides *(sea purslane) has a northern geographical limit in Britain and is restricted to suitable coastal habitats. (Maps produced using DMAP software by Alan Morton and provided by Biological Records Centre, Institute of Terrestrial Ecology, Monks Wood, Cambridgeshire)*

single lake, while at the other extreme some species are distributed naturally on all the major continents. Taxa which are distributed very widely are described as ***cosmopolitan***.

The species shown in Figure 14.3 occupies quite separate geographical areas. The range is thus discontinuous, or ***disjunct***. Such distributions are of great interest because they invite speculation as to how they have arisen. Some possible explanations are discussed later. It is not always clear when the term disjunct is appropriate: no species is truly continuously distributed in the sense that individuals occur very close together throughout the geographical range. In practice, biogeographers use their judgement when deciding whether a distribution is disjunct, although geographical separation is often so great that the use of the term cannot reasonably be disputed.

One of the guiding principles of biogeography is that the ranges of species are not static, but they expand, contract and shift in position over time. In general, the longer the timescales being considered, the greater the changes in range are likely to be. However, ranges can sometimes change very quickly (Figure 14.4), particularly when a species is introduced to a new geographical area to which it is well adapted. It is usually possible to distinguish an increase in range caused by a gradual expansion of the distributional boundary (as in Figure 14.4) from an increase in range caused by long-distance dispersal.

Explaining Species Ranges

The fact that a species is surviving within a particular geographical area means that the environmental conditions are suitable for all aspects of its life cycle. This is not such an

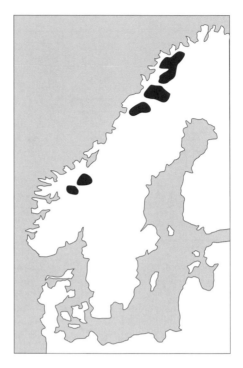

Figure 14.3   *The disjunct, or discontinuous distribution of the flowering plant* Campanula uniflora *in Norway. This has been caused by the survival of populations in unglaciated areas during the Pleistocene and subsequent failure of northern and southern populations to unite. (From Moore, D.M. (ed.) 1982* Green Planet: The Story of Plant Life on Earth. *Redrawn by permission of Cambridge University Press, Cambridge)*

obvious statement as it may seem. For example, a plant species may be able to grow vegetatively beyond the range where conditions are suitable for its sexual reproduction. If a particular species is absent from a certain area it should not be assumed that the species could not exist there: it could be that the species has not had the opportunity, or the time, to colonize the area in question. Explaining why a species is confined to its geographical range is no easy matter. This is because the environment of an organism is multifaceted and its various components interact in complex ways. To organize thoughts about the environmental dimension, a distinction can be drawn initially between the physical components (e.g. temperature, moisture) and the biotic components (e.g. predators, parasites, competitors) of an organism's environment.

The Physical Environment

Temperature

Although a species range may not be wholly explained by temperature regime, it is known, first, that all organisms are affected by temperature, second, that an organism can

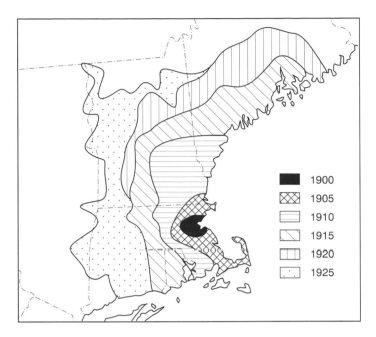

Figure 14.4   *Rapid range expansion of the moth* Lymantria dispar *(gypsy moth) in north-eastern USA after 1900. (Adapted from Brown, R. and Sheals, R. 1944 The present outlook on the gypsy moth problem.* Journal of Forestry *42: 393–407)*

survive only within a certain thermal range, and, third, that an organism performs less and less well as threshold temperatures are approached. For many organisms (e.g. fungi, bacteria, plants, insects) these principles can be demonstrated quite easily under controlled conditions by measuring performance over a range of temperatures (Figure 14.5a). Such experiments go some way to explaining the ecology of a species. They also help explain the geographical distribution of species, because in the real world individual species are more abundant and more successful, e.g. grow faster, leave more offspring, at certain parts of their geographical range than at other parts. In effect, the laboratory experiment is attempting to simulate the latitudinal, or altitudinal, temperature gradients that exist in the real world (Figure 14.5b).

In the hypothetical laboratory experiment (Figure 14.5a), the performance of individual organisms was measured over a range of *constant* temperatures. In the real world, though, temperatures fluctuate, usually both seasonally and diurnally. So laboratory findings provide only a general guide to geographical distributions. Also, the response of an organism to temperature usually varies according to its stage of development. For a particular plant species, the optimum temperature for seed germination could be 10°C, while the optimum temperature for flower production could be 25°C.

The relationship between temperature and the geographical distribution of a species can be explored using isotherms, because these provide a guide to threshold temperatures for species. The problem here is to characterize a temperature regime with a single parameter, so those which are thought to be most important are selected. For example, it

(a)

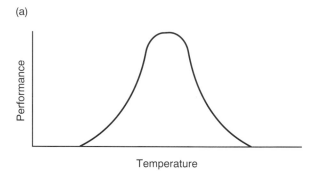

(b)

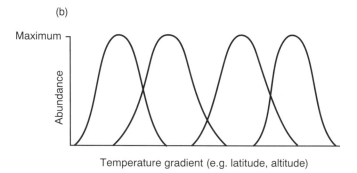

Figure 14.5 *(a) General model for the effect of temperature on an organism's performance (e.g. reproductive rate, growth rate). The model assumes an optimum temperature range and minimum and maximum thresholds. (b) Extrapolation of the temperature effect on performance to geographical distribution and abundance of four species along a temperature gradient (e.g. latitude, altitude)*

could be mean annual temperature, or mean minimum January temperature, or mean July temperature. It is important to appreciate that a good match between a distribution boundary and an isotherm is only a correlation and does not mean that temperature is the causal factor. Also, if low winter temperatures are associated with low summer temperatures, range extension into cooler climates may be prevented either by winter cold or inadequate heat during the summer months.

Establishing the mechanisms by which temperature determines distributional boundaries of species requires a thorough investigation of organisms at different stages of their developmental cycle. A study of this sort was carried out some years ago on the tree *Tilia cordata* (small-leaved lime), which does not successfully regenerate north of a certain area in Britain (Figure 14.2a). It was discovered that sexual reproduction was prevented in cooler conditions by inadequate development of the pollen tube. Seeds gathered from elsewhere, however, successfully established at these locations. In Finland, where higher summer temperatures permit adequate pollen tube growth, it is the slow development of seeds in the cooler days of late summer that sets the northern distributional limit for regeneration of the same species.

All species have potential distributional limits which are set by temperature. However, there is considerable variation between species in the relative importance of temperature in setting the actual distributional boundaries. In addition, differences occur between species in the stage of the life cycle at which temperature is most effective.

Moisture

For land organisms another key environmental variable is moisture. Water is essential for metabolism, it acts as a coolant (evaporation lowers surface temperature), and it is the principal medium for transporting nutrients and for voiding waste products. Many of the remarks made about temperature apply also to moisture. Again, research findings in the laboratory may provide a guide to distribution in the field. For example, experimentation may show the minimum amounts of moisture necessary for survival. However, moisture regimes are difficult to characterize with a single statistic. Total annual rainfall is often used for this purpose, but what is important is the availability of moisture for the organism being considered. This is affected by the seasonality of rainfall, its intensity, rates of evapotranspiration and soil conditions. Much of the rain that falls on an area within a year may therefore be largely ineffective as far as the organisms are concerned.

It is clear that organisms differ in their capacity to cope with very dry environments. However, there is not a great deal of variation between species of broadly similar type in their capacity to metabolize at low cellular moisture levels. Rather, explanations for species distributions along gradients of moisture availability are to be found in the differential capacity of species to obtain water from their environment, to conserve water, and to shut down metabolic processes in response to water shortages. A variety of adaptations are associated with plants which inhabit arid environments, including extensive root systems, high water storage capacity, small leaves and sunken stomata. A feature of certain desert plants is the type of photosynthesis known as crassulacean acid metabolism (Page 71). Recall that such plants take up carbon dioxide through open stomata at night and keep the stomata closed during the day when water loss is potentially much greater. Most animals in arid environments have the great advantage that they can confine their activities temporally and spatially so as to minimize water need and loss.

Temperature and moisture are key variables influencing the performance of organisms and the geography of species. In terms of mechanisms, however, these two variables combine and interact in a variety of ways. The case of air humidity and plants is one such example. As the temperature of air rises, so too does its capacity to hold moisture. In response to an increase in the evaporative demand of the atmosphere, plants tend to close their stomata, but species respond differently. Species which are confined to very humid situations often display an inability to control excessive water loss by stomatal closure when evaporative demand is high. Another example of the close relationship between the temperature and moisture relations of plants concerns desiccation damage. This is particularly associated with springtime in seasonal climates when high evaporative demand caused by high daytime temperatures combines with low soil temperatures to bring about excessive water deficits in the leaves and buds.

Photoperiod

Daylength, or **photoperiod**, affects a number of physiological processes, notably those involved with reproduction. It is therefore a potentially influential factor determining the range of a species. The breeding cycles of animals are largely determined by photoperiod, and natural selection has led to young usually being born at a time of the year when the probability of survival is greatest. Flowering of plants is another reproductive process frequently affected by photoperiod. Plants may be categorized broadly into three types with respect to their flowering behaviour. Some, called 'long-day' (or 'short-night') plants, do not flower unless daylength exceeds a minimum threshold; other plants ('short-day') do not flower unless daylength remains below a critical threshold; and flowering of some plants ('day-neutral') is independent of photoperiod.

The Biotic Environment – The Presence of Other Species

Discussion so far has been confined to the physical environment. The physical environment sets the potential range of an organism, the outside of the envelope in which populations of a species can maintain themselves. However, organisms of one species are continually interacting with those of other species. Some of these interactions have the effect of lowering the performance of an organism. Other interactions may actually enhance performance though, and in some cases may be essential. Beneficial associations between species include plants and their pollinating agents and plants and nitrogen-fixing bacteria.

The central question here is whether biotic interactions prevent species from realizing their potential geographical ranges. If this is the case, the actual, or **realized range** of a species will be less than the potential range set by physical environmental factors (Figure 14.6). Intuitively, it might be expected that biotic factors have some influence on geographical distributions. This is because the performance of organisms varies in

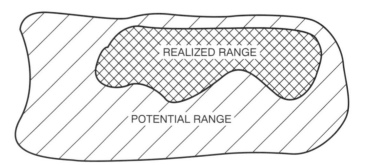

Figure 14.6   *The principle of potential and realized geographical ranges for a species. Physical environmental factors set the potential distributional limits but interactions with other species may prevent occupation of this area. Different factors may be involved at different parts of the range boundary. In this hypothetical example the northern range boundary is hardly influenced by other species but biotic factors are important in setting the southern boundary*

response to factors such as temperature and moisture, and it is therefore reasonable to assume that organisms are more vulnerable to harmful interactions with other species towards the limits of their range than in parts of their range where performance is much better. In addition to truncating species ranges at the margins there is also the possibility that species interactions themselves can in some circumstances be a major determinant of species distributions. The three major categories of interaction considered here are predation, interference and mutualism.

Predation

The term predation is commonly taken to mean one animal killing another, but it can be applied to a wider range of interactions involving the transfer of nutrients between organisms (Page 103). Used in this wider sense predation includes grazing of plants by herbivores, parasitism and insect parasitoids, as well as one animal killing and devouring another. There are two ways in which such interactions could influence species ranges. First, predation could prevent another species from occupying part of its potential range. Second, the range of a predator could be limited by the absence of a suitable prey species.

Although the effect of predation is to reduce the abundance and the performance of prey species, this is not to say that it is always a major factor in the control of abundance in populations. The effect of predation varies from one situation to another, and probably from time to time in a particular predator–prey relationship (Page 103). So it is impossible to generalize about the ecological role of predation, particularly when it includes a number of different types of interactions between species. For predation to be of major biogeographical significance, it must be demonstrated that the distribution of prey organisms is confined by the activities of predators. The potential for predation to influence geographical ranges has been demonstrated by introductions of predatory species, either deliberately or accidentally. Predatory fish have been introduced to lakes over much of North and Central America where they appear to have been responsible for range reductions in a number of other fish species lower in the food chain. The completion of the Welland Canal in Canada in 1829 permitted ships to by-pass Niagara Falls. The canal also permitted the migration of organisms into the upper Great Lakes. One organism, the fish-like sea lamprey, eventually had a devastating impact on native fish stocks. The introduction of insects for biological control has sometimes resulted in reductions in the range of the target organism, providing further evidence of the potential for predation to limit the geographical distributions of prey organisms. The problem with all these cases, however, is that they are rather artificial in the sense that they involve very rapid range expansions. They demonstrate the potential power of predation to control the biogeographical range of a species but do not provide evidence that ranges are normally controlled by predation. An experimental approach to test the efficacy of predation would be to remove a predator from an area and then determine whether the same area is colonized by other species known to be a food source for the predator. Even if predation rarely controls the distribution of prey species, it may increase the vulnerability of prey populations to physical environmental factors or to other biotic processes, and thereby contribute to the realized range of a species.

The extent to which the ranges of predators are determined by the presence of prey species depends largely on the dietary requirements of the predator. Clearly, for species with very specific requirements, and this applies to many insects and parasitic organisms, the geographical range of the food item may well determine the predator's realized range. However, this can only be determined by an investigation of the two species involved.

Interference

Species interactions other than predation which have a detrimental effect on at least one of the species are termed *interference*. One such interaction, ***competition***, occurs when an organism performs less well than its potential because it is deprived of resources by another organism. Competition can occur between organisms of the same species (i.e. *intraspecific*), but concern here is with *interspecific* competition. The resources for which organisms compete vary between types of organisms. Between plants, competition occurs principally for light, water and nutrients; between heterotrophic organisms competition may occur for food, and sometimes for space and territory. Although animals may display aggressive behaviour, competition is generally a rather passive process. It is likely that natural selection operates so as to reduce competition between species. As a generalization, it seems that the closer two species are in terms of their resource requirements, in the places and times they procure resources for example, then the more intense the competition between them.

Since the 1930s there have been heated debates among ecologists concerning the importance of competition in organizing ecological communities, and there is still no consensus. It is quite easy to demonstrate what appears to be a competitive effect under controlled conditions with two or three species, but much more difficult to do so under more realistic field conditions. Competition is probably very important in some situations, at certain times, but less so in others. In addition to competition other forms of interference occur in communities, including the release of chemicals by plants and fungi which inhibit the performance of other organisms. It is very difficult to evaluate the effects of such activities on the ranges of species, but in certain situations they may influence species performance.

Circumstantial evidence for the importance of interference behaviour in setting distributional limits is found where species with similar environmental tolerances have adjacent, but not overlapping, ranges. Such a distribution has been shown for kangaroo rats in south-western USA. Here, there is no evidence of physical discontinuities which would explain the pattern of distribution, and all the species have broadly similar environmental tolerances and requirements. Another example, also from south-western USA, involves chipmunk species. Two species are used here to convey the principles. One of these, *Eutamias umbrinus*, usually lives in closed coniferous forest of the higher mountain slopes, while the other, *Eutamias dorsalis*, inhabits the drier, open woodlands of the lower slopes. The former species is more arboreal than the latter, and in the tree canopy where it lives there is plentiful food. The chipmunk of the lower slopes is primarily ground-living and fiercely defends its food supply, which is relatively scarce. However, there are some mountains on which only one of the two species (it can be either one) occupies the entire elevational range, indicating that neither the physical environment nor the habitat can explain chipmunk distribution on mountains with both species. This leaves species interactions as the likely cause. Careful observation and experimentation have more or less confirmed such a hypothesis. It appears that the aggressive behaviour of the chipmunk from the open woodland is a deterrent to the species of the closed forest. In the closed forest canopy, however, the more arboreal species is so much more adept at procuring food that its territory is not invaded.

Mutualism

The term ***mutualism*** is used for interactions between species in which both (or all) the species involved derive some benefit. Mutualistic associations are very common in nature; for simplicity we deal here with cases involving two species, but mutualisms which involve more than two species have been discovered. For the two-species case, mutualistic associations can be obligatory for both partners, obligatory for one species but not the other, or obligatory for neither species. Additionally, mutualistic associations can be categorized on the basis of the type of benefits derived. The benefits are usually either nutritional, reproductive or protective, and each partner may derive different sorts of benefits. We have already met some examples of mutualism in this book. Mycorrhizal associations (Page 110) involving fungi and plant roots are nutritionally beneficial (sometimes obligatory) for the plant, while the fungus is provided with a supply of organic substances from the host. Certain plants live in close association with nitrogen-fixing bacteria (Page 121), which supply nitrogen to the host plant and receive organic matter in return. The majority of flowering plants are pollinated by animals (Page 172). The pollinating agent receives nutritional rewards in return for dispersing pollen and facilitating plant reproduction. The microbial residents of ruminant animals (Page 83) increase the availability of energy and protein to their host and are offered a satisfactory environment and supply of food in return. Another example of mutualism is that found between *Acacia* trees and ants in some parts of the world. Nutrient-rich nectaries situated on the stem attract ants, which in turn appear to reduce the level of herbivory by other insects. It is not difficult to appreciate that mutualistic associations provide some of the best examples of coevolution.

It is not possible to make categorical statements about the biogeographical role of mutualism. However, when one or both species in a mutualistic association is dependent upon the other, then clearly the range of one or both partners could be constrained. A contributory factor is the degree of specificity between the species involved. It could be that one organism requires the presence of another but there are a number of species that could carry out the role satisfactorily. Examining possible changes in mutualistic associations over the geographical range of a species would be an interesting biogeographical study. Mutualism, therefore, rather like predation and interference, involves quite complex interspecific interactions which may contribute to the realized ranges of species.

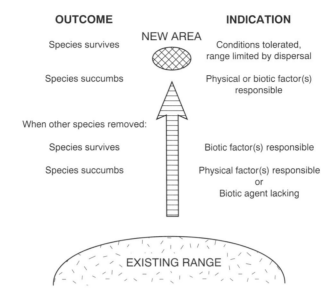

Figure 14.7 *Experimental approach to determining the relative importance of physical environmental factors and biotic interactions in determining the range of a species. The 'test' species is transferred to a new area and its fate is monitored*

Experimental Approaches to the Range of Species

Testing hypotheses concerning the relative importance of physical and biotic factors in determining the distribution of species is by no means easy. For some species, a useful approach would be to relocate individuals in a new area outside the existing species range (Figure 14.7). Survival in the new location would indicate that it is neither the physical environment, nor the activities of other organisms, that were preventing its movement to the new area. Instead it would seem that the organism has simply failed to disperse. If, however, the transplanted species died out in its new location, then either physical or biotic factors could be responsible. These two possibilities could be explored by removing all other organisms. If the species survived, it would seem that biotic factors were preventing its colonization of the new area. Further study might then reveal the nature of the biotic interactions responsible. However, if the species again succumbed following the removal of other species, it would seem likely that some aspect of the physical environment was preventing its colonization of the new area. An alternative possibility is that by removing all other species the organisms under examination were being deprived of one or more species necessary for their survival.

For an individual species, different factors may well be operating to determine distributional limits at different parts of the range boundary. Thus, for a plant species it may be low temperature that is controlling the higher latitudinal and altitudinal limits, but the lower latitudinal and altitudinal limits might be set by moisture availability and competition. Despite some interesting experimental work on which factors control distribution, the number of species examined remains very small. However, the reality of climatic change gives a new urgency to this type of work, particularly for species which pose a threat to human health, agriculture and wildlife.

Distributions Above the Rank of Species

Many of the principles introduced for the geographical distribution of species apply also to taxa of higher rank. However, because the overwhelming majority of genera contain more than one species, and most families contain several genera, the size of geographical ranges increases greatly as we move up the taxonomic hierarchy (Page 45). When mapped, the distributions of genera, families, etc. reveal continuous and disjunct distributions, as well as great variation in extent. Within the flowering plants some families, for example Gramineae (grasses), Compositae (daisy family), Leguminosae (e.g. beans, peas, acacias) and Cyperaceae (sedges), occur on all major continents. Other families have more restricted distributions. The Proteaceae is concentrated in the southern hemisphere, the Palmae is largely confined to the tropics, while the Cactaceae is confined to the Americas. At order level in the taxonomic hierarchy, geographical ranges are often very extensive, although there are still interesting biogeographical questions. For example, why are the monotreme mammals (echidna and platypus), which comprise an order, confined to Australia and New Guinea?

With each successive clustering in the taxonomic hierarchy, the degree of genetic variation within taxa greatly increases. Studies of the factors responsible for the distribution of taxa above the rank of species therefore place less emphasis on the current physical and biotic controls of distribution than on evolutionary lineages and geological and climatic events in the past. These themes are returned to later in the chapter.

Endemic Taxa

Taxa which have restricted distributions, regardless of rank, are said to be **endemic**. **Endemism** refers to the state of being endemic. When referring to a taxon as being endemic, it is necessary to specify the geographical area to which it is confined, so different areas can be compared using various criteria. Some geographical areas contain a high proportion of endemic taxa, while in other areas endemic taxa are very poorly represented. Species which are very restricted in distribution are inherently more vulnerable to extinction than species which occur widely. Thus endemic species, and areas which contain a high proportion of endemics, merit high priority for conservation. Two closely related aspects of endemism are introduced here: first, the circumstances that may lead to a species becoming an endemic and, second, the factors that lead to differences in the degree of endemism between geographical areas.

There are no rules governing the level of confinement necessary for a taxon to qualify as an endemic, but there are conventions. A species that occurred *only* throughout Europe and Asia would not have a distribution in any sense unusual, and would not normally be referred to as an endemic. In contrast, a species confined to a few small islands or a localized part of a continent would be described as endemic to these areas. At genus and family level, the term 'endemic' is applied to rather larger geographical areas: for example, the plant family Cactaceae is endemic to the Americas.

There are a number of possible explanations for the very restricted geographical distribution of a species. Some of these are itemized here, although in practice more than one factor could be responsible. One possibility is that the species formerly occupied a much greater geographical range, but over time the range has contracted. Such taxa are referred to as **palaeoendemics**. The tree *Sequoia sempervirens* (coast redwood), which is now confined to coastal groves from southern Oregon to central California, USA, is the sole survivor of a genus which was once distributed widely throughout Eurasia and North America. Alternatively, an endemic species may be a new species in evolutionary terms, and simply has not had sufficient time to occupy a broad geographical range. A species of this sort is termed a **neoendemic**. All species pass through such a phase in their evolutionary history, even though most become more widely dispersed with time.

An endemic species may be confined geographically because the area it occupies is surrounded by environmental conditions which it cannot tolerate. Obviously this situation is affected by the tolerance range of the species, its habitat requirements and its capacity for dispersal. In general, the greater the degree of specialization of a species, then the lower the probability that it will disperse. Hence, it is essentially isolation which is responsible for the restricted distribution. This 'island effect' is most convincingly demonstrated by true oceanic islands, but other examples are provided by isolated lakes and mountain tops. Mounts Kenya and Kilamanjaro in East Africa, for example, have some prominent endemic plant species. It is not only the degree of isolation that is important in such cases, but also the *period* of isolation. There is a tendency for endemism to increase with increased time of isolation because of the evolution of new species.

In referring to a species as being endemic to a certain area, the possibility exists that it is distributed more widely, but has simply not been recorded. This is much more likely for some types of organisms than others. Insects, for example, are much less well documented than the mammals. Similarly, some areas, such as the humid tropics, are less well recorded than most of the temperate world.

Because endemism can often be explained by environmental factors it is not surprising that geographical areas differ considerably in the proportion of endemic species they contain. The level of endemism in an area may sometimes be explained by a single factor, but the situation is often more complex. Isolation, both spatial and temporal, is one of the key factors. The Hawaiian Islands are extremely isolated, but in geological terms are quite recent, having arisen as a result of volcanic activity only about 20 Mya. These islands have a distinctive flora and fauna with a high proportion of endemic species. Originally, immigration of species must have been through long-distance dispersal, but thereafter much speciation occurred, probably due to the environmental heterogeneity of the islands. New Zealand, which has been isolated for some 80 million years, also has a high proportion of endemic taxa, including many genera. In contrast, Iceland has a relatively short history of isolation and an extremely low level of endemism. The Caribbean islands have some endemic species, but close proximity to the Americas has prevented the development of a biota rich in endemics. As the study of endemism inevitably involves consideration of speciation and extinction, we would expect environmental history to be important. Thus, the survival of certain plant species in

Madagascar and the Canary Isles may be due to the relative climatic stability of these islands during the Pleistocene when climatic fluctuations caused the demise of these plants on the African mainland.

Changes in the Geographical Distribution of Species

The Dispersal Process

For a species boundary to expand, there must be movement of complete organisms or propagules such as seeds and spores. This phenomenon, which is known as ***dispersal,*** is of great importance in biogeography. Because dispersal is so closely related to species distributions, some general principles are introduced here, but it should be understood that dispersal occurs continuously, usually without changes in a species range.

A convenient distinction can be made initially between truly active and truly passive dispersal. Active dispersal is best exemplified by mobile animals, particularly those that fly, swim or walk considerable distances. At the other extreme are organisms, such as flowering plants, fungi, algae and sessile animals, whose capacity for active movement is effectively limited to their own growth. For such organisms dispersal is passive, relying on agents of transport such as air currents, flowing water and more mobile organisms. Dispersal capacity varies greatly among organisms which move independently and also among organisms with little or no capacity for voluntary movement. Dispersal capacity also varies between different phases of the life cycle of individual species. Thus, the spores of ferns and fungi and the seeds of many plant species are readily dispersed by wind, and may survive immersion in water. Likewise, the resting stages of insects may be carried over long distances in the atmosphere. A capacity for voluntary movement is therefore no guarantee of rapid or widespread dispersal, while a lack of voluntary movement does not necessarily restrict an expansion of geographical range. The distinction between active and passive movement is not always marked. Many aquatic species, for example, can move independently to a degree but are also dispersed by water currents. An important biogeographical consequence of variation in dispersal capacity is that species distributions tend to change independently of each other, unless there is extreme host specificity. This means that the mix of species present in a certain area is liable to shift with time.

Dispersal may lead to the gradual expansion in the range of a species at its distributional boundary, or it may lead to the 'jumping' of an ecological barrier. What constitutes a barrier varies between types of organisms: oceans and mountains are effective barriers for terrestrial organisms, while landmasses similarly provide barriers for marine organisms. Long-distance dispersal is closely related to evolutionary processes because it may be followed by speciation (Page 38).

One piece of evidence for natural dispersal over long distances is the colonization of isolated volcanic islands, such as the Hawaiian islands in the Pacific Ocean. More recently, rapid recolonization by various species followed the volcanic eruptions which virtually destroyed all life on the Pacific island of Krakatau in the 1880s. The islands which resulted from these eruptions were covered by forest again after a couple of decades and had been colonized by hundreds of animal species. While some types of organisms are well equipped for long-distance dispersal, either actively or passively, dispersal of other organisms across ecological barriers is less easy to explain. For dispersal of terrestrial animals across water, 'rafting', on mats of vegetation dislodged from river banks, appears to be important. Although such passive dispersal clearly occurs, it should be regarded as a fairly infrequent and chancy event, and one with a progressively lower probability of success with increasing distance from a colonizing source.

If the transported species is to colonize a new area it must also establish itself and regenerate. For many species, particularly animals, two individuals of different sex are required. Even organisms with both male and female sex organs may not be self fertile, so at least two individuals are generally required for reproduction. Another point of relevance to colonization success is the existing level of occupancy by other species. In general, the probability of colonization success declines with an increase in species occupancy.

Studying Changes in Range

If the distributional limits of a certain species are known at different times in the past, an estimate can be made of the rate of dispersal. The availability of the relevant information varies greatly between different geographical areas and between different types of organisms. It also varies greatly according to the timescales involved. In some parts of the world, notably Europe and North America, there is a reasonable documentary record for the more familiar species during the recent past, but elsewhere such information is patchy. These records document some very rapid changes in species range during the last hundred years or so.

A historical picture of the geographical range of a species prior to the documentary record requires fossil evidence. As emphasized earlier (Pages 137–41), the fossil record is heavily biased towards organisms with hard body parts, and towards depositional environments. The historical geography of plant taxa during the past few tens of thousands of years relies almost exclusively on the preservation of pollen grains, specifically the distinctive outer case, or exine. When the technique of pollen analysis was described (Page 139), its value in establishing regional changes in vegetation was emphasized. In addition, by extracting and dating cores from suitable environments (e.g. peat bogs, lake sediments) in several different locations, it is possible to focus on individual taxa and record the dates in the past when they were present at particular locations, and also their contribution to the vegetation. The dispersal history of species can then be reconstructed, as in Figure 14.8. In this example, the two tree species migrated northward at different rates in response to a rise in temperature during the Holocene.

Climatic Change and Biogeography

One of the key features of Earth history, even over relatively short timescales, is changing climate. As all species respond to changes in temperature and moisture, climatic change inevitably results in a shift in the ranges of individual species. In fact, all species are subject to alterations in geographical range during their existence, caused mainly by climatic changes. The most recent 2 to 3 million years have been characterized by large temperature oscillations, giving rise to periodic intervals of extensive glacial cover. 'Ice age' events have profoundly influenced global biogeography and can often be invoked to

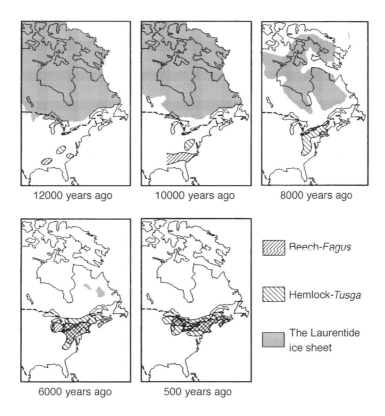

12000 years ago   10000 years ago   8000 years ago

6000 years ago   500 years ago

Beech-*Fagus*

Hemlock-*Tusga*

The Laurentide
ice sheet

Figure 14.8   *The dispersal of two tree species in North America in response to climatic warming. The range reconstructions are based on the abundance of pollen of the two taxa in different locations at various times in the past. Note that the two taxa migrated independently. The position of the ice sheet is also shown. (From Graham, R.W. and Grim, E.C. 1990 Effects of global climatic change on the patterns of terrestrial biological communities.* Trends in Ecology and Evolution *5: 289–292. Redrawn by permission of Elsevier Science, Oxford)*

explain species distributions. The general trend in the northern hemisphere was for species to move south in response to colder conditions and to move north again when temperatures increased. In reality the picture was much more complicated than this, with both the extent and configuration of the range of each species continually shifting in response to altered conditions.

Changes in species distributions during the Pleistocene and Holocene have been affected by topography and the effect of ice cover on sea level. In North America, where the orientation of mountain chains is predominantly north–south, species migrations tended to be of greater magnitude than in western and central Europe, where the east–west orientation of mountain chains provided a formidable barrier for organisms. However, not all parts of the northern landmasses were covered by snow and ice. The upper parts of some mountains are too high to have been glaciated, and thus provided a refuge for some organisms. Such unglaciated areas are called **nunataks**. Here, some species remained isolated, not only during glacial intervals, but after warmer conditions returned because they were unable to disperse across the new communities which established on the deglaciated landscape. This process has given rise to the disjunct distributions shown earlier in Figure 14.3.

The distributions of some species fragmented with alternating north–south migrations. For some species, populations became 'stranded' during southern migrations, and have remained isolated from the main part of the geographical range. This process also leads to disjunct distributions, as shown for the plant *Erica arborea* (Figure 14.9). We might expect these isolated populations to diverge increasingly over time, eventually giving rise to distinct species. Populations which are geographically isolated from the main part of the species range are known as **relicts**.

Changes in sea level can either facilitate or inhibit the dispersal of species. Falls in sea level, which were a consequence of continental ice sheet formation during the Pleistocene, facilitated the dispersal of species between present-day Australia and New Guinea, between Britain and continental Europe, and between Alaska and Siberia. The area between Alaska and Siberia, called Beringia, was exploited by the first humans to occupy the North American continent before the Bering Straits reformed. The worldwide rise in sea level which occurred during the first few thousand years of the Holocene re-established former barriers for land organisms.

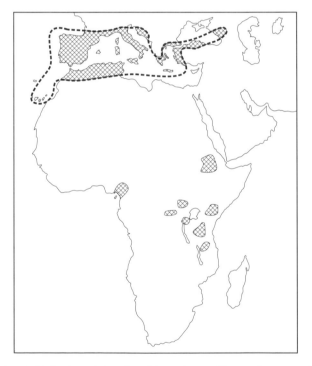

Figure 14.9   *Disjunct distribution of the plant* Erica arborea. *The southern populations became isolated at higher elevations following the general southward movement of the species during cooler intervals of the Pleistocene. A return to arid conditions in North Africa has maintained the disjunct distribution of this species. (From Moore, D.M. (ed.) 1982* Green Planet: The Story of Plant Life on Earth. *Redrawn by permission of Cambridge University Press, Cambridge)*

Geological Events and Biogeography

The distribution of taxa has been profoundly influenced by geological processes, notably continental movements and mountain building, both of which are manifestations of plate tectonics. Geological events can bring together previously isolated taxa, but also fragment continuous ranges, sometimes simultaneously. The coalescence of two formerly isolated land masses provides the opportunity for the dispersal of terrestrial species between them, but the newly enlarged land mass may form a barrier between a formerly continuous marine biota (Figure 14.10a). Conversely, the fragmentation of a land mass may cleave a continuous land biota into two parts which become increasingly isolated from each other, while the two formerly separated marine biotas can now potentially mix (Figure 14.10b).

Two examples will serve to illustrate such events. About 3 Mya, a mountain building episode united South America with Central and North America. This event led to a reciprocal dispersal of land mammals between two land masses which had been separated for some tens of millions of years. During these dispersals, often referred to as the Great American Interchange, many species from the north extended their ranges to the south, including certain animals (e.g. llama) regarded today as

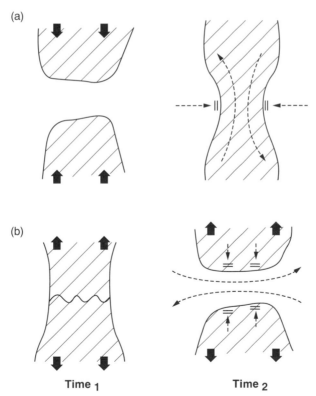

Figure 14.10 *Potential biogeographical consequences of continental movements. (a) Joining of continents facilitates movement of land biotas but isolates marine biotas. (b) splitting of continents isolates land biotas but facilitates mixing of marine biotas. Dashed arrows represent migrations of species*

typically South American. A number of South American mammals dispersed north, including the armadillo, porcupine and giant ground sloth. Palaeontological evidence reveals that before the two land masses came together, the number of mammalian families was about the same in the south and the north. It then increased temporarily in both before falling back to previous levels. Taxa from the north were more successful in the south than were taxa of southern ancestry in the north. Here, success is measured by the degree of diversification (radiation) within families and the rate of survival. The conventional wisdom for a long time was that differences in competitive ability were responsible for the changes. Also, as the 'invaders' from the north were placental mammals, and many of the southern species were marsupials (Page 174), the outcome was taken as evidence of the 'superiority' of the former. This rather simplistic view has now been largely abandoned. First, some of the South American taxa survived for a very long time indeed in ecological terms, and, furthermore, evidence for the degree to which ecologically comparable taxa replaced

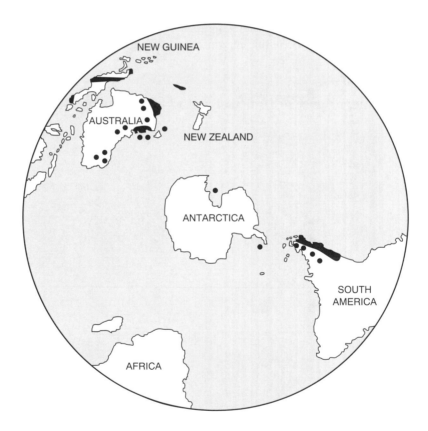

Figure 14.11 *The present distribution of the tree genus* Nothofagus *and the location of fossil finds (closed circles). The disjunct distribution of this genus is attributed to the fragmentation of Gondwana during the late Cretaceous. The various species, which occupy different landmasses, are called vicariants. (From Humphries, C. 1981 Biogeographical methods and the southern beeches. In: Forey P. (ed.) The Evolving Biosphere, pp. 283–297. Redrawn by permission of the British Museum (Natural History))*

each other is limited. Second, there is evidence that some of the South American taxa began to decline before the interchange. Third, there is evidence that the number of unfilled niches in South America was greater than in North America.

The second example illustrates fragmentation. Figure 14.11 shows the present-day distribution of the tree genus, *Nothofagus* (southern beech), and the location of fossil finds of this taxon. New Zealand, Tasmania and southern South America now have distinct *Nothofagus* species, but the distribution of the genus is disjunct. One possible explanation for the disjunct distribution is long-distance dispersal, but this can be discounted because *Nothofagus* seeds cannot survive in seawater. Before the concept of moving continents became generally accepted, some geologists postulated the former existence of land connections, which had long since disappeared beneath the sea. Now, plate tectonics provides an explanation for the present distributions. An important piece of evidence has been the discovery of *Nothofagus* fossils in Antarctica, indicating that this continent formerly experienced a much warmer climate than at present. South America, Australia, New Zealand and Antarctica once contributed to the southern continent Gondwana, which fragmented during the Cretaceous, thus dispersing and isolating the ancestors of the present species. Antarctica moved further south with the progressive loss of its vascular plants (Figure 11.9, Page 145).

The Relative Importance of Dispersal and Fragmentation

The previous discussion of possible explanations for the disjunct distribution of *Nothofagus* highlights one of the major sources of contention in historical biogeography. This is the relative importance of two theoretical models. One of these envisages long-distance dispersal across pre-existing ecological barriers; the other envisages that once continuous ranges have become fragmented by the erection of barriers to dispersal. The second of these models is known as *vicariance biogeography*, or *vicarianism*. Closely related taxa with a common ancestry are called *vicariants*. Earlier (Pages 38–40), these two models were introduced in the context of allopatric speciation, i.e. the formation of species from a common ancestor in geographically isolated regions. Some extreme proponents of either of the two models barely conceded that the other played any role at all. Now, however, most biogeographers acknowledge that both processes can occur, although the weight of evidence suggests vicarianism has had the greater influence on distributions. It is not difficult to appreciate why long-distance dispersal once seemed to be the most important process: it is simply because of the lack of an alternative credible mechanism. But mounting evidence during the 1960s in support of plate tectonic theory and continental movements provided a satisfactory mechanism for observed distributions of taxa.

Historical Biogeography

Because the ranges of taxa are continually changing, there is clearly an important geographical dimension to the history of taxa (phylogeny). This was hinted at on

(a)

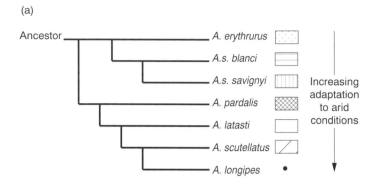

(b)

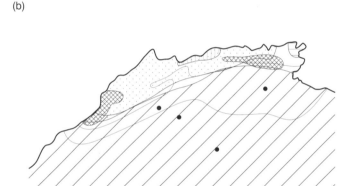

Figure 14.12 *Historical biogeography. (a) Proposed phylogeny of spiny-footed lizards (Acanthodactylus species) in North Africa. (b) The geographical ranges of the various species. The more primitive species are restricted to the relatively humid coastal area while the most derived species are found in very arid environments. (From Arnold, E. 1981 Competition, evolutionary change and montane distributions. In: Forey P. (ed.) The Evolving Biosphere, pp. 217–228. Redrawn by permission of the British Museum (Natural History))*

occasions during Part Three, as for example during the account of hominid evolution (Pages 179–82). The vital link between phylogeny and geographical distributions has been referred to more explicitly in the present chapter and will be further exemplified during discussions of floral and faunal zonation in the following chapter. Explaining present distributions of taxa requires the piecing together of evidence for the approximate timing of speciation and the geographical areas in which speciation occurred. This is based on fossils, with an increasing input from molecular biology based on the expected rates of change in key molecules. When the relevant fossils are scarce, reconstructions are very speculative. Historical biogeography therefore deals with the places where various taxa lived in the past as well as the evolutionary relationships between them. A proposed phylogeny for a closely related group of species, together with their present geographical distributions, is shown in Figure 14.12.

15

Biogeographical Zones

Two different approaches to zoning the biota are considered in this chapter. The first approach is based on the geographical distribution of plants and animals: in other words, taxonomic criteria are used. The second approach relies principally on the structural characteristics of vegetation, and is therefore confined to the terrestrial environment. Despite its rather descriptive connotations, the latter approach raises a number of issues concerning the temporal and spatial dynamics of the biosphere. Some of these issues are therefore also discussed in this chapter.

Floral and Faunal Zones

The question here is whether the geographical distribution of taxa is such that zones can be recognized, each containing distinctive assemblages of organisms. In this type of work it is usual to concentrate on one major taxonomic group and to deal with all members of that group simultaneously. Zonations based on flowering plants and mammals are dealt with here because these zonations are the most well known. The principles, however, are applicable to any group of organisms. Regionalizing floras and faunas, particularly at the global scale, relies mainly on genera and families. Working with species would be very difficult because of the huge numbers involved, while taxonomic ranks above family level (e.g. order and class) are usually too cosmopolitan to be helpful in differentiating zones. The emphasis here is on the principles underlying floral and faunal zonation: for more details concerning the taxonomic groups associated with the different zones some of the texts recommended at the end of Part Four should be consulted.

Looking for the Evidence

Europeans travelling to the tropics for the first time encounter many new families and genera of plants and animals, although some taxa on closer inspection appear to be quite familiar. The same is true for those travelling between Australia and South America and between Africa and North America. While such differences are readily apparent, the question is whether we can reasonably produce a zonation of the Earth's surface on the basis of the geographical distribution of plants and animals, an exercise which requires boundaries to be drawn between zones. If groups of families had perfectly coincident geographical ranges, and these groups were confined to particular parts of the world, then the task would be a relatively easy one. If, on the other hand, the various taxa were randomly distributed, or perfectly evenly distributed, there would be no objective basis for zonation. In reality neither of these two situations prevails. Rather, there is a strong tendency for some taxa and some combinations of taxa to be associated with certain regions of the world. The explanation for this lies largely in the configuration of continents in the past.

Initially, a handful of zones, each with a distinctive assemblage of plants or animals, and also distinctive absences, can be recognized. The terms ***realm***, ***region*** and ***kingdom*** are in common use for these primary zones, but in some schemes 'region' is also used as a subdivision of kingdoms and realms. (The choice of 'kingdom' is somewhat unfortunate because it is used in the sense of 'kingdoms of organisms'.) To avoid confusion, the neutral term 'zone' is used here for any area demarcated on taxonomic grounds. The handful of floral and faunal zones recognized initially can be progressively subdivided using more detailed taxonomic criteria.

A variety of criteria are used for zoning on taxonomic grounds. These include endemic taxa (Page 201), combinations of taxa, the number of genera within a family and number of species within a genus, and the absence of certain taxa. Zoning the world's flora and fauna is a somewhat imprecise science, particularly when it comes to locating boundaries between adjacent zones. Despite this, there is a fair degree of consensus as to how this should be done, particularly at the primary level. As might be expected, zones are set to a large extent by natural features providing barriers to dispersal. For land-based organisms, an expanse of ocean is the most obvious example. Other natural obstacles, such as mountain ranges and deserts, are climatically based. While introducing schemes for the zonation of mammals and flowering plants, some of the basic principles will be reinforced.

Faunal Zones

The first global zonation of animals to be of lasting influence – compiled by Philip Sclater in the 1850s – was based on the distribution of the avifauna (birds). It was followed in the 1870s by a zonation of mammals proposed by Alfred Russel Wallace. The general features of this scheme, which is broadly similar to Sclater's, have endured very well. Although there has not been complete agreement on the number of zones and the location of boundaries, the scheme shown in Figure 15.1 is widely accepted. In this scheme, North America (the Nearctic) and the Eurasian land mass (Palaearctic) form distinct zones. Not all biogeographers, however, consider that the faunal differences between the two major northern land masses are sufficiently great to justify a status equivalent to the other zones. The other zones are the African (sometimes called Ethiopian), the Neotropics (South America, most of Central America and the Caribbean), the Australian (including New Guinea), and the Oriental (embracing the Indian subcontinent, part of southern China and most of South-East Asia). The location of the

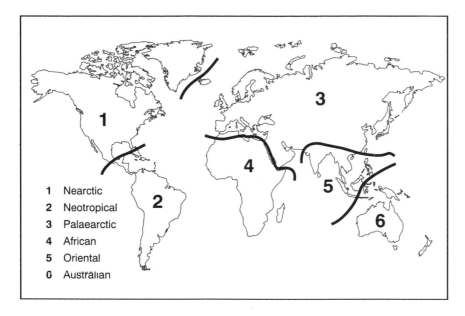

Figure 15.1   Faunal zones (realms or regions) based on the distribution of mammals. Although slightly
different zonations have been proposed, this basic structure is widely accepted.
Distinguishing features of each zone are as follows:
NEARCTIC. About 26 families, a few endemic; absence of certain families characterizes this region.
NEOTROPICAL. 32 families, about half endemic; order Edentata (includes sloths, armadillos and
anteaters) unique; combination of the families Camilidae (llama and vicuna) and Tapiridae (tapir);
distinctive monkey families; many widespread animal families absent.
PALAEARCTIC. 28 families, very few endemic; sharing of practically all families with at least one
other region is distinctive.
AFRICAN. 38 families, 12 endemic, mostly among rodents and insectivores, also hippopotamus
family; distinctive primates (including chimpanzee and gorilla).
ORIENTAL. Distinctive combination of families, 4 endemic including 2 primate families (gibbons and
orang-utan); a sharing of families with the Palaearctic.
AUSTRALIAN. Only 9 families, 8 endemic; overwhelming predominance of marsupial mammals;
unique presence of monotreme (egg-laying) mammals.
(After George, W. 1962 Animal Geography. Heinemann, London)

boundary between the Palaearctic and African zones varies between schemes, from the
North African coast to the southern Sahara. The distinguishing features of each of these
primary zones (listed in Figure 15.1) demonstrates how various criteria are used in this
kind of work.

The zonation of the mammals corresponds quite closely to the present configuration of
the continents. This correspondence arises from the timing of mammalian evolution in
relation to the final fragmentation of the continental land masses, particularly in the
southern hemisphere. Mammals, although present for much of the Mesozoic era,
underwent a great evolutionary divergence early in the Cenozoic era, after the demise of
the dinosaurs. The critical point here is that this occurred *after* the former southern
continent, Gondwana, had fragmented, so that subsequently mammalian faunas evolved
more or less in isolation on the new continents. The evolutionary divergence can be seen

today, particularly in South America and Australia, but also in the African and Oriental zones which have been isolated by mountains and deserts.

During the late Cenozoic, geological and climatic events further shaped the distribution of mammals. Some events facilitated animal movements between previously isolated land masses, as in the case of the interchange between North and South America following the formation of a land bridge about 3 Mya (Page 207). More recently, Pleistocene climatic changes have led to shifts in species ranges and contributed to a reduction in species diversity on the northern Eurasian and American land masses.

Floral Zones

The zonation of plants is less straightforward in many respects than that of mammals. Partly this is because there are around three times as many families of flowering plants as mammals (around 300 versus 100) and 10 times as many genera. It is also because the incidence of endemism is lower for plants at the family level. Furthermore, while only a handful of mammalian families have successfully colonized all the major continents, nearly a third of all plant families have done so. Consequently, the distribution of genera is much more important for plants than it is for mammals.

The foundations for floral zonation were laid in the early and middle decades of the 19th century when European botanists were becoming better acquainted with the plant life of Africa, the Americas, Asia and Australasia. Floral maps at the world scale became progressively refined during the later decades of the 19th century and a degree of consensus emerged concerning floral zones.

The two maps of floral zones in Figure 15.2 illustrate the kind of issues over which opinions differ. In both schemes the Holarctic zone embraces Eurasia, Greenland and North America. It is only in the very recent geological past that Eurasia and North America have been separated by a rise in sea level (which formed the modern Bering Sea), so a high degree of floristic similarity between these landmasses is to be expected. The Palaeotropics, another extensive zone, embraces most of Africa, Arabia, India and South-East Asia. Most of South and Central America and the Caribbean is sufficiently distinctive to form a separate zone. So far then the two schemes in Figure 15.2 are in broad agreement although there are small differences in the position of boundaries.

There is less agreement over the treatment of southern South America, southern Africa and Australasia (Figure 15.2). In one scheme these three areas form a single zone, indicating that the floras of the southern parts of South America and Africa are more closely related to each other than to more northerly floras in their own continents. These taxonomic affinities were noticed during the 19th century, and explained by former land bridges between the continents. In the other scheme there are six zones. The Australian flora and the South African 'Cape' flora are each deemed sufficiently distinct to form separate zones. The southern tip of South America and New Zealand form another zone, the Antarctic. This influential scheme, by the Russian botanist Armen Takhtajan, involves the division of some primary zones (which he called kingdoms) into subkingdoms and finally 37 floral regions.

In the floral schemes there is a degree of correspondence between the principal zones and the continents, but much less so than for the mammals. Again, the explanation is to

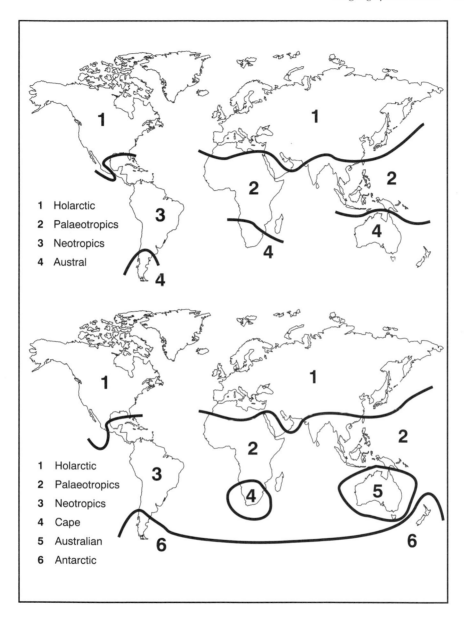

Figure 15.2   *Floral zones (realms, regions or kingdoms) based on the distribution of flowering plants. The points of difference between the two schemes are discussed in the text*

be sought largely in the timing of continental breakup in relation to the timing of evolutionary events. Despite the uncertainties surrounding the early evolution of the flowering plants (Page 172), it is clear that their early radiation occurred *before* the final fragmentation of Gondwana in the Cretaceous period. So it was possible for angiosperm taxa to migrate between what are now South America, Antarctica, Africa, India and

Australia. Movement between Gondwana and Laurasia would also have been possible through African connections. The southern parts of Africa and South America are now clearly differentiated from the more tropical areas to the north. India, which was once part of Gondwana, rafted northward during the Cenozoic with the almost complete loss of its southern floral associations.

Modern Approaches to Plant and Animal Zonation

While there is much agreement concerning the zonation of the world's fauna and flora, the process involved is rather subjective. Wallace, working in South-East Asia in the 19th century, used personal observation and the relatively slim records available. He observed the rapid transition from a marsupial-dominated mammalian fauna (the Australian zone) to one dominated by placental mammals, which included rhinoceros, elephant and tiger. This is the most famous of all biogeographical boundaries and was named the Wallace line, although subsequent studies have suggested shifts in its location. With time, regional lists of plant and animal taxa have greatly lengthened, and geographical ranges have became better known. However, the establishment of zones is still based largely on personal knowledge and intuition. Today, traditional approaches are complemented by more objective, quantitative methods. This is particularly the case when primary zones are successively subdivided using taxonomic criteria. Numerical values, called *coefficients of similarity* (or *dissimilarity*) can be calculated for any two prescribed areas using simple formulae. The values plugged into these formulae are usually the numbers of the taxa of interest which occur in each of the two areas, and the number of taxa shared between them. The values derived are then normally expressed on a percentage basis to facilitate comparison. A number of different boundaries can be chosen and the one providing the greatest degree of dissimilarity can be selected as the most appropriate to separate two zones. Despite such apparent objectivity, however, there is usually no unique solution to the problem. For example, different coefficients of similarity are in use, and they give different results. Although biogeographical zoning will always retain its subjective element, it is an important activity because it organizes biogeographical variation and it also contributes to a greater understanding of evolutionary relationships and environmental change in the past.

Vegetation Zones and Biomes

Overview

An alternative approach to zoning the terrestrial biota is based primarily on the overall structure, or *physiognomy*, of the vegetation. (Vegetation simply means the sum total of plants inhabiting a given area.) This approach requires a number of vegetation types to be recognized and their geographical distributions to be mapped. The maps usually depict *potential vegetation*, that is, the vegetation it is believed would be present in the absence of human activity. The names applied to the zones provide information about the structural characteristics of the vegetation, and often the climate in which they are found.

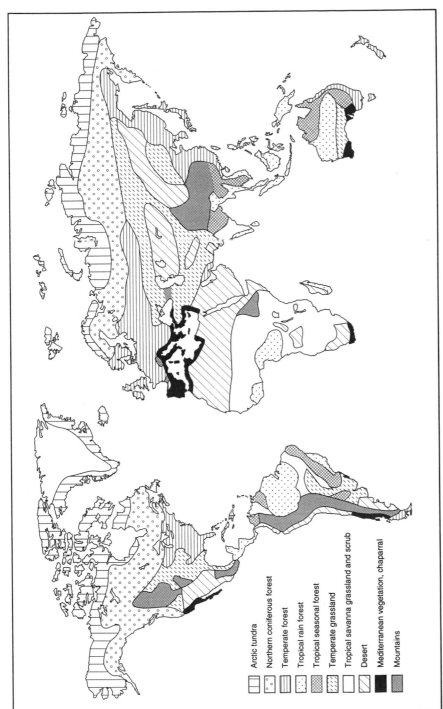

Figure 15.3 *World map of biomes or vegetation formations. The zones indicate potential vegetation. Structural features of vegetation are determined primarily by climate. (From Cox, C.B. and Moore, P.D. 1993 Biogeography: An Ecological and Evolutionary Approach, 5th edition. Redrawn by permission of Blackwell Science Ltd, Oxford)*

Arctic tundra

Northern coniferous forest

Temperate forest

Tropical rain forest

Tropical seasonal forest

Temperate grassland

Tropical savanna grassland and scrub

Desert

Mediterranean vegetation, chaparral

Mountains

A glance at any atlas will usually reveal a vegetation map of this sort. Vegetation zones are more or less coincident with biomes: the key difference is that the term 'biome' is used to imply consideration of all organisms, not just the plants, and also functional, as well as structural features of the biota. In practice, however, biomes and vegetation zones are equivalent, particularly at the global scale (Figure 15.3).

Criteria for Vegetation Zonation

The fairly clear distinction between trees, shrubs and herbaceous plants provides one obvious approach to differentiating vegetation types and mapping zones. The German scientist and philosopher Alexander von Humboldt is usually credited with laying the foundations for this type of study in the modern era. Humboldt travelled to South America as part of an expedition around the turn of the 19th century and made a number of important observations. One concerns the close relationship that exists between overall vegetation structure and climate; another is that similar structural features occur within unrelated species growing in similar climatic conditions. As European botanists assembled a more detailed picture of the world's vegetation during the 19th century, the link between vegetation structure and climate observed by Humboldt was more or less confirmed at the global scale. A number of other European scientists, particularly in Germany, contributed greatly to the development of phytogeography during the 19th and early 20th centuries. One was Oscar Drude, who applied the term *vegetation formation* to large areas of vegetation with broadly similar structural characteristics.

Numerous terms are used for vegetation types. *Forest* is often qualified by temperature (e.g. tropical, temperate and boreal forest; Figure 15.4) and by rainfall (e.g. tropical rain forest, tropical dry forest). The terms 'broadleaf' and 'coniferous' essentially make a taxonomic distinction, between forests dominated by angiosperms and gymnosperms respectively, although such trees differ also in overall morphology. Shrubs are essentially multi-stemmed woody plants of relatively low stature. Shrub-dominated vegetation is often referred to by local names. Thus in Britain, *heathland* is a standard term for vegetation dominated by plants of the family Ericaceae; the *chaparral* of California is a woody vegetation growing in mediterranean climates, and *garigue* and *maquis* denote shrub-dominated vegetation in mediterranean climates in southern Europe. The most common type of herbaceous vegetation is *grassland*, although other plant taxa usually grow in association with the grasses. Regional terms for grassland include *prairie* in North America, *pampa* in South America and *steppe* in south-eastern Europe and parts of Asia. Extensive areas of the warmer parts of the world are covered by *savanna(h)*, which denotes grassland with sparse trees. *Tundra* (from a Finnish term meaning 'treeless hill') implies vegetation of generally low stature in which combinations of dwarf shrubs, grasses, sedges, mosses and lichens are conspicuous. The physiognomy of *desert* vegetation varies considerably, but a discontinuous plant cover is normally considered a defining characteristic. However, while some desert areas are covered with barren sand or larger rock fragments, other parts are quite well vegetated with herbs, shrubs and even trees. When physiognomic types are subdivided into climatic categories, as in the case of tropical, temperate and boreal forests, this may reflect structural differences in vegetation between climatic zones. Typical temperate broad-leaf trees, such as oak, beech and ash, do differ in appearance from typical

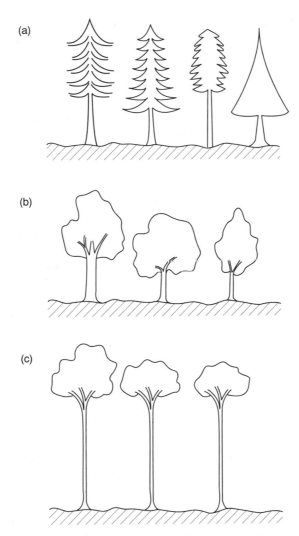

Figure 15.4 *Structural differences of trees characteristic of (a) boreal, (b) temperate and (c) tropical climates. (Drawing, Sandra Mather)*

tropical trees, for example those of the family Dipterocarpaceae of South-East Asia. Similarly, the trees dominating tropical and temperate forests differ from the coniferous (cone-bearing, needle-leaf) trees, such as the spruces, pines, firs and larches, that dominate the boreal forest zone (Figure 15.4).

Problems in Zoning Vegetation

Maps such as that in Figure 15.3 provide a general guide to the world's potential vegetation, but it is important to be aware of the problems inherent in their compilation and use. The number of zones identified on world maps varies between schemes, from just a handful to over 20. If the number is too small, valuable information may be lost, but if the number is too large, the maps are so complex that they are difficult to interpret unless reproduced in very large format. When only a few categories of vegetation are chosen for a world-scale map, it suggests a degree of homogeneity in the vegetation which is not evident at ground level. It may not be possible to show altitudinal changes in vegetation: for example, tropical mountains may be snow-capped for much of the year but such features are rarely shown on vegetation maps of world scale.

A second issue is the rather arbitrary way vegetation types are designated. For example, while the term 'forest' refers to tree-dominated vegetation, there are no rules about how dense the tree cover needs to be before the term is appropriate, and at what tree density 'savanna' would be more appropriate. Terms such as 'open forest', 'closed forest', 'woody savanna' and 'open savanna', chosen to characterize vegetation more closely, are largely a matter of judgement. A closely related issue is the location of boundaries between categories when the vegetation is continually changing spatially. This is not to deny the existence of enormous areas of vegetation which in general terms are structurally uniform, but there are also extensive areas where the vegetation occurs as a continuum in terms of both structure and species composition. If a continuum of tree densities exists, drawing boundaries between 'open forest' and 'closed forest' is an arbitrary process. Similarly, if it was decided to distinguish evergreen from deciduous forest there will usually be areas of mixed forest which do not fit well into either category. The problem of demarcating major vegetation zones is sometimes approached by recognizing transition areas (often called *ecotones*), but it is still necessary to decide where to draw the boundary separating the transition zone from the main vegetation categories. In general, the more intensively an area is studied, the greater the need seems to be for further categorization.

Some transitions between major vegetation types can be quite abrupt, presenting interesting questions about how plants with different physiognomies respond to their physical environment. The tree line, i.e. the latitude or altitude beyond which conditions do not permit tree growth, is a good example. Viewed from the air, the northern tree line in Canada and Russia can appear to be quite abrupt in places. A similar effect is sometimes seen on mountains. As the forest margin is approached in both situations, tree density tends to decrease, trees become more and more stunted and, at high altitude, tree growth is often more or less horizontal. The cause of tree lines has long attracted interest, and both experimental and historical evidence strongly implicate temperature as a critical factor. Forest has a greater structural diversity (or aerodynamic roughness) than vegetation nearer the ground, which means that leaf temperatures tend to track environmental temperatures more closely than is the case with lower-growing plants. Thus in cold weather tree leaves tend to be colder than leaves of plants of low stature. Also, it seems that trees are less successful than shorter plants in conserving moisture in late winter and spring, when the ground may be frozen. Thus water stress may also play a role along with temperature in determining tree lines. In other situations, tree density declines very gradually over a considerable distance so the term 'tree line' seems inappropriate. This is particularly the case with gradients of increasing aridity.

Regional and Local Vegetation Maps

So far, the discussion has emphasized vegetation zonation at the global level, and the differentiation of vegetation type has been based on relatively coarse structural features. The smaller the geographical area under study, the greater the opportunity to increase the number of vegetation categories recognized. Also, there is a tendency to incorporate plant names to denote vegetation types. Three examples of vegetation categorization at regional and local scales are shown to illustrate this sort of approach. The term 'tropical forest' is applied to extensive tracts of vegetation in the Amazonian Basin, West Africa, and South-East Asia and Australia, and it can imply a degree of uniformity which is not evident on the ground. British ecologist T.C. Whitmore proposed a categorization of forest types in South-East Asia which shows the considerable variation that exists in the region (Table 15.1). Differences in forest type are associated with variations in both altitude (climate) and soil conditions. The second example is the desert biome of the south-western United States and adjacent Mexico. A common scheme for differentiating this area, which embraces a range of climatic and vegetation types, is shown in Figure 15.5. Each of these regions is characterized by a distinctive assemblage of plants. This is an example of the close relationship that can exist between zonations based on floristic criteria (usually called *provinces* at this level) and those based on structural features. At a fine level of

Table 15.1 *A categorization of forest types in the tropics of the Far East. Note the influence of climate (topography), soil type, soil wetness and salinity on forest type. (From Whitmore, T.C. 1984 Tropical Rain Forests of the Far East, 2nd edition. Oxford University Press, Oxford)*

Tropical rain forest

Evergreen rain forest
Lower montane rain forest
Higher montane rain forest
Subalpine rain forest
Heath forest
Forest on limestone soils
Forest on ultrabasic soils
Beach vegetation
Mangrove forest
Brackish-water forest
Peat swamp forest
Freshwater swamp forest
Seasonal swamp forest
Semi-evergreen rain forest

Monsoon forest

Moist deciduous forest
Other dry seasonal forest

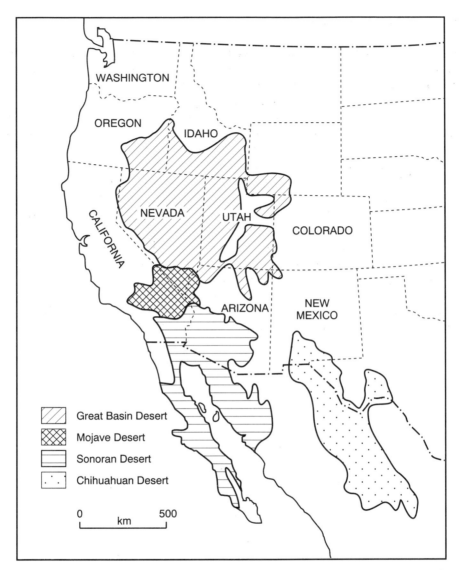

Figure 15.5 *Regional vegetation map showing the primary division of the desert area of south-western USA and adjacent Mexico. (Adapted from Shreve, F. 1942 The desert vegetation of North America.* The Botanical Review *8: 195–246)*

resolution these desert areas appear different because of the differences in the species composition. The third example is a relatively small area of the Rocky Mountains in the USA (Figure 15.6). Notice in this case that species names have been used in combination with physiognomic features: this indicates that the named taxa are dominant or otherwise conspicuous in the areas indicated, not that they are the only ones present. This pragmatic approach is commonly used in compiling vegetation maps at the local level.

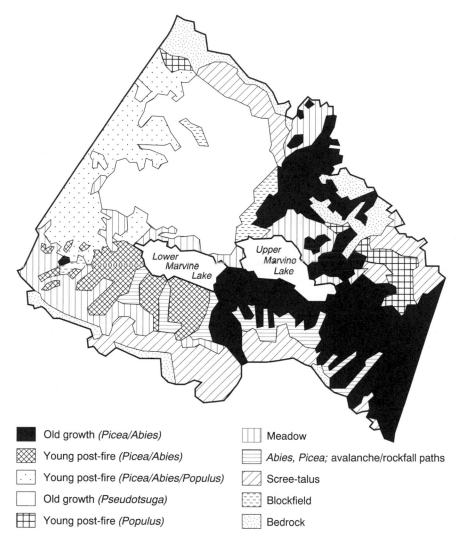

Figure 15.6 *A local vegetation map for an area of the Rocky Mountains in Colorado, USA. Note the variety of criteria used to differentiate zones. (From Veblen, T. et al 1994 Disturbance regime and disturbance interactions in a Rocky Mountain subalpine forest. Journal of Ecology 82: 125–135)*

Vegetation Mosaics and Disturbance

Inspection of vegetation, especially forest, but also shrublands and grasslands, often reveals a mosaic effect. This is particularly evident from the air. Such mosaics may be directly attributable to environmental variation, for example differences in moisture availability due to topography, or differences in soil chemistry due to parent materials. In addition, mosaics may be the product of natural **disturbance**. Disturbance means the sudden loss, or onset of loss, of living biomass over ecologically significant areas. Such disturbed areas range in size from a few hundred square metres in the case of the loss of a large tree to hundreds of square kilometres in the case of a major forest fire. The most important causes of physical disturbance are fire, wind, volcanic activity and landslides, lightning strikes, floods and ice-storms. It is now widely acknowledged that collectively such phenomena have a major effect on the world's vegetation. Disturbance can also be caused by other organisms. For example, elephants have caused extensive damage to trees in some parts of Africa, and insect outbreaks periodically cause massive defoliation in certain forest areas in North America. Furthermore, some pathogenic organisms may exacerbate the effects of other environmental factors to bring about tree mortality. Within regions in which disturbance is a major ecological factor, not all areas are necessarily affected equally. In fire-regime areas, floodplains are less susceptible than drier sites; where wind is a major factor, vulnerability to disturbance is affected by topography.

Fire is the most widespread natural disturbance agent and lightning is the principal source of ignition. Natural fires occur periodically over extensive areas of the world's coniferous forests, drier shrublands, grasslands and savannas. Return times for natural fire events vary: 15–30 years is typical for chaparral, while for boreal forest it may be over 200 years for major conflagrations. However, even with return times of hundreds of years fire has an influence on community characteristics. Within forests, low-intensity surface fires may occur quite frequently and they serve to remove litter and small plants. Fire suppression, however, which is so often a major policy objective in forest management, can lead to an accumulation of organic matter and the growth of young trees. When a fire does occur it is therefore more likely to move into the tree crowns. This will likely cause extensive loss of forest, and may also endanger people and property. Fire policy became a major public issue in the United States during 1988 when fires burnt extensive areas of forest in Yellowstone National Park. These fires reinforced the views of many ecologists concerning the ecological benefits of periodic burning in situations where fire is a natural agent.

Wind, particularly in the form of hurricanes and tornadoes, is an important disturbance agent in some parts of the world and, as with fire, the periodicity of major events varies from place to place. For the forests of the north-eastern United States, return times may average 50 years, but for forests in subtropical storm tracks such events occur every few years. The 'great storm', which did so much damage in southern Britain in 1987, provided a sharp reminder that few areas are immune from extreme events, even though return times may be very long.

Some disturbance events are associated with tectonic activity. Volcanic eruptions cause fires and eject debris of various sorts. Some ejected materials are inhospitable for plants and so colonization may be very slow, but in other situations vegetation establishes remarkably quickly. Much of the area affected by the Mount St Helens eruption of 1980 had a green cover by 1990. Landslides play an important role in the ecology of some forests located near plate margins, as for example in the Chilean Andes and parts of Japan.

There are two common explanations for the mosaic effect in vegetation subject to periodic disturbance. First, differences between blocks of vegetation may represent similar species assemblages in different stages of their growth cycle. This is most obvious when a forest is dominated by a single tree species occurring in even-aged stands. Thus, differences in appearance between blocks are associated with trees of different age. Second, differences between individual blocks may be caused by vegetation of different structural types. Good examples of this situation come from temperate deciduous forests in which disturbance is often followed by the successive dominance of the site by herbaceous plants, shrubs and, again, closed forest. It could take hundreds of years to restore the previous structure, and during this time the site could experience another disturbance. This is not to suggest that the forest necessarily represents a predetermined 'end point'. If prolonged waterlogging occurs, the forest could be transformed to bog. Changes in vegetation composition also frequently occur in gaps created by the loss of large individual trees, as in tropical humid forests, although vegetation changes are usually much slower and less conspicuous than when large areas of landscape are affected.

The process of vegetation change – which may be represented by different structures, different species, or both – is known as *succession*. Usually, succession on disturbed sites is described as *secondary*, meaning the site was previously occupied by vegetation. In situations where the site is a 'new' land surface, as in the case of volcanic ejecta, the term *primary* succession is used. (Other primary successional situations are deglaciated landscapes and sand dunes.) Succession merits a moment's consideration here because the topic has featured so prominently in the development of ecology. In fact, a theory of succession, proposed early in the 20th century, was the first unifying theory to emerge in the (then) young science of ecology. However, that rather deterministic model of succession has been largely abandoned in favour of theories that explain most vegetation successions in terms of plant characteristics such as dispersal capacity, growth rates, longevity and size. In some situations, disturbance is followed by little change in the species composition of the vegetation. This applies particularly to desert vegetation and grasslands where physical site properties are not drastically altered by disturbance.

Human Impacts on Vegetation

So far, the discussion of vegetation zones has focused on potential vegetation, and little reference has been made to the extensive areas appropriated for agriculture and extensive grazing by domesticated livestock. For example, intensive agriculture occupies most of the temperate forest zone covering western and central Europe, eastern North America and eastern China (Figure 15.3). Intensive agriculture represents an extreme case of habitat modification, but human influences in vegetation can be much less obvious. The fact is that there are few places on Earth that are 'natural' in the sense that they have been unaffected by human activity. This is not to say that the general features of the potential vegetation, including indigenous species, do not still cover extensive tracts of the planet. But all human activities, including the use of fire, management of grazing animals, and hunting and gathering, have ecological consequences. Even areas considered 'wilderness' from a Western perspective are not exempt from this generalization. The savannas and grasslands of East Africa, with vast herds of herbivores and their predators, give the impression of a truly natural environment. But, ironically, this is the region with the longest history of human occupation, and people still play an important ecological role through their use of fire and domesticated livestock. In fact, the long history of fire use in the African savanna, the North American plains and over much of Australia make it very difficult to disentangle the ecological effects of natural and anthropogenic fires.

Similarly, tropical forests have a long history of human occupation. These societies, living at low population densities, may not have had a major effect on the broad structural and functional features of their forest environment, but it is difficult to believe they have had no ecological impact.

The Uses of Vegetation Zonation

The world vegetation maps compiled during the 19th century were a major achievement considering the resources then available. They enhanced understanding of the world's geography and they provided an important context for the development of the new science of ecology in the closing years of the 19th century. These maps have been progressively refined during the 20th century as new techniques and more detailed surveys have provided a more complete picture of the world's vegetation. Vegetation survey remains an important activity in biogeography and ecology. However, far from being just a rather unfashionable background activity, the mapping of the biota is now seen as fundamentally important to an understanding of environmental processes. This is due largely to a growing realization that environmental understanding relies on the consideration of interactions between biotic and physical processes. As ecosystem types differ quantitatively in the ways in which they interact with the physical environment, the spatial distribution of biotic zones is of great importance. The influence of vegetation on the global carbon cycle (Pages 128–9), which is still not well quantified, and also on radiation and hydrological budgets, provide good examples of areas where vegetation geography is important.

One of the most enthusiastic proponents of a holistic approach to environmental issues is the British scientist James Lovelock, who is best known for the Gaia hypothesis. (The name Gaia was used by the Greeks for the goddess Earth.) Lovelock considers the biota and its environment to operate as a homeostatic system which opposes changes unfavourable for life processes. This is a truly radical proposal, going far beyond the undoubted capacity of organisms to influence their environment, as in the case of the rise in atmospheric oxygen which followed the evolution of water-splitting photosynthesis (Page 152). Aspects of the Gaia hypothesis remain very controversial, but the significance of complex feedback mechanisms between biotic and physical processes is not doubted. The lasting legacy of the Gaia hypothesis has been in promoting more interdisciplinary approaches to environmental issues.

Another factor which has stimulated renewed interest in vegetation geography is growing concern about the likely impacts of climatic change. A corollary of the close relationship between climate and vegetation is that vegetation zones should shift in response to changes in temperature and moisture availability. Ultimately, this is caused primarily by the migration of species in response to climatic shifts.

The introduction of satellite imagery during the last few decades has greatly enhanced understanding of spatial aspects of the biosphere. Aerial photography (another ***remote sensing*** technique) provides very useful information for vegetation survey but cannot be co-ordinated at the world scale in the way now possible using image generators located outside the Earth's atmosphere. The 'pictures' generated by space platforms rely on the optical properties of the vegetation and aquatic organisms. (Some features of radiation were introduced in Pages 63–5.) Essentially, solar radiation is received at the Earth's surface in a range of wavelengths. Green leaves strongly absorb radiation in the 400–700 nm range because of chlorophyll, the photosynthetic pigment. The greater the chlorophyll content per unit area, the greater the proportion of radiation in this wavelength range that is absorbed. However, radiation in the 700–1100 nm range is strongly reflected. Reflected radiation of red wavelengths (Channel 1 or C_1), and of near infrared wavelengths (Channel 2 or C_2), is measured to derive an index called the **Normalized Difference Vegetation Index** (**NDVI**), which in essence is an estimate of the amount of green tissue. The formula used to calculate the NDVI is:

$$(C_2 - C_1)/(C_2 + C_1)$$

The lower the values, the less the 'greenness' of the vegetation. As 'greenness' is related to the total amount of leaf tissue, and satellite imagery permits regular data collection, this technique provides the opportunity to estimate biomass and productivity much more speedily than traditional methods. It should also greatly assist attempts to monitor the response of vegetation to climatic change.

16

Geographical Aspects of Biodiversity

Biodiversity is a shorthand term for the total variability of life on Earth. The term itself is relatively new, but the concepts it embraces have a much longer history. For convenience we can identify three major elements of biodiversity. First, there is taxonomic diversity, which is usually represented in terms of the number of species. An important example was mentioned in Chapter 5 when the problem of estimating the total number of species on Earth was considered. Biodiversity can also be expressed as the number of genera, or families, particularly when diversity trends are reported over geological timescales. The second key element of biodiversity is genetic diversity within species. The loss of genetic diversity within species which have been domesticated for food production is particularly worrying because it reduces the potential to incorporate desirable traits such as disease and pest resistance into crops and livestock. Genetic erosion can also be a problem within 'wild' species because, as the gene pool becomes smaller, populations are less likely to be able to adapt to environmental challenges such as new strains of pathogens. The third major element of biodiversity is the variety of ecological community types. This includes not only the major biomes, but the immense variety of habitat types as well.

In practice, species diversity, genetic diversity and community diversity are closely interrelated because the destruction of communities can lead to genetic erosion and the loss of species. Protection of habitat of sufficient size for populations to be viable is perhaps the key objective of conservation.

The Several Dimensions of Biodiversity

While natural scientists have been interested in the various elements of biodiversity for several decades, more recently the term has become something of a 'buzzword' in political and socioeconomic arenas. The reasons for this are the widespread acknowledgement that human welfare is inextricably linked to biodiversity and the unequivocal evidence for the loss of biodiversity. The importance of biological diversity was highlighted in the United Nations sponsored report *Our Common Heritage* in the

Table 16.1   *Reasons for maintaining and enhancing biodiversity*

Ethical	Species have 'rights'
Aesthetic	Species and communities are a source of pleasure and enjoyment
Human welfare	Living species and communities are a resource, e.g. for tourism
	'Wild' relatives of domesticated species are a vital source of genetic variability
	Species are a unique source of chemical compounds of benefit to society, e.g. drugs, pesticides
	Species may be hunted or domesticated for food or fibre
	Species (particularly microorganisms) may be useful for environmental remediation
Ecological integrity	Loss of species may impair community function
Scientific value	Loss of species reduces information about ecology, evolution, systematics and Earth history

1980s and, particularly, in the deliberations at the United Nations Conference on Environment and Development ('the Earth Summit'), held in Rio de Janeiro in 1992. During the 1990s, biodiversity emerged as one of the key themes on the environmental agenda, as evidenced by the International Convention on Biological Diversity and the action plans produced by signatory nations. The nature of the arguments invoked for maintaining biodiversity are many and varied. They include aesthetics, ethics, economics, human health and welfare, and the integrity of ecosystems (Table 16.1). Although the major concern of this chapter is the ecological and biogeographical dimensions of biodiversity, it is human activities that are primarily responsible for the present high rate of species extinction. Attempts to arrest genetic erosion will be in vain if this is not recognized.

Representing Species Diversity

First, some basic principles concerning the use of the term 'diversity' in a biotic context are introduced, and then the representation of species diversity is discussed. Most people who work on species diversity concentrate on a particular group of organisms, e.g. fishes, plants or birds. The extent of the areas being studied varies greatly, depending on the objectives of the study. One person might be interested in the effect of soil type on plant species diversity within a fairly small area, while another might be interested in comparing bird or mammal diversity between tropical, temperate and arctic regions.

Whatever the spatial scale, the simplest measure of species diversity is the number of species of the chosen group. This is usually referred to as ***species richness***. If there are very large differences in species number, as often occurs when comparisons are made across climatic zones, this simple statistic can be adequate. But when numbers of species are not very dissimilar between areas, other aspects of diversity need to be considered. These usually involve a consideration of the relative contribution of each species as well as the total number present. Consider the case of two woodlands of similar area, each containing 1000 individual trees of 10 different species: in one woodland there are 100 individuals of each tree species, while in the other there are 910 individuals of one species and just 10 individuals of each of the other nine species. Species richness (10) is the same in both cases, but this simple statistic does not reflect the relative contributions of each species in the two communities. What is needed, therefore, is some other statistic which weights the species according to their representation in each community. For this purpose *diversity indices* are used, of which several are available. The choice of index depends largely on whether the investigator wishes to emphasize the species which are relatively abundant or those that are poorly represented. One way of presenting both the species richness of an area and the relative abundance of each species is with a *dominance–diversity curve* (Figure 16.1). This curve relates the order of abundance of each species (1st, 2nd, 3rd, etc.) to its abundance value. For animals and trees, the number of individuals is often a satisfactory measure of abundance, but for herbaceous vegetation another measure of abundance, e.g. cover, is generally used. While there are some drawbacks with this approach (it requires a fairly uniform habitat for example), it enables quite a lot of information to be presented in one diagram.

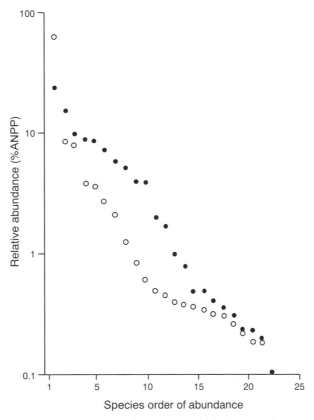

Figure 16.1   *Dominance-diversity curves for plants in two old fields in southern Ontario, Canada. Species are ranked according to their estimated contribution to annual above-ground net primary production (ANPP). Note the logarithmic scale on the vertical axis. Species richness is the same in both fields. In one field (open circles) a single species dominates the vegetation while in the other (closed circles) there is greater evenness of production between species. (Data collected by the author)*

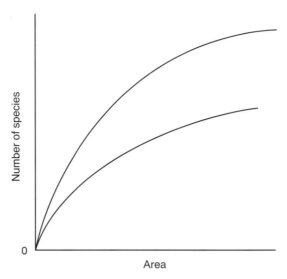

Figure 16.2   *Species–area curves. The horizontal axis could represent either areas of different size (e.g. oceanic islands, woodlands) or the intensity of sampling within a given area*

Dominance–diversity relationships raise the issue of the 'commonness' and the 'rarity' of species in a community. In general, the species of a particular group (e.g. plants, birds, fishes, mammals) are not represented equally (notwithstanding the earlier woodland example). The proportion of species which are abundant is typically very low, while the majority of the species are poorly represented. In other words dominance is concentrated in relatively few species.

Ecologists and biogeographers frequently examine the relationship between species number and the size of an area (Figure 16.2). There are two main types of *species–area relationships.* In one, the number of species is related to the size of the sampling unit within a reasonably uniform community. This relationship is often used to guide the size of sampling units (quadrats) in vegetation. The usual pattern is for species number to increase quite quickly initially as the area being sampled increases, but the curve gradually flattens as there are less and less species to be 'captured'. In reality the situation is rather more complex because 'uniform' communities rarely exist and some species will be extremely difficult to find. The species–area curve generated by such an exercise in effect represents differences in the intensity of sampling. Also, species–area curves are used to relate the number of species to the total area being investigated. (Whether the 'real' total number is known will depend on the intensity of sampling.) So species–area relationships could be constructed for lakes, islands, counties and nature reserves of different areal extent. Again, the general pattern is for species number to increase with the size of the area being examined, assuming that there are no other important variables influencing species diversity.

Whenever diversity values are being compared it is important to ensure that comparisons are valid, that like is being compared with like. To minimize the danger of spurious comparisons, three types of diversity – known as *alpha*, *beta* and *gamma* – are widely recognized. However, it must be conceded that the ways in which the terms are used varies widely, so this typology is only a guide. Alpha diversity refers essentially to diversity *within* localities, within uniform habitats for example. Gamma diversity, in contrast, refers to diversity in much larger, regional areas. Although not precisely defined in terms of areal extent (for example, what is a region?), the distinction is reasonably drawn in practice. Beta diversity is rather different in that it is not represented by a number signifying species richness, but by the turnover of species along an environmental gradient. It is often referred to as between-area diversity. A fairly straightforward way of dealing with beta diversity is to calculate it as the ratio of regional gamma diversity to the average alpha diversity of localities within the region. Despite the theoretical problems with these different types of diversity, the scheme serves as a reminder that caution is necessary when comparing diversity values.

Patterns of Diversity

Species richness is not constant from place to place, nor does it vary randomly. Rather, there are patterns, with different geographical and ecological situations being associated with characteristic levels of diversity. Some of these patterns are described in this section and some consideration is given to the theories proposed to account for them.

Most marked of the diversity patterns is a general increase in species diversity from the poles to the equator. The major exceptions to this latitudinal trend are the comparatively low diversity in arid climates and at high altitude. The latitudinal trend holds well for most major groups of organisms (e.g. plants, birds, fishes and insects) with the differences sometimes being in orders of magnitude. Thus, 10 ha of boreal forest contains just a handful of tree species, 10 ha of temperate forest typically contains some 20 tree species, but the same area of humid tropical forest may well support over 100, and sometimes nearer 300 tree species. Another general trend is for species richness to decline markedly over long altitudinal transects, which is associated with a general decline in temperature and an increase in rainfall. An exception to this generalization occurs on mountains in hot, arid climates: initially, species richness may increase with altitude, which is associated with an increase in rainfall, but, as moisture no longer becomes limiting and temperature falls still further, species diversity again declines.

Two other trends in species diversity relate to the size of habitats and their degree of isolation from potential colonizing sources. Both relationships have been explored well on oceanic islands. In the early 1960s two American ecologists, Robert MacArthur and Edward Wilson, proposed a theory of island biogeography which has been very influential. It arose from the observation that the relationship between the size of islands and the number of species they contain is quite consistent. When represented graphically on a logarithmic scale the two variables are linearly related (Figure 16.3a). Wilson's 'rule of thumb' is that a tenfold increase in area is associated with a doubling in species number, although the relationship varies between situations. MacArthur and Wilson proposed that each island has a maximum number of species which it can accommodate: the species number does not change over time but a change in species composition occurs due to the immigration of new species and extinction of residents. The theory has been applied to non-marine 'island' situations as well: lakes within a continental landmass and mountain tops are examples. The diversity–area relationship has clear implications for

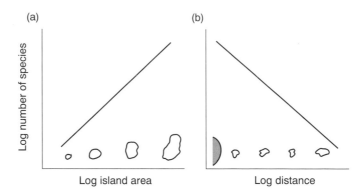

Figure 16.3   *General relationships between species richness and (a) island size, (b) distance of island from colonizing source. In (b) it is assumed that islands are of equal size. Linear relationships have often been shown when the number of species within a particular taxonomic group, obtained from a particular region, are logarithmically transformed*

conservation, particularly the selection and design of nature reserves. Importantly, it shows the magnitude of species loss that is to be expected as the area of suitable habitat declines.

The second general relationship is that species diversity on islands tends to decline with increasing distance of the island from its principal source of colonizing species (Figure 16.3b). In other words, the more remote the island the fewer the species. If the islands are of equal size, the species extinction rate should be the same on them all. However, the rate of immigration will be lower the further the island is located from its source of colonizing species. In examining this relationship in the field, all islands would ideally be of equal size, which never occurs naturally. Care must therefore be taken to avoid confounding island 'remoteness' with size.

Possible relationships between species diversity and biotic productivity have also attracted attention. Across geographical zones, a positive relationship is to be expected. For example, an increase in diversity is associated with the latitudinal increase in forest productivity from high latitudes to the tropics. Even within the more restricted climatic range of North America, tree species richness and evapotranspiration have been shown to be quite closely related. This is significant because evapotranspiration, which integrates both temperature and moisture, is correlated with primary productivity. There are, however, a few exceptions to the positive productivity–diversity relationship. Communities with low diversity, for example sedge or grass-dominated wetlands, can be highly productive. Also, some data sets have suggested a unimodal relationship, with maximum diversity occurring at intermediate levels of productivity (Figure 16.4a).

A number of theories have been proposed to account for diversity patterns, particularly the marked latitudinal gradient, but no one theory has proved entirely satisfactory. Older theories pointed to the greater stability of tropical regions over time and assumed that Pleistocene climatic changes brought about the extinction of many species and the dispersal of other species from higher to lower latitudes: given sufficient time, therefore, species should migrate back and speciation should occur markedly to increase diversity at higher latitudes. This idea is no longer favoured,

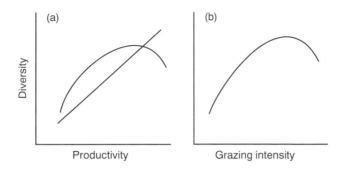

Figure 16.4   *Relationships found in some situations between species richness and (a) increasing productivity, (b) increasing grazing intensity*

partly because it is clear that the whole world was affected by Pleistocene glaciations. Interestingly, it has become clear that the extent of tropical forest shrank very markedly at times in response to periodic cooling and drying, and it is believed that these changes actually promoted speciation. Also, the latitudinal trend is not just a modern phenomenon. Another suggestion concerns the period of time that life processes are possible ('biotic time') expressed as a proportion of chronological time. Within the most recent thousand years for example, the total amount of time when conditions were suitable for growth, development and reproduction would be little less than a thousand years in the humid tropics but only 400 years in boreal forest. If the greater amount of 'biotic time' permits a faster rate of evolution then perhaps this could contribute to the greater diversity in the humid tropics than elsewhere.

More recent theories focus on the high productivity of the humid tropics, the relative constancy of temperature and generally more benign conditions for biotic activity year round. As pointed out above, tree species diversity has been shown to be related in a general way to primary productivity. There are theoretical reasons for assuming that the higher the annual primary production, the larger the number of viable populations that can be supported. This applies not only to the plants but to the heterotrophs as well. Climate, particularly its seasonal variation, may also contribute to the higher diversity of the humid tropics. In seasonal climates, organisms must be adapted to a wider range of physical environmental variables than is necessary in the tropics where temperature fluctuations over the year are usually small. The physical environment should therefore be a more important selective force in seasonal environments than in the tropics, where it is probably biotic interactions such as predation, parasitism, competition and mutualism that are the more potent evolutionary forces. The capacity of high-latitude species to tolerate a greater range of physical environmental conditions than species in the tropics is reflected in the larger geographical ranges they occupy.

The relationship between species richness and area of habitat has also been used to explore the latitudinal trend in diversity. Our cartographic representations of continental configuration usually overemphasize the land areas of higher latitudes; it is simply an artefact of the projections normally used for constructing world maps. The American ecologist Michael Rosenzweig calculated the true land areas occupied by five climatic zones (tropics, subtropics, temperate, boreal, tundra), choosing appropriate latitudes to mark the boundaries between adjacent zones. He found that around three and a half times as much land area is located in the tropical zone as in the next largest climatic zone, which is the tundra. Clearly there are no simple answers to the latitudinal trend in species diversity, although there are a number of factors that may promote higher diversity, especially when operating together.

Diversity and Ecosystem Processes

The maintenance and enhancement of species diversity almost defines ecological conservation. It is therefore very important to establish what factors influence species diversity at a local level. One such factor, habitat size, has already been mentioned. Other factors involve physical and biotic processes occurring in the community. Important variables include the type and intensity of both physical disturbance and grazing, and nutrient availability. Although there appears to be a generally positive relationship between productivity and diversity in communities over large geographical areas, this is not necessarily the case within individual communities. In fact, excessive nutrient enrichment tends to reduce species diversity, both on land and water. It appears that a minority of species are able to take advantage of the elevated nutrient levels and proceed to out-compete the other species.

Minor physical disturbance may encourage species diversity by reducing the uniformity of a habitat, while an absence of disturbance may have the reverse effect. Grazing also has a major influence on species diversity. Particularly important is the intensity of grazing. Many experiments suggest a unimodal relationship between plant diversity and grazing intensity (Figure 16.4b), although this relationship is influenced by variables such as the type of grazing animal, and the period of the year when grazing occurs. Thus the absence of grazing by rabbits in British sand dunes typically encourages the growth of a few coarse grasses, and eventually the invasion by woody plants. The presence of rabbits at relatively low population levels appears to constrain the growth of the more competitive grasses, allowing more plant species to co-exist. Above a certain threshold, however, diversity tends once again to decline because a more restricted group of species is adapted to the very disturbed and unstable conditions arising from the loss of vegetation (Figure 16.4b). A similar effect can be observed with large herbivores on rangeland.

Some years ago, American ecologist Robert Paine examined the consequences of removing starfish, the major predator, from areas of the intertidal zone in Washington State (USA). The result of relaxing grazing pressure was a decrease in species diversity among the prey organisms, principally shelled invertebrates, and the increasing abundance of one of these, the mussel. Again, predation appears to be operating through its effects on competitive relationships among the prey organisms. This type of work raises the issue of the relative ecological importance of species. For example, the deliberate exclusion of starfish had a disproportionately large effect on structure and function in the rocky intertidal community. The term *cornerstone species* is applied to those which have a controlling effect on community characteristics. For most communities, however, the relative ecological significance of individual species, and the consequences of their loss, remains largely unknown.

Further Reading – Part Four

Archibold, D.W. 1995 *Ecology of World Vegetation*, Chapman & Hall, London
(Very well illustrated overview of the different sorts of terrestrial and aquatic ecosystem types emphasizing functional aspects.)

Brown, J.H. 1996 *Biogeography*, 2nd edition. McGraw-Hill, London.
(Comprehensive treatment of geographical aspects of the biota; strong on the distribution of major taxonomic groups.)

Cox, C.B. and Moore, P.D. 1993 *Biogeography: An Ecological and Evolutionary Approach*, 5th edition. Blackwell Science, Oxford.
(Very good student text: the number of editions testifies to its popularity.)

Gaston, K.J. and Spicer, J.I. 1998 *Biodiversity: An Introduction*. Blackwell Science, Oxford.
(Useful brief introduction to various dimensions of the subject.)

Kent, M. and Coker, P. 1992 *Vegetation Description and Analysis*. John Wiley & Sons, Chichester.
(Comprehensive but sympathetic treatment of topics from first principles onwards – very useful reference for practitioners.)

Lovelock, J. 1987 *The Ages of Gaia: A Biography of Our Living Earth*. Oxford University Press, Oxford.
(A guide to the Gaia hypothesis by its proposer.)

Rosenzweig, M.L. 1995 *Species Diversity in Space and Time*. Cambridge University Press, Cambridge.
(Rigorous, comprehensive but readable discussion of all aspects of the subject.)

Walter, H. 1985 *Vegetation of the Earth: In Relation to Climate and the Eco-Physiological Conditions*, 3rd edition. Springer-Verlag, Heidelberg.
(Concise overview of the world's main vegetation formations emphasizing climatic differences and plant adaptations.)

Wilson, E.O. 1992 *The Diversity of Life*. Belknap Press, Cambridge, Massachusetts. (Also 1996 Penguin Books, London.)
(Highly enjoyable way of accessing complex ecological and biogeographical concepts. Recommended for evolutionary issues as well.)

Glossary

Adaptation   Any genetically determined characteristic (structural, functional or behavioural) that enhances survival and reproductive success in a particular situation.

Adaptive radiation   Major evolutionary diversification giving rise to new taxa.

Aeon   Largest formal division of geological time; the three aeons are the Archaean, the Proterozoic and the Phanerozoic.

Aerobic   Of an environment in which free oxygen is present, or of a metabolic process involving free oxygen.

Algae   Informal term covering a variety of photosynthetic unicellular or primitive multicellular organisms of (predominantly) aquatic environments.

Allele   One of the alternative forms in which a gene occurs.

Allochthonous   Of organic matter produced externally to a prescribed area, usually of water.

Allopatric   Occurring in different geographical ranges, as in speciation.

Alternation of generations   Alternation between diploid (the sporophyte) and haploid (the gametophyte) phases in the life cycle of plants, algae and a few animals.

Anaerobic   Of an environment with no free oxygen, or of a metabolic process not requiring free oxygen.

Anaerobic respiration   A type of energy metabolism of some bacteria in which oxygen is replaced by some other substance, e.g. nitrate.

Angiosperm   A flowering plant; a plant in which seeds develop from ovules within a closed ovary.

Anion   A negatively charged atom or group of atoms.

Artificial selection   Deliberate selection of individuals for breeding.

Asexual reproduction   Formation of a new individual organism without fusion of gametes.

Asteroid   Rocky structure orbiting the sun; size range approximately 1.0–350 metres.

Asthenosphere   Partially molten layer of the Earth's mantle on which the rigid plates of the less dense lithosphere 'float'.

Atom   Smallest entity into which a chemical element can be divided and still retain properties of that element.

Atomic number   The number of protons in an atomic nucleus; each element has a unique atomic number.

Autochthonous   Of organic matter produced within a prescribed area, usually of water.

Autotrophic   Of an organism, or type of metabolism, harnessing a non-biotic source of energy for manufacture of organic matter.

Banded iron formation   Iron-rich, laminated rock structure of Archaean and early Proterozoic times; the laminated appearance is largely due to variations in reduced and oxidized iron content.

Basal metabolism   All metabolic processes associated with normal functioning of an animal.

Benthic   Of the zone, or the organisms, at the bed of a water body.

Benthos   Community of organisms inhabiting the bed of a water body.

Binomial system   The accepted scheme for scientific naming of organisms using two names, the genus name and the specific epithet.

Biomass   General term for living organic matter, usually expressed as a quantity per unit area (e.g. $g\,m^{-2}$, $t\,ha^{-1}$).

Biome   Major division of the Earth's land biota based on structural and functional characteristics; as in desert biome and tundra biome.

Biota   Shorthand term used to refer to the living component of the environment.

Breed   Named, genetically distinct subgroup of a domesticated animal species.

Catalyst   A substance that enhances the rate of a chemical reaction but is not consumed during the process.

Cation   A positively charged atom or group of atoms.

Cell   The basic living unit of which all organisms are constructed.

Cell wall   Comparatively rigid layer surrounding cells of plants, certain protists and most bacteria.

Character   Any feature of an organism that is used for taxonomic purposes.

Chemosynthesis   An autotrophic mode of nutrition involving oxidation of simple inorganic entities to provide energy for organic matter synthesis from carbon dioxide.

Chlorophyll   Green pigment which is the primary site of light energy absorption in photosynthesis.

Chloroplast   Organelle in which chlorophyll is located within cells of photosynthetic eukaryotes.

Chromatid   A longitudinal half of a chromosome formed by replication of DNA in early stage of nuclear division; the chromosome is then made up of two identical chromatids.

Chromosome   Thread-like structure carrying genes; in eukaryotic cells located within the nucleus.

Codon   A sequence of three nucleotides (a triplet) coding for a particular amino acid or a 'stop' instruction in amino acid sequencing.

Coevolution   Evolution resulting from two taxa simultaneously exerting selection pressure on each other.

Community   All, or a specified subset, of the populations of species inhabiting a prescribed area.

Competition   Said to occur when an organism performs less well than its potential because resources (e.g. light, water, nutrients, food) are procured by other organism(s).

Compound   A molecule consisting of atoms of two or more elements held together in a definite ratio.

Condensation reaction   Chemical reaction involving the linking of two molecules with the elimination of water.

Constructive plate margin   Boundary between two lithospheric plates at which new crustal material is extruded.

Convergent evolution   Development of similar features within unrelated taxa subjected to similar selection pressures.

Cornerstone species   One with disproportionately large influence on organization of a community.

Cosmopolitan   Of a taxon with a geographically widespread distribution.

Crossing-over   Process by which chromosomes exchange alleles during the first division of meiosis.

Cultivar   Named, genetically distinct subgroup of a domesticated plant species.

Cytoplasm   The living part of a cell, excluding the nucleus in the case of eukaryotic cells.

Decomposition   The breakdown and loss of dead organic matter.

Denitrification   Biochemical process resulting in the release of gaseous nitrogen to the atmosphere.

Destructive plate margin   Boundary between two lithospheric plates where one plate descends under the other and is destroyed.

Detritus   The (little-altered) remains of living organisms.

Diagenesis   Alteration of rocks over time by heat and pressure.

Digestibility   The proportion of a foodstuff that traverses the wall of an animal's digestive tract.

Diploid   Of a eukaryotic nucleus, cell or organism containing two sets of chromosomes; diploid number denoted by $2n$.

Disjunct   Of a taxon distributed in geographically separate areas.

Dispersal   The movement of organisms or their propagules; required for expansion of the range of a species.

Dominant gene or allele   Allele expressed phenotypically whether occurring in homozygous state or in heterozygous state with its recessive partner.

Ecosystem   Any group of organisms together with the physical environment with which they are interacting; used also to refer to particular types, e.g. forest ecosystem, grassland ecosystem.

Ecotone   Transition zone separating two fairly uniform types of vegetation.

Ectotherm   An organism without special features for regulating body temperature.

Electromagnetic radiation   Radiation consisting of energy waves associated with electrical and magnetic fields; characteristics are related to wave frequency.

Electromagnetic spectrum   The range of wavelengths and frequencies over which electromagnetic waves are transmitted.

Element (chemical)   A substance made up of atoms with the same number of protons.

Endemic   Of a taxa restricted in distribution to a particular geographical area and occurring nowhere else.

Endergonic   Of a chemical reaction requiring an input of energy from an external source.

Endosperm   Nutrient storage tissue found in most angiosperm seeds.

Endotherm   An organism with adaptations for regulating body temperature; notably mammals and birds.

Energy   The capacity to do work.

Energy metabolism   Metabolic processes involved in the capture, release and use of energy by an organism.

Energy substrate   Chemical molecules which are broken down enzymatically to yield energy for metabolic purposes.

Enzymes   Proteins that catalyse chemical reactions.

Epilimnion   Relatively stable upper layer of low-density water in a stratified water body, usually a lake.

Era   Primary division of geological time in the Phanerozoic aeon; the three eras are the Palaeozoic, Mesozoic and Cenozoic.

Eukaryotic cell or organism   One containing membrane-bound organelles including a nucleus in which there are pairs of chromosomes.

Euphotic zone   Zone of water in which light energy is adequate for photosynthesis.

Eutrophic   Nutrient rich, especially of peat and water bodies.

Eutrophication   Nutrient enrichment; may be caused by natural processes or human activities (cultural eutrophication).

Evolution   Progressive change with time in the genetic composition of a population.

Exergonic   Of a chemical reaction that liberates energy as it proceeds.

Exine   The decay-resistant outer coat of a pollen grain or a spore.

Fermentation   An energy-yielding metabolic pathway not requiring oxygen; gives rise to a variety of by-products.

Fertilization   Union of gametes with formation of diploid zygote.

Fitness   A measure of the capacity of a genotype to leave its genes to future generations.

Flower   The reproductive structure of an angiosperm.

Food chain and food web   Refers to the movement of energy and chemical matter through a community of organisms; represented diagrammatically.

Fossil   Remains or other tangible evidence of an organism's existence in former times.

Founder effect   Process whereby a population establishes in a new geographical area and quickly diverges from its parent population on account of individuals containing only a fraction of the genes of the total population.

Fruit   Mature ovary of a flowering plant (angiosperm); contains the seeds.

Gamete   Sex cell; a special haploid cell or nucleus which unites with one of opposite sex to produce a (diploid) zygote.

Gametophyte (generation)   Haploid, gamete-bearing, phase of a plant's life cycle; may be dominant phase, as in mosses, but usually small; may be dependent or independent of sporophyte.

Gene   Sequence of DNA nucleotides which codes for a particular polypeptide or an RNA molecule. Genes provide information for structure and function in organisms and are passed to successive generations in reproduction.

Gene flow   The movement of genes (strictly alleles) within and between populations.

Gene frequency   The relative abundance of genes (strictly alleles) in a population.

Gene pool   The total complement of genes in a population.

Genetic code   The universal genetic language made up of DNA triplets, each of which codes for a particular amino acid or a stopping instruction in amino acid sequencing.

Genetic engineering   The artificial transfer of pieces of DNA from one organism to another.

Genome   The total genetic information in an organism's nucleus.

Genotype   The particular combination of genes (strictly alleles) of an individual organism or cell.

Geological timescale   The formal division of time into named intervals; based primarily on the fossil record.

Glycolysis   First part of energy-generating processes of respiration and fermentation. Can proceed with or without oxygen.

Guild   Group of species exploiting a common resource in similar ways.

Gymnosperm   A flowerless seed plant in which seeds lie unprotected, not within fruits; notably the conifers.

Haploid   Of a eukaryotic nucleus, cell or organism with only one set of chromosomes; haploid number denoted by *n*.

Heterotrophic   Of an organism, or mode of nutrition, dependent on an external supply of preformed organic substances.

Heterozygous   Having different alleles for a given trait on a pair of homologous chromosomes.

Hominid   Informally, of taxa considered more human-like than ape-like.

Homologous chromosomes   The two chromosomes in a pair having identical gene sequences; diploid nuclei have the two homologues of each chromosome pair, haploid nuclei have only one of the homologues.

Homozygous   Having identical alleles for a particular trait on a pair of homologous chromosomes.

Humus   Chemically complex and much altered mixture of organic remains found in soil horizons and at soil surface.

Hybrid   Offspring of two parents known to be genetically unlike in some respect; as in case of different genetic lines, varieties and species.

Hydrogen bond   A weak kind of chemical bond involving hydrogen and (usually) two nitrogen or oxygen atoms. Important for holding molecules of DNA and proteins together and in linking water molecules.

Hydrolysis   Chemical reaction involving the splitting of one molecule into two with the addition of hydrogen and hydroxyl groups from water to the products of the reaction.

Hydrothermal vent   Site of hot-water spring on the ocean floor; associated with constructive plate margins.

Hypha (pl. hyphae)   Filamentous structure which is part of a fungus.

Hypolimnion   Lower layer of relatively high-density water in a stratified water body, usually a lake.

Ice age   Informal term referring to long interval of unusually extensive snow and ice cover.

Index fossil   Fossil taxon used as reliable indication of age of rocks in which it is found.

Interference   Any activity of one organism, other than consumption, that reduces the performance of another organism; includes competition.

Interglacial   A comparatively long warmer phase of an ice age when considerable glacial retreat occurs.

Interstadial   A comparatively brief warmer phase during an ice age.

Ion   An atom, or group of atoms, carrying a net electrical charge on account of unequal numbers of protons and electrons.

Irradiance   Amount of radiant energy received by a surface, measured in terms of energy per unit area per unit time.

Isotope   One of two or more forms of the same element with a particular number of neutrons in the nucleus; isotopes of the same element thus have different mass numbers.

Joule   Internationally recognized unit of work or energy.

Leaf area duration (LAD)   The integral of the leaf area index and time.

Leaf area index (LAI)   The area of leaf tissue per unit area of land surface.

Leaf area ratio (LAR)   The amount of leaf area per (usually) unit weight of a plant.

Life cycle   Genetically determined developmental pattern of an organism.

Lithosphere   Rigid outer layer of the Earth; comprises crust and outer layer of mantle, and fragmented into plates which 'float' on partially molten asthenosphere.

Maintenance diet   The amount of food necessary to maintain an organism at constant weight.

Mantle   That part of the Earth between the crust and the core.

Mass extinction   Informal term for the disappearance of a significant proportion of taxa in a short interval of geological time.

Meiosis   A process involving two successive nuclear divisions during which the chromosome number in a nucleus is halved and there is opportunity for assortment of chromosomes and genetic recombination.

Metabolic pathway   A sequence of enzyme-controlled biochemical reactions.

Metabolism   The sum-total of chemical reactions occurring in a living cell, tissue or organism.

Metabolizable energy   That part of ingested food energy available to an animal for metabolic purposes.

Micrometre (μm)   One millionth of a metre (10^{-6} metre).

Mid-oceanic ridge   Narrow submarine mountain chain – occasionally emergent – associated with constructive plate margins; e.g. Mid-Atlantic Ridge.

Mimicry   Increased resemblance (usually form, colour or behaviour) of one type of organism to another type; usually a predator avoidance adaptation.

Mineralization   Process by which elements held within organic matter are released in inorganic (mineral) form; occurs in soil and water during decomposition.

Mitochondrion (pl. mitochondria)   Intracellular organelle which is the major site of aerobic respiration (oxidative metabolism); found in all but a few eukaryotic organisms.

Mitosis   A nuclear or cell division that results in the formation of two daughter nuclei or cells with identical number of chromosomes and identical genotype as the original; usually accompanied by cell division.

Molecule   A stable chemical entity held together by chemical bonds and consisting of two or more atoms of the same or of different elements; a single molecule of a particular compound cannot be further divided and still retain the properties of that compound.

Moneran   A member of the (prokaryotic) kingdom Monera; effectively a bacterium.

Mutualism   Interactions between species in which both (or all) the species included derive some benefit.

Mutation   A change in chromosomal DNA.

Mycorrhiza (pl. mycorrhizae)   An association between a fungus and the root of a plant.

Nanometre (nm)   One-billionth of a metre (10^{-9} metre).

Natural selection   Differential reproduction among genotypes in a population in which there is variation between individuals and a potential for increase in number of individuals. Major mechanism for evolution.

Net assimilation rate (NAR)   The rate of carbon uptake per unit leaf area in photosynthesis.

Neutron   Uncharged particle present in all atomic nuclei except common isotope of hydrogen.

Nitrification   The conversion, by bacteria, of ammonium ions, via nitrite, to nitrate.

Nucleus   (1) Atomic: positively charged central core of an atom, containing at least one proton and (except for hydrogen) at least one neutron; accounts for tiny fraction of an atom's volume but most of its mass. (2) Compartment in a eukaryotic cell containing the chromosomes.

Nutrient   A biotically essential chemical element, but also applied to any substance essential for life processes.

Oligotrophic   Nutrient poor, especially of peat and water bodies.

Ombrogenous   Of areas, particularly peat, to which all water (and nutrient) inputs are from the atmosphere.

Organ   Part of an organism with a well-defined structure and function.

Organelle   A membrane-bound intracellular structure (e.g. nucleus, mitochondrion) which is the site of particular cellular functions; confined to eukaryotic cells.

Ovule   Structure in seed plants comprising female gametophyte (including egg) and covering tissue; develops into the seed following fertilization.

Oxidation   Chemical reaction involving the loss of electrons from a substance (which is thus oxidized). Metabolic oxidations often involve the addition of oxygen or loss of hydrogen.

Oxidative metabolism   Energy-yielding process involving free oxygen; essentially respiration.

Parallel evolution   The development of similar adaptations in closely related taxa due to similar selection pressures.

Parasite   Organism living on or in, and deriving its nutrition from, another living organism.

Pathogen   A (usually) biotic agent (e.g. bacterium, fungus, virus) which induces disease.

Peat   The physically and chemically transformed remains of vegetation; its accumulation is due to the prolonged inhibition of decomposition processes.

Pelagic   Of open water environments and organisms.

Period   Primary division of time within the three geological eras of the Phanerozoic aeon.

pH   A measure of the acidity or alkalinity of a substance; expressed on a logarithmic scale of 1–14 in which 7 denotes neutrality; the lower the value the greater the acidity.

Phenetic classification   A classification of organisms based solely on resemblance and without deliberate reference to evolutionary considerations.

Phenotype   The features of form, function and behaviour of an organism; an expression of interaction between genotype and environment.

Photon   A discrete quantity of energy; as in case of electromagnetic radiation.

Photorespiration   Light-induced biochemical process resulting in release of carbon dioxide from C_3 plants.

Photosynthesis Biochemical and biophysical process involving the synthesis of energy-rich organic molecules from carbon dioxide and a hydrogen donor (usually water) using light as a source of energy.

Photosynthetically active radiation (PAR) The range of wavelengths of the electromagnetic spectrum absorbed by chlorophyll and used in photosynthesis; approximately 400–700 nanometres.

Phylogenetic classification A classification of organisms based on evolutionary relationships.

Physiognomy Study of overall morphological features, e.g. of vegetation; used as criterion for categorizing vegetation.

Physiology The study of function of organisms.

Phytoplankton General term referring to microscopic photosynthetic organisms, mostly unicellular algae, in open water.

Plate Major unit of the lithosphere; plates are separated by different types of plate margins.

Plate margin Linear zone separating the plates which make up the Earth's lithosphere.

Plate tectonics The study of movements of the Earth's lithospheric plates.

Pollen Male (micro)spores of seed plants; carries the male gametophyte and is transported by wind, animals or, sometimes, water.

Pollen tube The male gametophyte of seed plants; tube-like structure that develops as angiosperm pollen grain germinates on a receptive stigma; carries the male gametes to the site of fertilization in the female gametophyte.

Polymer A large molecule made up of much smaller molecules of similar type linked together to form a chain, e.g. polysaccharide.

Polyploid An organism having at least three times the haploid number of chromosomes; common in plants, rare in animals.

Population A group of organisms of the same species inhabiting a prescribed area.

Potential energy Energy in a potentially usable form.

Predation The consumption of living tissue by another organism; commonly used to imply capture of one animal by another animal.

Prey Any organism that is the food source of another organism; use sometimes confined to animals.

Primary production Organic matter produced by autotrophic, principally photosynthetic organisms, but strictly chemosynthetic organisms also.

Primary productivity The rate at which organic matter is accumulated by autotrophic organisms; expressed on a per unit area per unit time basis.

Prokaryotic cell or organism One without duplicated chromosomes or membrane-bound organelles; effectively a bacterium.

Protist A member of the eukaryotic kingdom Protista; most are microscopic unicellular organisms.

Protoplast That part of the cell in which metabolism occurs; in eukaryotes differentiated into nucleus and cytoplasm.

Protozoa General term for a group of unicellular 'animal-like' organisms now placed within the kingdom Protista.

Radioisotope An unstable isotope that spontaneously disintegrates by the emission of particles and/or radiation.

Recessive gene or allele   In heterozygous state, allele whose expression is masked by alternative, dominant allele and therefore does not contribute to phenotype.

Reduction   A chemical reaction involving the gain of electrons or hydrogen by a substance (which is thus reduced); term includes the removal of oxygen from a substance.

Relict   Of a species or community separated by a major ecological barrier from its main area of distribution.

Reproduction   The formation of a new organism by either sexual or asexual means.

Reproductive isolation   The cessation of gene flow between all members of a population due to reproductive barriers such as geographical isolation and breeding incompatibility.

Respiration   A series of biochemical reactions involving the release of energy from organic substrates for energy-demanding activities; usually refers to oxidative metabolism, but see anaerobic respiration.

Ribosome   Subcellular structure, comprising protein and RNA, where polypeptides are produced.

Rumen   Much enlarged stomach of many types of mammalian herbivores in which microbial populations anaerobically break down fibrous plant material and synthesize amino acids.

Ruminant   Any large herbivorous mammal possessing a rumen.

Sea-floor spreading   The movement of crustal material either side of, and away from, a constructive plate margin on the ocean floor as new material is extruded; responsible for changing configuration of the continents.

Secondary metabolite   A biochemical substance not directly involved in an organism's own metabolism; usually affects its relationship with other organisms.

Secondary production   Organic matter of heterotrophic organisms.

Secondary productivity   The rate of organic matter accumulation by (i.e. growth of) heterotrophic organisms; expressed on a per unit area per unit time basis.

Seed   The fully mature ovule of gymnosperms and angiosperms; contains the embryo and (usually) a nutrient reserve.

Selection pressure   Measure of the effectiveness of environment to change gene frequency in a population.

Sessile   Of an organism fixed in one position and effectively immobile.

Sex chromosome   Chromosome determining sex of an individual organism; differ in type between males and females; possessed by most animals and some plants.

Sexual reproduction   The production of a new individual by the union of two haploid gametes.

Solution   A mixture formed by dissolving a substance (the solute) in a liquid.

Somatic cells   All cells of an organism with the exception of the spores and gametes.

Speciation   Processes which lead to an increase in the number of species.

Spore   Haploid cell of plants from which gametophyte develops.

Sporophyte (generation)   Diploid phase of a plant's life cycle on which spores are produced; alternates with gametophyte generation.

Stadial   A cold phase during an ice age.

Stigma   Part of the female flower of angiosperms which is receptive to pollen grains.

Stomate (pl. stomata)   Apparatus for gas exchange on (usually) plant leaf surface; comprises a pore (stoma) and surrounding guard cells; pore size varies according to water status of guard cells.

Succession   Of vegetation, change in species composition over time in a particular area.

Stratified   Of a water body in which distinct layering is evident; due to density differences in temperature and/or salinity.

Stromatolite   Pillar-like limestone or, more rarely, siliceous structure up to a few metres in diameter with alternating organic-rich and organic-poor layers; former largely associated with cyanobacteria; prominent in Proterozoic aeon.

Subduction   The descent of one lithospheric plate under another where two plates converge.

Sympatric   Occurring in the same geographical range, as in speciation when a new species arises in the same geographical range as its immediate ancestor.

Systematics   The study of all aspects of relationships between organisms.

Taxon (pl. taxa)   A named group of organisms of any taxonomic rank.

Taxonomy   That branch of systematics dealing with the classification of organisms.

Thermocline   Layer of water in which temperature gradient is pronounced.

Tissue   A mass of cells which share structural and functional features.

Trace element   A chemical element required by an organism in tiny amounts for normal functioning.

Transcription   First stage of protein synthesis; involves 'reading' of section of chromosomal DNA and formation of complementary strand of messenger RNA which carries the information to the site of protein synthesis.

Translation   Second stage of protein synthesis; involves decoding information on messenger RNA molecule and linking of amino acids to form a polypeptide at a ribosome.

Translocation   Transport of soluble substances around a plant.

Transpiration   The evaporative loss of water from the aerial parts (shoot) of a plant.

Triplet   A sequence of three nucleotide bases on a DNA or messenger RNA molecule.

Trophic level   A clearly defined stage in a food chain, e.g. primary producers–herbivores–carnivores.

Ultraviolet radiation   Electromagnetic radiation in wavelength range 10–400 nanometres.

Ungulate   General term for a large, hoofed herbivore.

Upwelling   Upward movement of water from depth that occurs in some oceanic areas; important mechanism for nutrient transfer.

Vacuole   Fluid-filled cavity characteristic of plant cells; often occupies much of a plant cell's internal volume.

Vascular tissue   Bundles of elongated cells which conduct water and inorganic and organic substances in solution around plants.

Vertical evolution   Change in gene frequency across the entire range of a species; may lead to a new species replacing another.

Vicariant   A taxon whose geographical distribution is due to the formation of a major ecological barrier which separates a formerly continuous geographical range.

Virus   Life form comprising nucleic acid and (usually) protein coat; reproduction is confined to living cells in which a variety of responses, including many diseases, are induced.

Volatilization   Conversion of chemical substances to vapour phase (gas) by high temperature, as in a fire.

Water potential   The potential energy of water molecules; used as a measure of water status of plant tissue and soil; water potential is lowered with solute addition to pure water.

Zooplankton   General term for tiny animals and other non-photosynthetic organisms of open water which have little or no capacity for independent movement; includes juvenile stage of many organisms which later become free swimmers.

Zygote   The diploid product of the union between male and female gametes; the first cell of a sexually produced individual.

Index